The Functions of Unnatural Death in Stephen King

The Functions of Unnatural Death in Stephen King

Murder, Sickness, and Plots

Rebecca Frost

LEXINGTON BOOKS
Lanham • Boulder • New York • London

Published by Lexington Books
An imprint of The Rowman & Littlefield Publishing Group, Inc.
4501 Forbes Boulevard, Suite 200, Lanham, Maryland 20706
www.rowman.com

86-90 Paul Street, London EC2A 4NE

Copyright © 2022 by The Rowman & Littlefield Publishing Group, Inc.

All rights reserved. No part of this book may be reproduced in any form or by any electronic or mechanical means, including information storage and retrieval systems, without written permission from the publisher, except by a reviewer who may quote passages in a review.

British Library Cataloguing in Publication Information Available

Library of Congress Cataloging-in-Publication Data

Names: Frost, Rebecca, 1985- author.
Title: The functions of unnatural death in Stephen King : murder, sickness, and plots / Rebecca Frost.
Description: Lanham, Maryland : Lexington Books, [2022] | Includes bibliographical references and index. | Summary: "The Functions of Unnatural Death in Stephen King: Murder, Sickness, and Plots examines the function of death in over thirty of King's works to parse out the ways the master of horror plays with the idea of death and approaches it from multiple angles"— Provided by publisher.
Identifiers: LCCN 2021058562 (print) | LCCN 2021058563 (ebook) | ISBN 9781793646217 (cloth) | ISBN 9781793646224 (epub) | ISBN 9781793646231 (paperback)
Subjects: LCSH: King, Stephen, 1947—Criticism and interpretation. | Death in literature. | Horror tales—Authorship. | LCGFT: Literary criticism.
Classification: LCC PS3561.I483 Z6657 2022 (print) | LCC PS3561.I483 (ebook) | DDC 813/.54 dc23/eng/20211220
LC record available at https://lccn.loc.gov/2021058562
LC ebook record available at https://lccn.loc.gov/2021058563

To Karen and Colin: some of my happy to make you happy.

Contents

Acknowledgments ix

Introduction: "Death Is When the Monsters Get You" 1

Chapter One: "It's Not Really Her Anymore": Creating the Threat 9

Chapter Two: "You Know About the Cycle?": To Perpetuate the Monster 23

Chapter Three: "People Are Mortal": To Build Suspense 39

Chapter Four: "I Saved My Book by Blowing Approximately Half Its Major Characters to Smithereens": To Narrow the Focus 61

Chapter Five: "Question: Death, Where Is Thy Sting? Answer: Every-Fucking-Where": To Urge the Characters on to Action 65

Chapter Six: "More Than Any of Us Probably Know, She Hurt": As Revenge 79

Chapter Seven: "What If He Has a Helper?": As Renfield 91

Chapter Eight: "I Want to Die Well": As Heroic Sacrifice 107

Chapter Nine: "It Could Destroy Everything": To Restore Order 125

Conclusion: "It Seemed to Mean Something": Confronting Death and Multifaceted Horror 147

Bibliography 187

Index 191

About the Author 197

Acknowledgments

Thanks go first and foremost to Patrick McAleer and Philip Simpson, who initially welcomed me into the PCA/ACA Stephen King Area in 2014. I appreciate everyone I've met through the national conferences. Thank you for being willing to share your scholarship and helping me hone my own.

I would like to thank my reviewer for pointing out strengths of my initial draft and making suggestions for improvements.

Thank you to my ever-encouraging constant supporters: Angela Badke, Tom Blessing, Zach Blessing, Isaac Flint, Stephanie Flint, Colleen Hix, Rae Hix, Jesse Koenig, Angela Musser, Michelle Wright-Blessing.

And, of course, thank you to my parents, who are slightly less iffy about Stephen King than they are about serial killers; and Eric, who has finally started reading some of them so he can follow my ramblings.

Introduction

"Death Is When the Monsters Get You"

When I was out to dinner with my husband a few years ago, our conversation landed on Stephen King and, for some reason, death. At the time he had not read any of King's books, so he asked me if there were any that did *not* include death. Since we live in the Upper Peninsula of Michigan, and because the restaurant we had chosen was far up the Keweenaw Peninsula, right on the shore of Lake Superior, and out of cell phone range, I had to make a mental list of all of King's titles and search them for death. My conclusion that night was that I could think of one of his novels that did not have anyone die in it, but only one.

There is an abundance of death in King's works because he writes within the horror genre, one he has studied closely in his own nonfiction *Danse Macabre*. Focusing on movies, King nevertheless explores horror's relationship with death, separating the way adults and children approach it. Horror movies, King argues, "allow us to regain our childish perspective on death,"[1] removing some of the taboos so that we can get up close and investigate. He relates a specific incident from his childhood, his own first real encounter with death in the form of a dead cat and the experiments he and some of his friends performed on it. They approached death with curiosity instead of fear.

As an adult, King has continued this approach in his storytelling. By engaging with fictional deaths in multiple ways, and using those deaths to guide his plotlines, King continues to poke at the dead cat and marvel at the maggots instead of withdrawing in fear and disgust. Twenty-first-century Americans hold death—especially the death of other human beings—at a distance, having moved away from personally preparing their loved ones for the grave toward commercializing the process with funeral homes and undertakers. When loved ones die, their bodies are surrendered, chemically processed, and carefully prepared for the final viewing. If families are not particularly religious, then they may believe that death is the end, or have no idea if anything comes next.

If the death is a result of old age or at the end of a long illness, it might be considered more of a blessing than a curse. Sudden, unexpected death, however, is a different story. When someone is, as they say, cut down in the prime of life, the horror is not just of the situation that caused the death, but of all the potential that has been eliminated.

Even within the worlds created by Stephen King, death is still largely The End. There are only rare instances when the horror is compounded with human spirits captured either by supernatural beings or their own hatred to continue inflicting pain on the living. Death as the sudden end of the anticipated life, especially when a character is either young or instrumental to the plot of the book, holds its own horror, whether the death itself is drawn out or sudden. Even though King himself argues that "sometimes dead is better,"[2] the alternative then must be truly horrific, because living is best of all.

King's Constant Readers would be hard-pressed to name novels, novellas, or short stories in which none of his characters die, because death is a constant in his works. Although death can be expected—and new favorite characters' fates can be a cause for worry—the deaths themselves are not all the same. Death can be anticipated, but it does not always occur in the same manner, in the same element of the narrative, or to the expected characters. Part of the horror is that, like in life, an unnatural death can occur at any moment and affect any character.

This book therefore seeks to parse out the multiple ways in which King's narratives make use of unnatural deaths, especially in relation to horror and suspense within the stories, as he continues his "ongoing investigation"[3] into the subject that began with a child approaching a dead cat.

UNNATURAL DEATHS

This book focuses on "unnatural deaths" as opposed to "murder" because not all of King's unnatural deaths can be categorized that way. If the focus were narrowed to "murder," then *Cujo* could not be a topic of discussion, because dogs are incapable of homicide. In fact, King emphasizes throughout the book that Cujo himself was a good dog and only killed people as a reaction to his rabies infection. Cujo would never have hurt people without the outside viral influence, and even then, dogs lack the planning capabilities and moral structure for their actions to be deemed "murder."

The plot of *Cujo*, however, treats the dog's rabid attacks as a kind of serial murder to build the suspense. Readers are aware from the time Cujo chases a rabbit down a hole and encounters a bat that Cujo is pre-rabid, which sets up both expectation for the narrative and suspense because readers know more than the book's characters. When Cujo's master, the boy Brett Camber, tells his mother Charity that he believes Cujo might be sick, Charity has her own reasons for not investigating this claim further. All of this works to increase the tension and the reader's knowledge of what happens when a dog, especially a big Saint Bernard, goes rabid, even before Cujo kills the Cambers' neighbor and then father Joe Camber himself.

Cujo positions the dog in the same monstrous category as Castle Rock's other famous serial killer, Frank Dodd, who much more traditionally fulfills that role. Although caught by a psychic, Dodd was a human through and through, committing murders in his hometown—and elsewhere—over several years and living his normal life between them: the textbook definition of a serial killer. Dodd is described in terms of inhuman monstrosity, while Cujo is simply not human, but the narrative suspense created by the series of deaths functions very similarly within the novels.

Other books that involve violence enacted upon humans by nonhumans, such as *The Tommyknockers* or *Under the Dome*, would also have to be excluded from this discussion if this book narrowly clung to the idea of "murder" over "unnatural death." Murder is defined as an act between humans. When a human kills a nonhuman there are specific terms, just as when a nonhuman animal kills a human. Unnatural deaths between humans and nonhumans are known as hunting, attacks, or mauling, depending on the predator/prey configuration.

While nonhuman animals such as dogs are generally considered to be lower in cognitive, emotional, and ethical ability than humans, no such similar judgment can be passed for the Tommyknockers or the nameless alien children in *Under the Dome*. The Tommyknockers themselves are long dead, their influence coming passively from their ship and the way the hull interacts with Earth's atmosphere, while the aliens in *Under the Dome* are compared to children playing with ants and a magnifying glass. "Murder" occurs when both parties are considered to be equals, and the actor can be reasonably expected by greater society to see his or her victim as similar to the self instead of Other. Granted, the killer himself might be sociopathic and not see the connection, but wider society can make it all the same.

MASS, SPREE, AND SERIAL MURDER

Deaths in King's works rarely come alone. The horror is, of course, increased by the number of deaths. If the threat is neutralized, then the narrative shifts to one of recovery and restoration. An active threat allows the horror to continue. However, not all multiple murders are created equal. The most common divisions of multiple murders enacted by the same person or people are mass, spree, and serial murders.

If more than one person is murdered at a single time, in a single location, then this is known as a mass murder. These include bombings, such as the bomb in the closet in Boulder or the atomic bomb in Las Vegas in *The Stand*, or the meth lab explosion and resulting fire in *Under the Dome*. Each has a single event that causes multiple deaths in a short amount of time, without changing location.

A spree murder falls between mass murder and serial murder in that, although multiple people are killed, the location changes. Lloyd Henreid and Andrew "Poke" Freeman of *The Stand* are spree killers when readers first encounter them. They have murdered the man who was supposed to cut them in on a robbery and then others any time their current vehicle needed replacing. Lloyd and Poke were not, however, secretive about their "TRI-STATE KILL SPREE,"[4] having left enough evidence in abandoned vehicles to be identified. Although they were not listening to the radio, the news was already reporting on them before their capture. Their identities were not a secret, and they did not attempt to return to their normal lives between murders.

Serial killers, such as Castle Rock's infamous Frank Dodd or Bob Anderson in "A Good Marriage," commit multiple murders, in multiple locations, across a longer span of time. Between these murders, the serial killer returns to his normal, everyday life so that even those closest to him—including Sheriff George Bannerman or Bob's own wife, Darcy—are unaware that they know the perpetrator of these crimes. Although the exact number of separate murders necessary for someone to be labeled a serial killer has changed, most recently in 2005 being reduced to two if they are at separate times and locations,[5] it is this return to "normal" life between the murders that fully distinguishes the serial killer from other mass murderers.

This is also why the figure of the serial killer is more often the center of a longer thriller or suspense narrative. A mass murder occurs and is finished within a relatively short amount of time, although the uncertainty and aftermath of the event may last longer. Spree killers are frequently identified early on and the danger is known both to readers and to characters within the story. Serial killers extend the narrative and the suspense, because popular knowledge indicates that they will keep killing until they are caught, and that they are very good at hiding their true identities. General serial killer narratives are structured for readers to also play along in attempting to identify the killer as the narrative unfolds, but suspense can be heightened when the reader is aware of the threat while other characters remain ignorant.

Although each of these categories is generally used for a particular narrative purpose, King does not always follow such conventions. Neither Frank Dodd nor Bob Anderson has his story told in the traditional serial killer narrative, as will be discussed in later chapters. While mass murders are also frequently used as instigating events that set up characters to then parcel out motive and deal with emotional and physical aftereffects, King does not always use mass murder this way. Part of the creation—and manipulation—of the horror is the subversion of reader expectations and the deliberate narrative moves meant to keep readers guessing.

NARRATIVE FUNCTION

There are three general points in the plot in which King introduces these deaths, and this book organizes discussions around these locations. Moving chronologically through a plot, the deaths are generally not included in the exposition. However long or short this section might be, it introduces the reader to the world before the horror occurs. In most of King's works, this world is meant to be recognizable as "the real world" in which we currently live, and readers are expected to make these associations and connections.[6] The horror ensues when the natural, anticipated order of things is subverted.

The location of the horror matters to the story, since "plot sequences fall into a hierarchy"[7] dictated by generic convention. Readers who come to generic texts have expectations of what those texts will offer and how the narrative will be constructed. At times King follows the more common generic constructions of horror, but at others he subverts these conventions. Indeed, Jerome Bruner argues that "a tale must be about how an implicit canonical script has been breached, violated, or deviated from"[8] to be worth telling. King's varied uses of death within his plots allows him to explore the various narrative functions of what, at first blush, seems to be a single occurrence.

King makes full use of the fact that the structure of narrative itself "tends to establish a confusion between consecutiveness and consequence, between time sequence and logic."[9] Although he most frequently constructs his narratives chronologically, he completely controls the speed at which readers, characters, or both at the same time, uncover important information. These varied reveals play into the suspension/curiosity/surprise trio that Meir Sternberg deems the "three master functions"[10] of a narrative, allowing readers to know things before the characters themselves uncover them, or to wonder along with the characters, or to be completely blindsided by events or new information that neither they nor the characters anticipated. Although it is considered poor storytelling for characters to possess important information and be allowed to keep it from the reader through the narrative's construction, readers are frequently allowed knowledge that the main characters do not possess to lead to suspense: when will the characters discover it? And, of course: how many will suffer or die before this information is learned?

It is difficult, then, to speak of a single function of death within King's works because there is no one reason for his characters to die. It is easier to move chronologically through the narratives themselves to divide the deaths first by their location within the book and then to examine commonalities of similarly positioned deaths.

The first plot location where unnatural death makes an appearance is during the introduction of conflict. The death itself can be the inciting incident that directs the rest of the plot, as seen in chapter 1. The initial deaths set up the conflict that faces the main characters who spend the majority of the story attempting to restore order or correct the problems introduced by these deaths. These are unexpected deaths that have no instigation further back in history, unlike those in chapter 2. The horror of the deaths in chapter 2 comes in that they do not stand alone, but that they have happened before—and, unless the situation is drastically changed, will happen again. The threat is therefore not only to the lives of those who have died already within the plot and the others who might before the book is over, but also to future generations.

The second plot location for unnatural deaths in King's works is during the rising action, driving the characters toward the climax. This includes deaths like those in chapter 3, where the deaths themselves work to increase tension for the reader. The main characters do not have all the information that readers possess, and thus might not be aware of the dangers awaiting them in the future. Indeed, by simply knowing that this is a Stephen King book, readers have a better grasp on the threats and possibilities awaiting the characters who, outside of *The Dark Tower*, do not realize they are characters created by Sai King. Chapter 4 discusses the deaths that King uses as an author in order to reduce his cast of characters to a more manageable number. This is a technique that he has admitted to in *On Writing*, specifically referencing a plot element in *The Stand*, but his penchant for large-cast books means that this is not the only time he has drastically reduced his named characters before the climax of a book. Chapter 5 looks at the stories in which the main characters have been hesitating over what they should do next and are driven onward specifically because of a death or deaths within the plot. These are not deaths that warn the reader alone, but deaths that immediately influence the main characters' direction for the rest of the book.

The third place King frequently uses unnatural death is in the climax of the book itself. Chapter 6 addresses the deaths purposefully caused by the main characters to solve their problems. Whatever else has happened in the plot has driven them to use death as their solution, however temporary or problematic it might be. Part of this might involve the deaths in chapter 7, in which the supernatural threat's human sidekick must be eliminated prior to confronting the main threat. Unlike Dracula's human accomplice, the Renfields in King rarely feel an attack of conscience, and they are killed not by their masters but by the main characters. Aligning themselves with the threat to protect themselves from death in fact results in their own deaths. Chapter 8 also finds its roots in traditional narratives as good men—and at least one woman—die to save the others. These generally occur at the plot's climax, once again spurring the surviving main characters on to action, now in memory of their fallen comrades. Chapter 9 addresses the ways in which deaths must occur either at the climax or during the falling action for the resolution to properly take place. Any remaining threat needs to be addressed here so that order can be restored—although of course the horror is increased if, during the resolution, the threat is shown to still be active.

During the resolution itself, like in the exposition, death rarely, if ever, occurs. The most horrific event is an indication that the threat has not in fact been defeated and that the danger might come again. The horror of the resolution in King is not death itself, but the lingering possibility of future deaths.

The conclusion reviews this cavalcade of death to highlight the complexities of what, at first blush, seems to be a single plot point. Whether King is following or subverting generic expectations for horror, the character deaths he writes are rarely chosen to simply rid the book of a character who has outlived their use for the author. Deaths are more frequently important events meant to drive the plot forward in some way, but even those ways are many.

Death, especially unnatural death, is horrific and a staple of the genre, but it loses its punch and meaning if the deaths are not purposeful within the plot. King, the Master of Horror, uses death in multiple ways and in different elements of his plots to serve several distinct narrative purposes. This is not to say that there is absolutely no senseless death in King, or that he always has high literary reasoning for killing off a character, but rather that unnatural death in and of itself has a complicated function within his stories. King uses unnatural death in ways that both align with and subvert reader expectations, all in the name of creating horror and continuing to poke at death. As he has observed, "we make up horrors to help us cope with the real ones,"[11] and death is the most universal horror.

NOTES

1. Stephen King, *Danse Macabre* (New York: Berkley Books, 1983), 198.
2. Stephen King, *Pet Sematary* (New York: Pocket Books, 1983), 216.
3. King, *Danse Macabre*, 197.
4. Stephen King, *The Stand* (New York: Anchor Books, 1990), 117.
5. Peter Vronsky, *Sons of Cain: A History of Serial Killers from the Stone Age to the Present* (New York: Berkley, 2019), 19.

6. Peter Lamarque and Stein Haugam Olsen, *Truth, Fiction, and Literature: A Philosophical Perspective* (Oxford: Clarendon Press, 1994), 337.

7. Meir Sternberg, "Telling in Time (II): Chronology, Narrative, Teleology," *Poetics Today* 13, no. 3. (1992): 476.

8. Jerome Bruner, "The Narrative Construction of Reality," *Critical Inquiry* 18, no. 1 (1991): 11.

9. Roland Barthes, *Pleasure of the Text* (New York: Hill and Wang, 1975), 251.

10. Sternberg, "Telling in Time (II)," 534.

11. King, *Danse Macabre*, 13.

Chapter One

"It's Not Really Her Anymore"
Creating the Threat

Death in Stephen King's works is present at, or even before, the beginning of his stories. Characters face not simply impending death but are threatened by the long dead—or undead. It does not take mass murder, or even the murder of a famous figure, to affect King's characters, since "even one person's breach of morality can affect the lives of an entire city or nation."[1] It is possible for a single death to have an impact even generations after the death occurred so that King's characters have fallen out of touch with the history that has led to the events within the plot.

These long—or even recently—dead might be vampires in *'Salem's Lot*; ghosts haunting either the Overlook Hotel in Colorado or Duma Key in Florida; or a malevolent spirit seeking revenge along family lines in Maine. In these situations, the main characters must learn about the circumstances surrounding the deaths to combat the threat against their own lives. They played no personal role in these characters' deaths but are forced to face the consequences all the same.

Other early deaths occur in the opening scenes or chapters of King's work and set up the main characters to face the consequences, whether or not they themselves played a role in those deaths. Jessie Burlingame of *Gerald's Game* and Morris Bellamy of *Finders Keepers* are more active than most, causing a death and committing murder within the opening scene. Each must then deal with the consequences of the death caused, Jessie much more quickly than Bellamy, in attempts to save both their lives and their original life goals.

The deaths that take place early in Luke's plot arc in *The Institute* and before Red meets Andy Dufresne in "Rita Hayworth and Shawshank Redemption" were not caused by the main characters but put them in dire straits all the same. Luke's parents were murdered during his kidnapping, making him a person of suspicion should he ever escape his kidnappers, and Andy Dufresne ends up in prison with Red after being convicted for the double murder of his wife and her lover. Both Luke and Dufresne face the challenge of surviving, and then escaping, imprisonment, clinging to their own basic innocence.

In contrast to these openings where the main characters encounter death either accidentally or as a twist of fate, the four boys in "The Body" purposefully decide to seek out a dead body, "taking a significant step toward maturity in searching for a first exposure to death."[2] Perhaps King's adult characters have already encountered death, or perhaps the suspense of knowingly moving toward another's death is increased when the characters themselves are young and innocent, but the boys in "The Body" are prime examples of King's child characters expressing simple curiosity about death.

Yet another character stumbles upon a long-dead ghost haunting a bathroom in "Sneakers," undergoing his own maturation process in spite of already legally being an adult. Others, as a group, encounter the sudden disappearance and presumed death of almost all of the passengers on their red-eye flight in "The Langoliers." Although these characters were not the cause of these deaths, and any lingering spirits do not seem to want to do them harm, they have to learn from them in order to move forward with their lives in a meaningful way.

FACING THE ALREADY DEAD

'Salem's Lot, King's second published novel, focuses on a small town in Maine undergoing a twentieth-century vampire invasion. The vampire himself, Kurt Barlow, is not only already undead before the novel begins, but "is a personification of the fundamental unrepresentable Gothic horror, death."[3] This real-life vampire follows many rules and restrictions present in narratives of fictional vampires, including the need to feed on human blood, thereby creating more vampires. It is not just Barlow's presence, but so many characters' insistence on "common sense explanations"[4] for the strange happenings within the town, that lead to so many deaths—or perhaps undeaths.

The first to die, suffering a true death, is in fact a dog found hanging on the cemetery gates. *'Salem's Lot* thus subverts the usual "hierarchy of death"[5] by making the first occurrence so distant and impersonal. Although the violent death of an animal is sad and disturbing in an abstract way, the dog was not known to the book's central characters. As the story continues and the deaths continue, they move ever closer to the circle of the book's heroes. It would be impossible for everyone to stay safe in a town where each night means a growth of the vampire population.

As in so many of King's books, Barlow's identity as a supernatural creature helps him increase the amount of damage he can spread. Although Susan Norton is a central character who has been present for discussions of vampires, she refuses to accept this explanation for what is happening to her hometown. Instead of relying on the others for help or even safety in numbers, she strikes out on her own, carrying only a flimsy wooden picket as a nod to the vampire theory. She may as well have gone completely unprepared, considering how quickly she is taken prisoner and "metamorphoses from a sweetly inept helpmate to an equally inept vampire"[6] when Barlow finds her after dark. Instead of assisting the book's central heroes, the now-undead Susan must be staked through the heart and become another obstacle on their way to victory.

Susan dies because of her lack of belief in the supernatural, but even full acceptance is no guarantee of survival. Jimmy Cody, a local physician, shows a much greater capacity for belief than even the book's resident writer, but Cody does not live to see the last page. Knowing that Barlow's inhuman helper has been dispatched, Cody puts too much stock in the idea that vampires are helpless and unguarded during the daytime. He literally falls into a passive trap set by the town's vampires to prevent any of the vampire hunters from finding Barlow's new hiding place. By concentrating on the fact that vampires cannot be out in the sunlight, Cody failed to consider any nonhuman forms of protection they might have put in place.

While Susan's death weakens the central group largely because of emotional attachments, Cody's is a blow because of his actual usefulness in combating the bloodsucking threat to the town. As Tony Magistrale points out, the central characters are battling not only Barlow, but the "mega character"[7] of the town itself. Only this small group is at all prepared or willing to fight back against this newest invasion, and the vampires manage to pick them off one by one, making their circle even smaller. Although the Lot is threatened by the undead figure that has so recently arrived, it was already crumbling from the inside and therefore made a perfect location for Barlow's infiltration.

The supernatural element in *The Shining* is also clearly associated with a location—the Overlook Hotel—but the danger is not a general threat to all mortals who visit, unlike the vampire-infested Lot. The Overlook wants young Danny Torrance specifically because he "shines" with a psychic power, and the hotel has multiple methods to secure him. Although one of those methods involves using Danny's living father against him, many of the threats within the Overlook are people who have died there, generally through suicide.

The situation in Colorado is different from the one in *'Salem's Lot* because the Lot is overrun with vampires: a threat that can be found in books on a library shelf. There is a name for what is happening in the Lot, although one associated with myth and legend and therefore removed from reality. The Overlook, on the other hand, is more nebulous and difficult to name. There is simply some sort of force that preys on the shining and can manipulate people like Delbert Grady and Jack Torrance into murder. The threat is not something that has come from the outside and descended on the place but rather, the hotel "literally is the protagonist"[8] of this narrative. The place and the threat are one.

Jack is not vulnerable because of his refusal to believe, the way Susan Norton was, but rather because of his damaged self-image. Through his alcoholism and his anger, Jack has lost many of the aspects of his life that he considered to be key to his worth: he has been unable to finish writing his play or publish much recently, and he lost his job at a New England prep school. His position as winter caretaker at the Overlook came about thanks to a favor done by one of his old drinking buddies, and this is Jack's last chance to make something of himself. If for whatever reason he cannot keep the job, he would have to send Wendy and Danny to live with her mother and see himself as a failure in all aspects of his life.

The Overlook preys on Jack's desires both to write something serious and to lash out at the world that has done so much looking down its nose at him. When he discovers that the hotel's basement is full of old documents, most in boxes and some neatly organized into a scrapbook, he dreams of writing a tell-all about the Overlook revealing the seedier deaths and goings-on from its past. In Jack's mind, the Hotel has chosen him to be its biographer, placing him high in a position of honor and making him "an intimate and integral part of the Overlook's ongoing history."[9] Jack wants to feel special and have his genius and talents recognized, and the force powering the Overlook is more than willing to play to his vanity so that it can get inside him and use him to kill Danny, because the undead prove to be unable to complete this task.

The threat from the Overlook, unlike the danger in *'Salem's Lot*, does not come solely from the previous deaths. The hotel can use inanimate objects—the hedge creatures, the fire hose, and the clock, to name a few—to scare or intimidate its guests. Danny and Jack are the main focus of these moments, not all of which are attacks, and Danny especially quickly divides the Overlook and its grounds into areas that are "safe" and "not safe."

Even though he is so young, Danny is the first one to grasp the danger of their situation. Because of the shining, though, he knows how important this job is to his daddy, and even if he could have convinced Wendy to take him away, he waits too long and the three Torrances get snowed in. Jack is blinded to the danger, again due to his alcoholism, anger, and issues of self-image. Wendy sees the least of the supernatural events within the hotel and is personally only threatened by the still-living Jack. Although she can see some of the remnants of one of the long-ago parties on a night when the elevator runs itself, proving that at least some of the Overlook's actions are real and not induced hallucinations, she does not see—or get threatened by—any of the ghosts. For nearly too long, Wendy believes that the only threat to Danny is his own father. Like Susan Norton, she clings to the known world, although Wendy certainly has her reasons. She knows that Jack could hurt Danny in his anger because he has hurt Danny in the past.

Wendy, as has been pointed out previously, is a largely passive abused wife who could not bring herself to leave her husband even after Jack broke Danny's arm. Both Wendy and Jack candidly admit this event to Danny's pediatrician early in the book, agreeing that they had danced around the idea of divorce but are now on better terms. This scene both demonstrates the power of Danny's shine and, coming in that moment, is meant to show the optimism of Jack's trajectory: although he lost his teaching job, there is still the potential of the winter at the Overlook to be just what he needs to complete his play, and his wife is still at his side and once again in love with him. Despite the events of the past, "there is still a glimmer of hope"[10] for the family's future.

This potential is necessary for the full horror of the situation to be realized, although nothing can be done to save Jack. Once the narrative has begun, everything is in place "to pull the characters along"[11] toward their predetermined end. Isolated in the Overlook Hotel, the Torrances are doomed to endure what the lingering spirits have in store for them, and their survival is not guaranteed.

The threat in *Duma Key* is more in line with the Overlook Hotel than the Lot's vampires, because there is no established mythos attached to the undead. Edgar Freemantle, lately of St. Paul, Minnesota, left his former life as a building contractor after an accident on a job site. He lost both his arm and his marriage, because the long-term results of his head injury included violent mood swings. Edgar, like Jack, must contend with a violent temper.

And Edgar, like Jack, leaves his old life behind to relocate. Rather than a possessed hotel, Edgar chooses to take his geographical cure on a Florida island called Duma Key. During his first night in his rented house, he sees—and sketches—a ship out on the Gulf. It is his first look at what he comes to learn is the ship of the dead, but far from his last. That ship, run by an entity called "Perse," is responsible for Edgar's incredible artistic output. Indeed, John Sears argues that *Duma Key* presents a "theory of artistic inspiration as a form of possession by the dead."[12]

It is never entirely explained what Perse is, although her physical representation is of a china doll, and she has control over the people nearby. If any of those people show artistic talent, she uses them through their paintings and drawings. Those artworks, as Edgar learns after a night of automatic painting, can literally kill. In her previous bid for power, Perse used her artist in order to kill others to join Perse's ship of the dead. Those killed by Perse rise again and threaten Edgar.

Unlike in *'Salem's Lot*, these risen undead are not the overarching threat in and of themselves. They are not mindlessly feeding, but specifically targeting Edgar because of his talent on behalf of Perse. In this they are more in line with the undead from *The Shining*, who worked under the influence of the Overlook to fulfill the whims of a higher power. While the Overlook wanted Danny and was just playing with Jack to get to his son, it seems that Perse specifically wants Edgar—and she is not above using his love for his daughter against him. Perse manages to use one of Edgar's paintings to influence its new owner to kill Ilse Freemantle, Edgar's favorite daughter, and therefore induce him, in his grief, to draw his now-dead daughter on the beach.

After Perse's defeat seems certain, this sand Ilse rises to tempt her father to join Perse's ship of the dead. Edgar is forced to confront not only the reality of his daughter's murder but also his own role in it and his current precarious situation. Any hope of reconciliation with his ex-wife is now gone, since she, like Edgar, blames him for Ilse's death. Edgar had up until then managed to avoid being press-ganged into joining the ship of the dead, but in his tight focus on the issue at hand he, like Jimmy Cody, overlooked a fatal detail. The horror in these in-text deaths is that, by focusing on the pre-narrative dead, these characters have caused preventable deaths and have opened new ways of being threatened.

A further parallel with *The Shining* comes when the stories of the undead must be told through documents from the past because, while libraries may have sections devoted to the vampire mythos, the threat here is local and distinct. Some of these are newspaper articles, such as when Edgar's friend discovers the headline declaring Elizabeth's older twin sisters "ARE GONE."[13] The other important documents are little Libbet's drawings, which speak to Edgar much in the way the old receipts in the Overlook's basement enchanted Jack. These documents from the past, especially those from before the important pre-narrative deaths, provide key information for the readers, even if the main characters do not recognize their value. Jack, for example, has his own reasons to ignore any possible threat coming from the Overlook, while Edgar is content to ride out the mystery of his newfound talent and not question it. They are not the only characters to turn a blind eye to the danger that accompanies their perceived benefits.

Bag of Bones shifts the original threat further, making it both more and therefore somehow less human. Like Perse, the threat itself can be named, but unlike the strange china doll—or possibly goddess—the family curse plaguing author Mike Noonan originated with the murder of a human woman. On the day when a group of young men gang-raped Sara Tidwell, they also drowned her son and then murdered her. Since then, the descendants of those men have been forced to drown some of their own children after ritualistically dressing those children in the colors Sara herself had been wearing that day:

red and white. The theme is not that people can be possessed before or after death to become monsters, but that "monsters live inside ordinary people."[14] After Sara's murder, whatever remained of her—her spirit or soul—was able to open itself to embrace something monstrous.

The tension of information shared and withheld comes in the way "King structures the novel by carefully controlling the flow of information to the reader."[15] Mike's late wife Jo, whose death opens the book, apparently had a wealth of information, but she died before revealing it to her husband. When Mike finally starts trying to uncover what his wife knew, he is blocked not only by the reticence of the locals living on TR-90, but the years that have passed since Jo's research. Because she kept it such a secret, and because Jo's memory is still painful to him, Mike's attempts at uncovering what really happened to Sara proceed only in fits and starts.

Here the deaths are tied to a location, Dark Score Lake, in large part because the family lines have remained in the same town. Sara's strength is greatest at the lake, since both she and her son ended up buried at its edge, near the house Mike now owns. When Jo Noonan began to uncover this, she stopped suggesting that they go to the lake house. Her fear of the family curse was so great that she did not tell Mike that she finally suspected she might be pregnant.

Mike does not face the issue of needing to convince other people that this supernatural danger is real. Many of the other descendants, and even people who simply live in the same town, understand that *something* is going on, and that they should not meddle with it. Although they might not know the full story, they understand that something is "revisiting the sins of the fathers on their children,"[16] and they do not want to make the situation worse. They have lived near the lake their entire lives and they know what must be done.

It is Mike himself who needs convincing of the supernatural truth. Jo did not tell him what she had discovered because she feared that he would not listen to her. Part of it was Mike's involvement with his writing at the time she uncovered the curse, but part of it places Mike in the same position as Ben Mears: the authors, used to creating whole worlds out of their heads, are most stubborn about accepting such unscientific or inexplicable elements in real life.

Mike falls here into the same categories as the Torrance family and Edgar Fremantle in that there is no solid mythos on which he can draw to either identify or destroy the threat. He cannot explain the situation to someone else using a single word like "vampire," and he has no way of knowing what might repel or destroy the threat. His guidance comes through several disturbing dreams, some of which are more like visions, and the messages Jo manages to sneak him. It takes Mike a while to decode them, but he gets there eventually.

Bag of Bones presents readers with a combination of deaths at the beginning of the narrative. Sara's death long before Mike's birth lays the groundwork for the overarching threat of the family curse. Jo's death, in chapter 1, sets Mike up with a number of more immediate personal challenges.

In these books, King presents his characters with a threat based on deaths that occurred long before the events of the narrative. These dead, or somehow undead, people threaten the lives and mental stability of the main characters, although the protagonists may or may not have known them in life. The original deaths are not witnessed in "real time," and are shown only through flashbacks or visions if experienced at all. There is another category of death early in the narrative, however, when the initial death is *part* of the main story and sets up the characters for their struggle.

DYING IN THE OPENING SCENES

In *Gerald's Game*, it is the death of Gerald Burlingame that puts his wife in her own tight place. Dead of a heart attack by the end of chapter 1, Gerald has handcuffed Jessie to the headboard of the bed in their lake home, using police-grade handcuffs and leaving the keys far out of her reach. In a sex game gone wrong, it is the unbound man who dies, but Jessie's prospects are dim. She is very nearly crucified in that position, unable to extract her hands, free the other ends of the cuffs, or alert anyone to her predicament. It is a "modernized"[17] Gothic scenario of the trapped woman, but the husband who terrorized her is now dead and her prison is the bed itself instead of the entire house.

Jessie is therefore in physical danger of dying of thirst or perhaps suffocating because of her position. Stuck with only herself and the voices inside her head, she is also in danger of her own thoughts and memories, long suppressed, having to do with sex, shame, and the men in her life. Present-day Jessie remains tethered to that bed while her thoughts take her down the darkest parts of memory lane, until she concludes that she is indeed desperate enough to break the water glass, slit her wrist for the lubricating blood, and nearly de-glove one of her hands so she can escape. By that point she is in such a state that she believes she has hallucinated the sole human intruder into their lake house.

None of this would have happened had Gerald lived. His death was not a happenstance heart attack, but rather the result of Jessie's own actions. After being handcuffed to the bed, Jessie realized that she did not in fact want to engage in this sex play. At first Gerald treated her protests like they were part of a game but, after she realized that he knew exactly what she meant and intended on having sex with her anyway, she kicked him in the stomach and the groin. He managed to gasp one word—"heart"[18]—before falling off the bed and dying. If Jessie had not kicked him—if she had submitted to marital rape—then she would not have been trapped by the handcuffs. In this moment, though, Jessie "refuses to be victimized"[19] by her husband and ends up putting herself through a longer ordeal.

Gerald's death, unintentionally caused by Jessie, leaves her stranded and desperate to the point where she opts for potential suicide by exsanguination and a pages-long description of how her flesh peels back from her hand as she frees herself. She needs the entire book of being stuck on that bed, alone with her thoughts and all the voices inside of her head, to reach the point where she is inventive and brave enough to attempt it. Had Gerald not died, the story would have gone in a vastly different direction, and Jessie might have been allowed to leave her past unexamined.

A similar early death sets the stage for *Finders Keepers*, the second novel in the Bill Hodges trilogy, although this one is intentional murder. Morris Bellamy, one of King's fanatic number one fans, leads a break-in at the house of reclusive author John Rothstein that was meant to be a robbery but turned into murder. As George Beahm points out, "[t]his would normally be the end of any story,"[20] but the book is not in fact about Rothstein. It centers around fan obsession instead of the author character, and Bellamy's story picks up decades later concerning Rothstein's unpublished works instead of Rothstein himself.

Unlike Jessie Burlingame, Bellamy could not have reasonably avoided this entire run of events if he had kept himself from murder. The length of time covered by his narrative is measured in decades instead of days and involves far more people. Even if Bellamy had left Rothstein alive, he still found himself in prison shortly after burying the trunk of stolen goods, which meant protagonist Peter Saubers could still have discovered it later. The used-book seller would not have been able to hold murder over Bellamy's head—and *he* might have survived, as well—but, as soon as the notebooks were stolen and buried, there was the danger of someone else finding them. Rothstein's death adds a further complication, but it seems more incidental to the instigating moment rather than being the sole cause of the plot's conflict.

The deaths at the beginning of Luke Ellis's storyline in *The Institute* are integral to the plot and therefore drive Luke's actions for several reasons. When teams from the Institute go out to kidnap telekinetic or telepathic children, they murder anyone else in the house as a matter of course. The children are told that their families are fine and waiting for them, and that they will be returned home after their memories have been wiped, able to resume their normal lives. While most children, young and scared, at least pretend to accept this story, Luke is a genius and sees through this lie immediately as being highly improbable.

Luke suspects that his parents must be dead, but he does not seek to confirm this for himself immediately. Although he discovers a way around the internet blocks put on the laptop the Institute gives him, and although he realizes that they might discover this deception at any moment, it takes Luke a long time to convince himself to check his hometown newspapers. Although he *suspects* that his parents must be dead, he knows the value of hope and does not want to verify it. When Luke does finally read the headlines for himself, confirming both his parents' deaths and his own position as suspect, this knowledge helps him make up his mind to escape the Institute and reveal it to the world. By controlling the flow of information, King allows the Ellises' murders to occur twice within the plot: first for the readers, who witness them as they happen, and again later for Luke himself, giving their deaths a second function of spurring him on to action.

RESPONDING TO DEATH IN A SHORTER FORMAT

Although novels allow King's characters more time to react to substantial deaths that occur either before the narrative begins or in the opening scenes, his short stories and novellas also pit his characters against these instigating forces. Like his novels, they run the gamut from being realistic to dealing with the supernatural, giving a wide array of reactions and emotions in addressing these early deaths. While his characters must determine the meanings of those deaths more quickly than in his novels, their relationships with those deaths are no less complicated for the shorter word count.

"Rita Hayworth and Shawshank Redemption" is the story of Andy Dufresne's imprisonment for the murder of his wife and her lover. The double murder is what lands Andy in Shawshank Prison in the first place and makes his path cross with the narrator's. Red chronicles Andy's stay in prison, gradually befriending him and coming around to the conclusion that Andy's protestations of innocence are truthful. His wife and her lover were murdered by someone else, but Andy was the one put on trial and the one sentenced for their deaths.

The novella is a story of an unjustly imprisoned man fighting first to survive and then to escape. The double murder, committed before Red met Andy and long before he began writing this story, is the root cause of all narrative events. While the murder in Red's past is one for which he was indeed responsible, adding a layer of growth and change as Red's orientation to his past shifts, the fact of Andy's innocence not only allows others to root for his escape, but provides Andy with the motivation to maintain both his sanity and his calm in the meantime.

The pre-narrative death in "The Body" likewise was not caused by the main characters, but the body of the boy who had gotten lost in the woods and was hit by a train becomes a site of contention between narrator Gordie and his friends and the local bullies. Each friend group had the idea of being the ones to "discover" the dead boy, and Gordie's group, being younger, set off on foot on a multiday journey to see their first dead body. The boys view it as an adventure and a part of growing up, and as an adult recalling the journey, Gordie outlines the divisions within their friendships and the way in which their lives will soon diverge.

Unlike Andy Dufresne, the boys are adventuring toward a death instead of attempting to deal with the legal consequences following one. Although Gordie has a relatively happy ending, the way Andy is assumed to after his escape, the other boys meet untimely deaths between the date of the walk and when Gordie sits down to write about it. "The Body" takes place over a matter of days and descriptions of what happened to the boys after they found it and confronted the bullies come as part of the falling action, rather than the way "Rita Hayworth and Shawshank Redemption" focuses entirely on the consequences of the deaths. The boys' approach to, and fascination with, death is markedly different from the way Andy was described as being cold and distant, both at his trial and while in prison.

King's short story "Sneakers" also focuses more on the journey toward understanding a pre-narrative death than dealing with the aftermath. John Tell slowly comes to realize that the sneakers he has seen in the third-floor men's room of a recording studio belong to a man who was murdered decades previously. At first terrified at the thought of seeing a ghost, he eventually learns that the famous producer he has been idolizing was in fact that man's murderer. Although Tell had been feeling increasingly ambivalent about the producer after being on the receiving end of a sexual pass, this understanding allows Tell to act instead of simply reacting and to quit his job.

Older than the boys in "The Body," Tell's overall confrontation is not necessarily with death but with the complexities and flaws of people who are generally revered. All the same, Tell, too, grows and matures because of his interaction with this death. One of his coworkers, a man who will leave the room during confrontations and cannot say a bad word against the producer without stuttering, can explain the sneakers but does not understand them on the same level as Tell. While Tell leaves his job, striking out into the unknown with even less of a plan than Andy Dufresne escaping from prison, the other man simply stays.

In these three examples, the killings, whether in the form of bodies or a ghost, create the central tension as the characters react to the various forms of death and the immediate consequences of those deaths. In "The Langoliers," the deaths that occur at the start of the novella are shocking and horrific, but not the central conflict facing the surviving members of Flight 29. Although the central characters awake in chapter 1 to discover that the other people on the plane have disappeared, their main concern is surviving in the strange new world awaiting them when they land. Only when they manage to refuel the plane for the return flight do they have to consider the meaning of those disappearances, leading to a situation discussed here in chapter 8.

These characters are not going to be arrested for murder, and there are no bodies or ghosts to see, fight over, or reveal dark pasts. The disappearances—and suspected deaths—of the other passengers are a side effect of the main threat, instead of being the threat itself. They have to deal with the meaning of the deaths in a way closer in line with John Tell's relationship with the mysterious sneakers, piecing together what this strange occurrence means for them in their own continued lives. It is a striking scene of mass death without the gore, made all the more suspenseful by the fact that the protagonists awake mid-flight without pilots or crew. These initial deaths are, however, shunted aside in the face of the dangers and strangeness they find upon landing, and only come to the forefront again when they are just shy of returning to their own world and time and restoring order.

ONLY THE BEGINNING

Deaths that occur before the story starts are generally more likely to be the direct cause of deaths within the story itself, while deaths shown during the opening chapters tend more toward setting the main characters up for future challenges. The Overlook's ghosts, the vampire Kurt Barlow, Perse and those who work on the ship of the dead, and Sara Tidwell with her curse on the families all present the main characters with a threat because of previous death. The Overlook, Perse, and Sara Tidwell want to kill certain people because they are, in their own way, special. This will increase their power. Barlow is not looking to kill people, but rather to turn them into the undead and thereby spread the threat through numerous hungry new vampires. The dead here are the threat, and in some cases "no real peaceful resolution is possible."[21] Destruction is optimal, but sometimes the threat endures.

When a death occurs early on in a character's story, then that death sets up problems for the main character later. It is not ghosts, however, that threaten Jessie Burlingame, Peter Saubers, Luke Ellis, Andy Dufresne, the boys of "The Body," or the survivors of "The Langoliers," even if this final threat is indeed in some way supernatural. Although Jessie must do battle with her own thoughts and memories to overcome her manacled dilemma after her husband's death, Peter, Luke, Andy, and Gordie and his friends are facing very human foes outside of themselves. Bellamy is out to kill Peter because of how much he risked—and how many people he killed—for the contents of that trunk, while Luke's parents were merely collateral damage as part of the workings of the Institute. Andy must survive prison, Gordie's group has to face local bullies, and the survivors of the red-eye flight have to contend with the new world in which their plane lands. John Tell of "Sneakers" finds himself facing a ghost, but this is not an Overlook ghost or one of Perse's slaves. The ghost appears to teach him something and push him toward a new level of understanding, but not to threaten him.

By and large, the characters dealing with these early deaths are adults, or groups in which children can follow the leadership and example of adults. The outlier here is "The Body," in which Tony Magistrale points out that "King implies that for children the mystery of death is even more complicated than it is for adults, for in their confusion and innocence children often assume a measure of personal responsibility."[22] Part of this complication comes in the boys' conscious decision to seek out death—again, the death of another and not their own—and part comes through their isolation from others, specifically adult others. The groups in *'Salem's Lot* and "The Langoliers" include a child, but in each case a remarkable child capable not only of learning from adults, but also of teaching them. The boys in "The Body" only have each other and therefore make their own decision to journey toward death and their own maturity without consulting, or seeking help from, grown-ups.

These early deaths differ, though, from deaths that happen in the beginning of the narrative but are part of a series. Although some of the already mentioned deaths cause a series through a long-running curse or sense of vengeance, they do not perform the same function as early deaths that are themselves a part or continuation of a series. These are the subject of the next chapter.

NOTES

1. Jonathon P. Davis, *Stephen King's America* (Bowling Green, OH: Bowling Green State University Popular Press, 1994), 47.

2. Davis, *Stephen King's America*, 55.

3. John Sears, *Stephen King's Gothic* (Cardiff, University of Wales Press, 2011), 197.

4. Joseph Reino, *Stephen King: The First Decade,* Carrie *to* Pet Sematary (Boston: Twayne Publishers, 1988), 7.

5. James E. Hicks, "Stephen King's Creation of Horror in *'Salem's Lot*: A Prolegomenon Towards a New Hermeneutic of the Gothic Novel," *The Gothic World*

of Stephen King: Landscape of Nightmares (Bowling Green, OH: Bowling Green State University Popular Press, 1987), 78.

6. Mary Pharr, "Partners in the Danse: Women in Stephen King's Fiction," *The Dark Descent: Essays Defining Stephen King's Horrorscape* (New York: Greenwood Press, 1992), 23.

7. Tony Magistrale, *Stephen King: The Second Decade, Danse Macabre to the Dark Half* (New York: Twayne Publishers, 1992), 82.

8. Heidi Strengell, *Dissecting Stephen King, From the Gothic to Literary Naturalism* (Madison: The University of Wisconsin Press, 2005), 88.

9. Magistrale, *Stephen King: America's Storyteller* (Santa Barbara: Praeger, 2010), 112.

10. Davis, *Stephen King's America*, 26.

11. Sharon A. Russell, *Stephen King: A Critical Companion* (Westport, CT: Greenwood Press, 1996), 48.

12. Sears, *Stephen King's Gothic*, 224.

13. Stephen King, *Duma Key* (New York: Pocket Books, 2008), 171.

14. Strengell, *Dissecting Stephen King*, 92.

15. Sharon A. Russell, *Revisiting Stephen King: A Critical Companion* (Westport, CT: Greenwood Press, 2002), 93.

16. Strengell, *Dissecting Stephen King*, 88.

17. Strengell, *Dissecting Stephen King*, 48.

18. Stephen King, *Gerald's Game* (New York: Signet Books, 1992), 37.

19. Kimberly Beal, "Monsters at Home: Representations of Domestic and Sexual Abuse in *Gerald's Game*, *Dolores Claiborne*, and *Rose Madder*," *The Modern Stephen King Canon: Beyond Horror* (Lanham, MD: Lexington Books, 2019), 67.

20. Beahm, *The Stephen King Companion: Four Decades of Fear from the Master of Horror* (New York: Thomas Dunne Books, 2015), 451.

21. Russell, *Revisiting Stephen King*, 95.

22. Magistrale, *Stephen King: The Second Decade, Danse Macabre to the Dark Half*, 92.

Chapter Two
"You Know About the Cycle?"
To Perpetuate the Monster

The deaths discussed in this chapter are themselves part of a series—that is, the killers discussed would likely be labeled as serial killers, were they human. The FBI's definition of "serial killer" has changed since the term was first publicized in the 1970s, but generally refers to multiple murders enacted by the same person, spread out over time and place so that the killer can return to "normal" life between events.[1] Supernatural creatures do not exactly have a "normal" life to which they can return, but King has multiple examples of nonhuman serial killers with their own agendas for serial murder who "consciously decide to kill presumably lesser beings for not just nourishment but also for pleasure."[2]

Because these deaths are part of a series, and often also part of a cycle, some have usually occurred before the story even begins. Frequently one of these murders stands out and marks the start of the narrative. While it is only one of many, there is something about the death to distinguish it from the others. It has a personal impact on the novel's main characters and draws them to not only identify the killer, but also to connect it to previous murders. Even though others within the narrative may not see these connections, it is up to the main characters to recognize that the threat is in fact serial and that the monster they face has done this before. This makes the antagonist more dangerous, since it has clearly already figured out how to continue its cycle, and because the main characters must then realize that the monster has no plans to stop. If they are unable to identify it, and kill it, more and more people will die.

Here, "King's trust in close-knit communities"[3] emerges again and again as groups unite to confront, and hopefully defeat, these creatures. Such dangers should not be faced alone. In *It*, "The Library Policeman," *The Outsider*, *Doctor Sleep*, *The Long Walk*, and *The Institute*, groups of people either gather or are thrown together to rely on each other for support during their ordeal. The two cases where a single person attempts to confront the danger alone—"N." and "Bad Little Kid"—do not end in triumph. Rather, instead of defeating the evil, each individual seems only capable of passing on knowledge of the threat and, therefore, the threat itself.

This cycle of the monster allows for, and generally demands, a more in-depth backstory. Because this creature is not now, and perhaps never was, human, its origins must be explored and understood so that the main characters can identify its weaknesses and figure out how best to confront it. Readers are often privy to much more information than the main characters, and therefore more fully aware of the dangers the main characters face, especially if they approach the monster believing it to be merely human. This creates suspense as readers work with more information than the protagonists have uncovered and provides readers with an explanation for why the cycle must happen. These monsters, with their sequences of death, are merely here to feed.

SERIAL-KILLING CREATURES

King's most famous supernatural serial killer is arguably Pennywise the Dancing Clown, one of the names of "It." Derry, Maine, is one of King's fictional cities that is frequently revisited in subsequent novels and short stories. In *It*, we learn that Derry is different from other places. It seems to be filled with "greater levels of mayhem and violence"[4] than other cities of similar size and makeup. Gruesome acts of mass murder not only occur on an apparently regular basis in Derry but are also ignored with astonishing consistency. Something seems to urge Derry's citizens to either look the other way or even willingly participate when it comes to axe murder, shooting a couple of cars of outlaws in broad daylight, or setting fire to the only local speakeasy that will accept nonwhite patrons. Violent death enacted by one group of people on another, including children "facing the horrors created by adults,"[5] is apparently an open secret in Derry, as is the cycle.

The main characters in *It*—the seven members of the Losers' Club—first live through one of these dangerous cycles at age eleven in 1958. The town has enough recognition of the danger to its children to implement a curfew, and various members of the Losers are shown having conversations with their parents about being home in time for supper and making sure to never play alone. Multiple children have gone missing or been discovered dead in bizarre situations, and the parents give lip service to the threat while at the same time do not know where their children go or what they get up to during their long days of summer vacation.

The adults, including the chief of police, discuss the various murders and dismiss them as being the work of an itinerant bum or two, since "rationality prevents the adults from accessing the whole truth."[6] The murderer is certainly not an upstanding Derry citizen and thus has moved on, although there is always the possibility that another homicidal vagrant might decide to stop in Derry for a while. "Only the children are fully aware that there is something more sinister going on,"[7] and that the threat has not left Derry. In fact, the monster has been there since long before the town was first founded.

What the older citizens of Derry know, and what the Losers learn, is that the cycle of violence in Derry kicks into high gear every twenty-seven years with a particularly harsh stretch of violence and missing or murdered children that lasts at least fourteen months. The first cycle the Losers experience began in the fall of 1957 with the death of Georgie Denbrough. Taking the paper boat his big brother, Bill—leader of the Losers—made him, Georgie went out to sail it along the streets in the rain. He was discovered dead by a sewer grate with his arm pulled off. As the Losers discover, the cycle needs a particularly gruesome event to mark its beginning and another large slaughter to mark the end. Although these endpoint events might involve adults more than children, it is children who are Its "perfect victims."[8]

It opens with Georgie's death in 1957. Although the novel jumps around chronologically, at times covering the child Losers in 1958, the adult Losers in 1985, and reproducing segments of Mike Hanlon's research from the years in between, the next chronological event to be narrated is the last day of school in the summer of 1958. By that time other children have died, including at least one that some of the Losers knew personally. The curfew is in place, parents sign up to drive children home from evening activities, and the school bullies appear to be more of a threat than whatever is killing the children. For a town that seems to have a mad child murderer on the loose, Derry as a whole is rather calm and complacent. It has, of course, been through such things before.

Tony Magistrale suggests that Derry is willing to turn away from acts of violence because "the town must somehow compensate for its past moral transgressions by sacrificing a part of its future,"[9] but the relationship between Derry and the mysterious cycle goes deeper. When Bill Denbrough returns to Derry in 1985, his taxi ride across town allows him to see how Derry has flourished in the intervening decades. Traffic has increased greatly because of the number of banks that have sprung up, Derry has a large and popular mall, and Derry Home Hospital has grown up astonishingly to the point where Bill compares it to a college campus. Derry is not, in fact, suffering because of its relationship with the creature dwelling underneath the sewers. For the mere sacrifice of a handful of children every generation, Derry can thrive.

The children who disappear or are found dead during late 1957 and 1958 are thus not only part of a series relegated to those few months, but to a cycle that can be traced back for centuries. This is not a human serial killer, but an "evil which originates from outside"[10]—not just from outside the individuals, but from outside Earth itself. The creature variously known as Pennywise the Dancing Clown, Robert Gray, or simply It is in fact alien, and thus has a longer life span than any human. It wakes long enough to increase the violence in Derry and eat of the city's children, then sleeps until the next generation is born so It can start again.

Although Georgie's death opens the novel and begins a cycle, he is not the first but, in actuality, a continuation. Georgie's murder is followed in the narrative by that of Adrian Mellon in 1984. Mellon, like Georgie, was the casualty that began one of Its cycles. His place as the second narrated death is the first indication that there is indeed a cycle and suggests a connection between his death and Georgie's. The addition of a clown in each scenario—in the sewer grate where he pulled off Georgie's arm, or in the canal where he began to eat Mellon's flesh—strengthens this connection. By this point, though, readers understand that, while Mellon might be the first in a new cycle, he is not *the* first. This could cause readers to question whether Georgie might not have been, either.

Mike Hanlon later points out to the others that, although Adrian Mellon is legally an adult, he was in fact a very *childlike* adult. King "never fully explains why the children of Derry are Pennywise's primary prey,"[11] but speculation is given that states it is a child's imagination—and a child's ability to sum up fear in a single image—that leads to this focus. Each of the Losers can recount their first encounter with It and the specific, curated form It took at the time, and King even shows It killing two other children under different guises. Many of these images are drawn from the movies: the mummy, the creature from the Black Lagoon, and the teenage werewolf, for example, but others are more personalized. Eddie Corcoran and Bill Denbrough are both haunted by their dead little brothers, and Mike Hanlon's encounter with It as a large bird is explained to the reader as a latent memory from when Mike was just a tiny baby.

The fears of the children, then, are concentrated and summed up into a single form that It can assume to terrify them. Many of the children, like Adrian Mellon, were partially eaten, but It decides to terrorize them before killing them. This apparently adds to the flavor of Its meals, which are plentiful. Despite the curfew and the apparent parental concern, all the Losers and Its other child victims are alone at the time of their first encounters. These are not always at night, and not always in out-of-the-way places. Richie Tozier sees It take the form of the large plastic Paul Bunyan statue that is prominently displayed in town, and Ben Hanscom saw It on the canal on his way home from school. It seems that Derry conspires to isolate Its most likely prey, urging any nearby adults to turn away.

Karen Thoens goes further to argue that the mothers in the novel "mirror the monsters their children combat."[12] The mothers are distant, not stopping abuse from the fathers, or not realizing their children are in fact loners, or willingly increasing the disconnect between the generations because they feel they do not understand their children. The parents who truly care about their children move away from Derry when the cycle ramps up again, but the Losers—and the dead children—have parents who are complacent and only ask their children to be back by dinner. By the time any of the mothers would be calling the police, their children could be long dead.

Derry, then, does not wish to rid itself of It. Instead, the town aids and abets the monster living beneath it, in exchange for the success Pennywise seems to offer. Those who help It can prosper. Even the six Losers who eventually left Derry have all become successful in their chosen careers, very young in life. Only Mike Hanlon, who both defied It and then remained in Derry, does not benefit from Its power. Pennywise must understand in some way that It can be hurt, even before the Losers injure It in 1958, because It functions as a symbiote rather than a parasite. Instead of just feeding on Derry's children, It also offers the adults something in turn in order to keep the peace and allow them to continually look away.

The danger—and concern for the Losers, as well as the rest of Derry's children—increases throughout the novel as all of this is revealed. The Losers are threatened not only by this strange clown but also by school bullies, who act unchecked by adult authority. Their troubled relationships with their parents are revealed slowly, and Stan Uris's parents are never actually seen at all. The narrator reveals that the danger is not in fact from an itinerant murderer, as the adults of Derry conclude, but from something that lives within Derry . . . and, eventually, that Derry fully supports. The only adults shown standing up to It are the Losers. All others quite literally make themselves scarce when trouble approaches, increasing readers' fear for the children of Derry above and beyond what even the Losers might know.

Pennywise is not King's only early face-changing monster that feeds on children's fear before going into hibernation. Ardelia Lortz of "The Library Policeman" does not kill all the children she feeds on, but she does seem to need at least two murders to enter into her period of hibernation. Because the novella's heroes have little information to go on, they can only assume that Ardelia steals faces from known people, relocates to places those people have never lived, and sets up shop as the new librarian so she can terrify children during story hour. Like Pennywise, she is seen in the same small town before and just after her current hibernation, although the heroes theorize that she would leave Iowa as soon as she acquired her new identity. In this she has more in common with King's Outsider than It, although all of these creatures depend on their changing outward appearances to keep them supplied with terrified victims.

The Outsider—the titular figure of the 2018 novel—shares many similarities with Pennywise and Ardelia Lortz. This new menace can also change its face, although the Outsider does so by collecting DNA from people and then assuming their shape, down to their fingerprints. In this way, the Outsider makes victims of adults as well as children, taking on the guise of an unsuspecting adult to horrifically murder a child. The Outsider leaves forensic evidence at the scene of the crime, ensuring that the framed adult will quickly be identified, and feeds not only on the child's body, but on the emotions that swirl within the community during the ensuing investigation and trial.

The Outsider, unlike Pennywise, is not limited to a single location and in fact makes use of his changing appearance to travel between murders. He is suspected to have specifically chosen Terry Maitland as his next face while in Ohio because Maitland would be returning to Oklahoma. Thus, the similarities between child murders would not be noted—although, even if they had, the suspect in Ohio completed suicide and would not have been alive to kill Frankie Peterson. With the way the Outsider so clearly frames someone and the high death rate of the accused murderers, identifying the child murders as part of a series requires a supernatural explanation.

While Pennywise has the support of Derry's grown-ups in Its pursuit of sustenance, the Outsider also benefits from the worldview of the adults it encounters. Most of them are unlike returning King character Holly Gibney and therefore more like detective Ralph Anderson or lawyer Bill Samuels, willing to put their faith in scientific evidence and to dismiss anything that cannot be so proven. The forensic evidence, after all, was strong enough for Ralph to order Maitland's public arrest without even an initial interview or a query as to an alibi. The prosecution was *certain* they had their man, and the Outsider's habit of walking around and clearly showing another face, speaking to as many witnesses as possible, just cemented their identification. All of Flint City knows Coach T, so if multiple witnesses placed Maitland near the scene of the crime or in bloodstained clothes, then it had to be Terry Maitland they saw.

As this information is uncovered or presented by Holly, the suspense increases because of concerns for the Outsider's next adult victim, Claude Bolton. Maitland was an upstanding member of the community known for his work with children, and the crowds were still after his blood. Bolton, a bouncer at a strip club, is a former addict who has a record. If he were to be accused of any sort of crime, public reaction could be even more immediate and violent. Further, considering the Outsider's presumed modus operandi, a child would have to die to put Claude in danger. It is imperative that the team find the Outsider and kill him before he can continue his series of horrific murders.

The suspense is increased because, although the Constant Reader may agree with Holly's assessment that the child-killer is supernatural, the men, led by Ralph, are much more skeptical. The slow reveal of the way Frankie Peterson died, combined with the multiple deaths that follow his murder, all lead to anticipation and fear that the Outsider will strike again before Ralph can accept the possibility of its existence. Ralph already feels guilt over Terry Maitland's death at the hands of Frankie's older brother and the fact that he was the one who had to kill Ollie Peterson, and it is clear that he would also feel responsible for any future deaths that he should have been able to prevent.

Ralph's resistance mimics that of Loser Stan Uris and, in a similar way, threatens the protagonist groups' possibilities of success. Although all the Losers are terrified during their various engagements with It, Stan is the one who most resists the very *idea* of Its existence. Ralph needs to be fully on board before their group approaches the Outsider, and similar scenes take place between Holly and Ralph, and Bill and Stan, as each leader argues that, if the doubtful member of the group refuses to believe, then all is lost. Ralph and Stan can accept the belief and drop the conditional, at least for the initial moment of confrontation. When faced with the return of the monster, Stan chooses suicide over a second battle. Ralph has yet to be put in such a situation.

The added tension of needing to convince others of a cyclical, supernormal pattern of death is also present in *Doctor Sleep*, although the main characters in this text have something not present in *It* or *The Outsider*: supernatural powers of their own. *Doctor Sleep* is a sequel to *The Shining*, in which a haunted hotel wanted young Danny Torrance because of his psychic powers. Now an adult, Dan uses his "shine" mainly to assist hospice patients during the times of their deaths. He has met a few others who also shine—unlike the Outsider, he knows for certain he is not the only one—but not until he meets Abra Stone does he encounter someone whose shine far surpasses his own. Unfortunately for Abra, there is a group of people known as the True Knot who are also looking for children with the shine so they can kill them and eat their essence.

The True, like the Outsider, travels to kill. King emphasizes that they are overlookable, forming caravans of their supersized campers like so many others already on the road. They are able to use their own powers to track down the proper children, known to the True as "steamheads," so that they can torture them and capture the "steam" that emerges prior to their deaths. They then feed on this steam to keep themselves young and strong. Much of the True's interactions with steam involves a sort of sanitized distance as the group breathes in steam released from a metal canister. One murder is, however, shown in progress. It is an event so horrific that young Abra, halfway across the country, witnesses the murder of the kid she calls "the baseball boy." She rouses her parents from her nightmare and even reaches out to Dan in her terror. The baseball boy, later named as Bradley Trevor, has enough of the shining to be an excellent ballplayer, able to anticipate pitches before they come at him. The True has not taken steam in a long time, and they first kidnap Bradley, and then murder him, slowly and painfully, to take the steam that comes off him. Brad, terrified, begs the True not to hurt him, and then, pitifully and horrifically, after he has already ruptured his vocal cords with screaming, whispers, "Please kill me."[13] It is a brutal scene in which the narrator ever so gently explains that pain purifies the steam, and that the True have to eat.

It is also a scene that shows the reader the fate of any steamhead child who crosses the True, and because the narrative has already introduced young Abra Stone and her impressive shine, it shows the readers exactly what fate the True would have for Abra when they find her. The fact that she can spy on the murder, and that the group's leader has *seen* her spying, increases the tension further. Now Rose and the True know that Abra exists and this, coupled with the narrative's explanation that the True is running low on steam, sets up the long game of cat and mouse. Rose decides to let Abra age a while longer, perhaps to get stronger, but she still marks Abra for future consumption.

In their torture of their child-meals, the True Knot is similar to It. It—a creature who has never been human and therefore purely feeds on what is and has always been Other—seems to need the fear of the child to make a nutritious meal. The True Knot, however, can feed upon the steam released by any dying person. It seems, as Patrick McAleer points out, that "the added pleasure involved [with the torture] is an unnecessary one"[14] purely meant to flavor the meal. The True *could* survive on murder—or terrorist attacks—alone, but instead *chooses* to murder children and torture them for a long time first. Whatever they might be now, the True used to be human, and were children very like the ones they mutilate for long hours. There is no empathy between the True and their victims.

Much like in *It*, it takes a child to look past the horror of the murders and decide upon action. It is Abra, not Dan or any of his friends who know the situation, "who decides to avenge the children"[15] the True have murdered. Dan is horrified at the idea, but also afraid for himself, and for Abra. Although he is an adult now, Dan instead of Danny, he worries about how tasty of a meal he himself will make. Even though Abra is the one who saw the murder of the baseball boy, Dan plays the grown-up card and insists that she does not believe the full extent of the danger of letting the True know that she exists. These child murders are terrible, but Dan, like Derry, searches for justifications to look away.

The True also has the advantage over It and the Outsider by being able to add new members to its group as it finds them. Although It is shown to be female, and to have laid numerous eggs, none of them seem to be viable. Perhaps, in time, It might have a child that lives, but the threat Stan Uris recognizes in 1958 has not come to pass by 1985. The Outsider, during his final confrontation, asks Holly eagerly if she has met another like him. She has not then, although she finds another variation later, in the novella "If It Bleeds." It and the Outsider, however, see themselves as alone in the universe, especially after It marks the death of Its counterpart, the Turtle. They are inhuman freaks, forced to wander alone and lonely, with every human face permanently Other.

It might be rare for the True to find a new member but, as seen early on with the turning of Snakebite Andi, it is indeed a possibility. They are selective, offering initiation only to people who have powers that can help them, but they are also a group dependent on each other in ways that are usually only seen in King's protagonist ka-tets: multiple characters banded together for a single purpose. His main characters frequently form groups to compensate for each other's weaknesses and offer their strengths, but the antagonist is more often summed up in a single Big Bad. The True Knot is made of multiple people, and although Rose the Hat is their leader and feels a personal grudge against Abra, the other members are necessary to fulfill Rose's plan.

The child murders enacted by the True, then, are not lonely acts of one creature intent on survival. The group works together, normalizing the process and following their leader because the other option—expulsion—would rob them of this food. Although they are not completely immortal and invulnerable, taking steam allows them to live for centuries, rolling back their biological clocks. Being separated from the group means leaving behind those who can track and find steamheads, as well as access to Rose's canisters of stored steam. Survival for the Outsider might be tied to being alone and unrecognized, but survival for those who have been turned by the True means staying with the True.

THE HUMAN MONSTER

The above examples of serial death—indeed, serial murder—in King involve supernatural murderers who either have never been, or no longer are, human. Their purpose in enacting these series of murders, in both the short term and long term, is literally self-preservation. Each feeds on some aspect of the murder and its aftermath, usually tainted with strong emotions of fear and pain, to strengthen itself in order to continue living. Although the True eat steam, both It and the Outsider are shown to use their teeth on their victims, and body parts are noted in both cases as being missing and presumably eaten. The purpose of these murders, shorter cycles within a longer series, is to continue the life span of the murderers.

Another of King's works—one of his earliest novels, although not published first—concerns an annual occurrence of multiple murder presented not to prolong a living creature, but somehow an entire social system. *The Long Walk* was originally published under King's pseudonym, Richard Bachman, and has since been first collected with other Bachman books and then reprinted under King's name. It concerns a televised national competition in which 100 boys ages thirteen to nineteen begin walking south from the Canadian border at 9 o'clock on May 1 and must continue moving at a minimum of four miles an hour until only one boy is left. The method of "buying a ticket" or being taken out of the Walk is not revealed until the first Walker, Curley, falls below speed for a fatal fourth time. Although all the Walkers and spectators were perfectly clear on the rules from the beginning, the narrative, told from Walker Raymond Garraty's point of view, reveals that the boys and the crowd all gasp as though they had not, in fact, known. Readers, who have not been given any background information on the Walk, only know about the rule concerning falling below speed.

Before Curley is shot and killed, none of the boys involved have specifically come out and said that "buying a ticket" in fact means being shot by the soldiers who have been accompanying them. This happens on a public street, in front of an audience, and during a competition overseen by someone known only as the Major. Garraty has already remembered that his father called the Major "a society-supported sociopath"[16] but without any further explanation for the label, so Curley's death is a complete shock to the reader. Constant Readers who have come to the book later, after Bachman was revealed to be King, might suspect such a thing before it happens, but the brutality of a boy being shot by a soldier as part of a competition is stark and sobering.

Like in the other books mentioned, the realization that this first death is in fact part of a series leads readers to fear for the lives of the other characters. The meaning of earlier discussions—that boys who gather up four warnings will be out of the Walk—takes on new levels as readers realize that this means ninety-nine boys will have to be shot before the Walk can be concluded. It is a race with a finish line that advances at a steady four miles an hour with ever-changing dangers.

There is no secrecy about the Walk. Bets are placed on Walkers each year, in Vegas and at high schools, and there is constant television coverage from downstate Maine until the end. At least two of the boys, Garraty himself and a Walker named Stebbins, have personally seen segments of the Walk in the past. Although they discuss how they ended up here, watching other boys die and waiting for their own bullet, "moral questions regarding the legitimacy of the state's actions are never raised."[17] The Walk is indeed state-sponsored, and passing the aptitude test to get the chance to die on national television is an honor. The Walkers receive musket salutes and cringe as jets fly over in formation, and the crowd cheers both the Walkers and the Major.

Although told in third person, the narrative is limited to the thoughts and feelings of Garraty himself. The other boys he meets—those who last long enough to become friends—are observed from the outside with descriptions of their physical appearance and through their own dialogue, but the book is told through Garraty and Garraty alone. This creates an interesting interplay of tension when it seems that Garraty will receive his bullet and the Walk will continue without him, since readers will be able to see how many pages are still left in the book. If Garraty were to die at that moment, a narrative shift would need to occur to fill up the rest of the text.

One of the differences between *The Long Walk* and *It, Doctor Sleep*, and *The Outsider* is the way in which the characters who will die are introduced before the moment of their deaths. Many of the children in *It* are only mentioned when they are already corpses, as is Frankie Peterson in *The Outsider*. Bradley Trevor, the baseball boy in *Doctor Sleep*, has a short introduction before his murder, but it is condensed. Readers do not follow Bradley throughout his daily life and form a close connection to him before the True find him. In fact, readers are only introduced to Brad via the True, and thus are already aware of what his fate must be.

The Long Walk allows Garraty and therefore readers to form relationships with various other boys in the Walk so that they, like Garraty, can begin to fear seeing those friends die. Curley might be only a name and a number, brought to Garraty's and readers' attention only because he has been receiving warnings, but readers are drawn into the lives of a handful of other Walkers through their conversations with Garraty on the road. Garraty's small group, known as the Musketeers, is fleshed out more complexly as they discuss how and why they ended up on this road with the imperative to walk or die. The deaths, especially of Garraty's final competitors, are quicker than that of Bradley Trevor, but more emotionally resonating because readers more fully understand what has been lost.

The Walk, being a nationally televised event, operates on a strict schedule, more like Its cycle than the Outsider or the True Knot. Although no children are eaten, the citizens in this world, like the inhabitants of Derry, have agreed to sacrifice part of their future to some greater concept. The Major stands in as representative for the governmental and social structures that allow the Walk to persist, and even the Walkers continue to cheer him after hours and miles on the road. The Major somehow provides for them in the way It provided for Derry, allowing for prosperity and upward mobility as long as the proper sacrifice is made.

The background for the Walk—the social structures, the actual events of what is described as "the Change," and the morality of such an event—is never questioned. For the boys, this is simply how things have always been, the way Derry has always made room for It and Its violent tendencies. This is not an intrusion of the new or of some kind of Outsider who must be ousted and defeated, but part of the cycle of life in this dreary new America. Although ninety-nine boys, or perhaps the full 100, will die each year, there are still multitudes willing to line up to take the aptitude test and hope to see their name come out of the drum.

This presentation is turned on its head in *The Institute*, where children of both genders are forcefully taken from their homes to serve a faceless organization that neither explains their purpose nor admits that the end result will be the children's deaths. While the Major's face and the Walk itself is televised and nationally supported, the Institute must be hidden away in the Maine wilderness and kept a secret. The Walkers' deaths are noted, cheered, and bet upon, but the children who find themselves waking up in the Institute are framed as potential murderers instead of public heroes and only make headlines when they are accused of breaking the law.

In neither case do the children seem to fully understand their role in supporting the larger organization. The apparent glitz and glamor of being one of the Walkers, as well as the possibility of the Prize, draws hundreds of boys to the aptitude test each year, although the discussions the Walkers have on the road show that they are not entirely sure what was being tested. Only at the very end of *The Institute*, and then because the children have led an uprising and survived, does someone attempt to explain that these children, too, serve the larger state. They are also meant to be seen as dying heroes' deaths, even if their passing and their bodies must be hidden.

Even though there are no elements of the supernatural in *The Long Walk*, these cyclical deaths still function to feed and perpetuate the monster. It is still a nearly faceless creature, represented by the Major in his khakis and reflective sunglasses, but a more realistic one: the government and social structures instead of an alien, an Outsider, or a group of no-longer-human beings. The governmental structure in *The Institute* is likewise entirely human, although the lives sacrificed to keep it functioning are children who themselves possess supernatural powers.

NARRATIVE AS SERIAL KILLER

Although in many cases the narrative's deaths literally feed the monster in some way, two of King's short stories—"N." from *Just After Sunset* and "Bad Little Kid," collected in *Bazaar of Bad Dreams*—shift the purpose of death and perpetuation. In each case, the point-of-view character listens as another character tells an unbelievable story. Psychiatrist John Bonsaint treats a patient who believes that he is protecting Earth against an invasion from another plane by his obsessive behaviors, and lawyer Leonard Bradley listens to his client's death-row confession about why he murdered a small child who had been hounding him all his life and bringing death in his wake. Neither listener initially believes the story he is told.

The danger in "N." is centered around the stones in a place called Ackerman Field, and the creature attempting to break through from its universe to ours seems to be limited to this single location as a portal. Like It, Cthun appears to be limited geographically, although N. can take action to keep the world in balance while he is away from the field. After N. first tells John his story and then completes suicide, John starts the same obsessive behaviors he witnessed in N. The danger of Ackerman Field is clearly serial because, by the end of the short story, not only John but his sister have also engaged in the rituals and completed suicide, and yet another person is ready to go investigate. The field and the rituals necessary to contain Cthun do not feed on the deaths, but they sap sanity and energy if Cthun is to be kept at bay.

The seriality in "Bad Little Kid" is not as clear. Although the death-row prisoner tells a story in which the kid wearing a propeller beanie appears at multiple times in his life, causing various deaths, there is only one transfer of apparent madness. At the end of the short story, after the prisoner's execution, the lawyer returns to his car to find a propeller beanie waiting for him. Readers are left to assume what happens next.

In each of these stories, it is the sharing of the tale that perpetuates the threat—or the madness—and death seems to be a side effect. Being made aware of Ackerman Field and the impending invasion compels the listener to take responsibility for protecting Earth against Cthun. Although the story can be passed along verbally while one such guardian is alive, the person on the receiving end does not seem compelled to act until after the guardian has died. But guardianship, like hearing the story of the bad little kid, comes with a death sentence, and the danger begins when the current sufferer decides to tell his story and pass it on.

FEEDING THE MONSTER

The purpose of the cyclical deaths mentioned in this chapter is one of continuation, but not necessarily growth. The monster, whether it is an alien, a librarian, an Outsider, the True Knot, or the state, must be fed so that it will not wither away and disappear. The cycles of death are therefore maintenance and not necessarily escalation. The readers fear for the characters when the characters themselves are part of the group on which the monster feeds, or when the characters—often foolishly—decide to confront the monster and end its cycle.

Frequently the monster's actions make up a sort of fractal composed of smaller cycles within larger cycles. Pennywise murders a series of children as part of Its overall series of waking and sleeping. Ardelia Lortz feeds on children's fear when she is awake, and only needs their deaths when it comes time for her hibernation. The Outsider has periods of rest between committing murders and causing more fear and death to erupt around each of these murders. Even the Major oversees a series of murders on an annual basis, starting each year on May 1 at 9 a.m. Only the Institute has implemented an ongoing cycle of acquisition and death, continually kidnapping the proper children to replace the ones who have died. Although the main characters are generally driven to act because of the threats to a single person's life, or a single person's death, that single person is only one of many.

In these examples, the serial victims are children, or the childlike, preyed upon by adults—or at least Others in the form of adults. They are "the embodiment of the adult world that strives to swallow its young,"[18] a common theme in King's works and repeated multiple times within each of these narratives. Children have talents and aspects that are threatening both to human adults and to supernatural adult-appearing creatures, including their imaginations and innocence. King's adult heroes must frequently return to a state of childhood in order to triumph over these creatures, confronting both the darkness in their own pasts and the losses inherent in transitioning from childhood to adulthood.

In contrast, the monster in "Bad Little Kid" appears to be childlike. His attacks on the prisoner start during boyhood but, while the bad little kid always appears to be a little kid, the prisoner grows into adulthood. After living through his own vicious cycle, the prisoner both murders the little kid and passes on the persecution to the one who hears his story. This is similar to "N." in which the series of deaths occurs in the form of suicides completed by those who have heard a story about a certain place and who begin to feel an obsession with patrolling that place and keeping horrible creatures from passing through it from their world into ours. In "N.," the deaths are not of innocent bystanders, but of the self-proclaimed protectors who want to prevent widespread death and horror. Even closed, that portal takes its toll.

Killing to perpetuate a monster is not the only reason King's characters might experience a cycle of death. Just as an intentional, scheduled series of deaths, such as those seen within this chapter, can build suspense as readers fear for the lives of their favorite characters, so can other types of serial death. The lack of predictability serves to heighten the suspense even further since it does not give readers a chance to relax and characters a moment of relative safety.

NOTES

1. Vronsky, *Sons of Cain*, 19.
2. Patrick McAleer "Untangling the True Knot: Stephen King's (Accidental) Vegan Manifesto in Doctor Sleep," *The Modern Stephen King Canon: Beyond Horror* (Lanham, MD: Lexington Books, 2019), 219.
3. Strengell, *Dissecting Stephen King*, 199.
4. Tony Magistrale, *Landscape of Fear: Stephen King's American Gothic* (Madison: Popular Press, 1988), 110.
5. Sara Martin Alegre, "Nightmares of Childhood: The Child and the Monster in Four Novels by Stephen King," *Atlantis* 23, no. 1 (2001): 112.
6. Cory R. Goehring, "Seven Children and *It*: Stephen King's *It* as Children's Story." *The Many Lives of IT: Essays on the Stephen King Horror Franchise* (Jefferson, NC: McFarland & Company, Inc, 2020), 22.
7. Jennifer Jenkins, "Fantasy in Fiction: The Double-Edged Sword," *Stephen King's Modern Macabre: Essays on the Later Works* (Jefferson, NC: McFarland & Company, Inc., 2014), 17.
8. Strengell, *Dissecting Stephen King*, 209.
9. Tony Magistrale, *Stephen King: The Second Decade, Danse Macabre to the Dark Half*, 45.
10. Russell, *Stephen King: A Critical Companion*, 125.
11. Magistrale, *Stephen King: The Second Decade*, 106.
12. Karen Thoens, "*It*: A Sexual Fantasy," *Imagining the Worst: Stephen King and the Representation of Women* (Westport, CT: Greenwood Press, 1998), 134.
13. Stephen King, *Doctor Sleep* (New York: Scribner, 2013), 166.
14. McAleer, "Untangling the True Knot," 229
15. Clotilde Landais, "Reading *Joyland* and *Doctor Sleep* as Complementary Stories," *Stephen King's Contemporary Classics: Reflections on the Modern Master of Horror* (Lanham, MD: Rowman & Littlefield, 2015), 43.
16. King, *The Long Walk* (New York: Signet Books, 1979. Reissued 1999), 17.
17. Magistrale *Stephen King: The Second Decade*, 49.
18. Davis, *Stephen King's America*, 51.

Chapter Three
"People Are Mortal"
To Build Suspense

In the previous chapter, the serial deaths within King's works were meant specifically to feed a monster and perpetuate a cycle. There was a clear purpose for all of them, centered around the continuation of an evil. This means that, although readers may not agree with the reasoning behind the deaths, they were able to understand why these deaths had to happen. The monster simply felt that the lives of its victims were insignificant compared to its own existence.

This chapter deals with King's works in which the deaths themselves form a series, but without the same underlying purpose of perpetuating a cycle. These deaths, often caused by the same person or supernatural being, are not necessarily part of an ongoing, repeating sequence. They may in fact be the only time that this series of deaths will occur. Unlike in the previous chapter, readers are left without the historical touchpoint of knowing that such things have happened before, and without the looming threat that such things will happen again. Instead of covering cycles that last centuries, or events that are known to recur annually, these threats are more localized and operate on shorter time lines. For all of that, they are no less gripping, since serial death is, in itself, a suspenseful narrative.

For stories like *Cujo* and *Christine*, the suspense comes in the form of earlier deaths of less-sympathetic characters. While the details are unknown to the central—and more well-liked—figures, readers follow along as either the rabid dog or the possessed car kills viciously and violently. They thus have more information than the central characters and are well aware of the possibility of their favorite characters' deaths and just how gruesome they might be. In *Christine*, the worry is not just for those who may have angered the car, but for Arnie, who, after an initial increase in social standing, "deteriorates rapidly once Christine begins her rampage of revenge."[1] Even though Arnie may have bought and paid for his fate, the narration makes him sympathetic and another site of reader concern.

In "The Mist," on the other hand, readers are not allowed to see or know more than the narrator. Because the strange mist covers everything, including all but glimpses of the monsters lurking outside, the narrator and readers alike are confronted with "the terror of the unknown"[2] alongside only a few isolated examples of known or suspected death. At first people walk out into the mist, never to be seen again, but then deaths begin to show the survivors exactly how dangerous the world has become, both inside and out.

At times the serial killer is in fact a human being, like Frank Dodd in *The Dead Zone* or Bob "Beadie" Anderson in "A Good Marriage." Dodd is considered to be such a standard serial killer that he plays only a small role in the book, which is in fact Johnny Smith's story, and not Dodd's.[3] The serial killer narrative is itself part of a series proving the veracity of Smith's visions and the extent of his power. Anderson, on the other hand, is the central concern for his wife, who has just discovered his other identity. The serial murders have already happened by the time the novella begins, but Darcy's knowledge of them is new and must be dealt with.

Then there are the deaths that occur around a certain location or quickly near the narrative's main characters. In *Pet Sematary*, the road running in front of Louis's house is hungry, killing pets and people alike and causing the story of the strange burying grounds to be spread. The alien invasion in *Dreamcatcher* allows readers and two of the main characters an in-depth, immediate glimpse into what happens to humans who ingest some of the extraterrestrial spores, arming them with knowledge of the symptoms and dread/anticipation when other characters start presenting with them. *Duma Key*, another magical and destructive location like the pet sematary, uses murder to test the strength and reach of its powers, and then to attempt to drive the main character to do its bidding.

Once again, readers frequently find themselves with more information than the characters possess. This is instrumental in creating the suspense and differentiating it from surprise, in which the readers also did not possess the necessary information to expect what was coming. Readers are frequently privy to scenes of death through the eyes of the characters who are being killed, and information of those deaths is not always communicated to the other characters. Readers are therefore able to anticipate the danger that the main characters will face, as well as their trajectory toward these confrontations. By witnessing what happens to others when they cross paths with the threat, readers are treated to a real-time sample of what may await their favorite characters, and yet they are helpless to stop those characters from the decisions that will place them in danger.

NONHUMAN SERIAL KILLERS

Cujo is not classified as the story of a serial killer because a dog—in this case, a rabid Saint Bernard—cannot commit murder. King mentions multiple times that, had Cujo not encountered a rabid bat, the dog would never have hurt anyone. Flashbacks show just how gentle a giant Cujo is, carrying a small boy around on his back for rides, obeying commands, and generally being a good dog.

The tension of the narrative builds in part because readers are aware of Cujo's health as soon as he encounters the bat. The other plot elements build to leave Donna Trenton and her four-year-old son, Tad, stranded in the Cambers' dooryard, trapped in a car that refuses to start as a fully rabid Cujo terrorizes them. Because the Cambers and Vic Trenton are out of town, Donna and Tad are left for days during the hottest part of the year so far. By the time Donna's Pinto comes to rest by the Cambers' garage, though, Cujo has already started his series of murders.

The first victim, initially noticed only by Cujo and the readers, is Gary Pervier. He lives alone, and the only visitor he expects is Joe Camber. Pervier also knows Cujo, and at first does not react when the dog comes to visit. Too late, Pervier realizes that Cujo is rabid, but he is savaged and dies before he can call for help. When Joe comes to see Pervier, Cujo emerges from the relative dark and coolness of the cellar and kills Joe before he, too, can reach the phone. Readers thus understand that no one is home at the Camber place, and that Cujo has deteriorated so far that he will kill people, including those who have always been kind to him.

When Donna manages to coax the Pinto into the Cambers' dooryard, readers therefore already know to fear for her long before she realizes the problem. The brutal deaths of Pervier and Joe cause readers to fear for Donna, who has been unfaithful and thus, according to the rules of the horror genre, must be punished for illicit sex; and Tad, who is only four years old and innocent.

Donna's attempts to reach the Camber house and hopefully find the door unlocked have been curtailed by Cujo, who has injured her legs and belly and infected her with rabies. The time of possible rescue is limited therefore not only by Tad's rapidly deteriorating condition, but by Donna's weakness and the spread of the virus. Although Cujo is ill and worsening, he is not failing fast enough. When Sheriff George Bannerman finally decides to take a drive out to the Cambers' just to follow up questions about the Trentons' missing Pinto, readers—even those who have not encountered later novels about Castle Rock and therefore already know Bannerman's fate—hope the man will live and best the dog, but the feeling is tempered by the character's complete lack of knowledge.

Bannerman, then, becomes Cujo's third victim, this one killed in front of two witnesses. Instead of only imagining what Cujo might do to her and her son, Donna has a full visual example. On the one hand, there is hope, since someone will notice Bannerman's absence and come looking for him; but on the other, Bannerman had a gun and was still killed by the rabid dog.

Cujo's first two kills—Gary Pervier and Joe Camber—came early in the disease's progression, before his nervous system had been too severely weakened. Although they work to instill suspense for the reader because these deaths demonstrate Cujo's inability to stop himself, there is still the hope that the virus might ravage the big dog quickly enough that his collapse will come before Donna or Tad's death. By killing Bannerman, as well—a large man who was, after all, armed—King shows both Donna and his readers that Cujo is still lively enough to remain a threat.

The arrival of Bannerman, and his quick glimpse inside the baking Pinto, also allows an outside description of the situation Donna and Tad find themselves in. Donna's "focus is always on preserving Tad,"[4] noting how dry his lips are, how much his voice croaks, and when he has a seizure, but she does not concentrate on the changes in her own condition. Her concern for her son above and beyond herself is, perhaps, her one redeeming quality in a novel that does not present her as sympathetic, but Bannerman's shock at Donna's condition reveals exactly how little time is left. Perhaps Donna can be forgiven for attempting to wait Cujo out so far, but if she is going to act, it must be soon.

Unable to know that others are already on the way, Donna "decides that she cannot wait for a white knight to rescue her"[5] and exits the car for the last time. She grabs for Brett Camber's old baseball bat, which she had first spotted much earlier, but the taped handle had made her fear it might not be strong enough as a weapon. The bat does wobble and then break in her hands, but Donna manages to beat Cujo to death just as her husband arrives—and asks her how long their son has been dead. Although finally spurred into action after Bannerman's death, and certain that Tad had been alive when she left the car, Donna is faced with the fact that she could not, in the end, save her son. In what Tony Magistrale calls "King's most pessimistic book,"[6] the price for Donna's affair seems to be the life of her only child. King himself does not confirm that Tad's death was the consequence of his mother's sexual promiscuity but, at the end of the book, "the sins are there and Tad is not."[7]

The first two deaths caused by Cujo's teeth and claws are, as King himself has worded it in *The Stand*, "No great loss."[8] Neither Pervier nor Joe Camber is an upstanding citizen, and Charity has already been seen mulling over the fact that her life and Brett's would be better without Joe. The concern raised by Joe entering Pervier's place is not, therefore, on par with the concern felt for Sheriff Bannerman, Donna, or especially Tad. For readers to truly feel the suspense and appreciate the tension, the life of a "good" or "innocent" person must also be at stake.

King uses the same narrative structure of a nonhuman killing multiple humans in series in *Christine*, when the killer is now an inexplicably sentient car. Like Cujo, she cannot be said to truly be a serial killer—a label given to human murderers of other humans—but Christine has an intent that Cujo lacks. While King stresses that Cujo, when in his right mind, had always done his best to be a good dog, Christine has no such moral standards. Cujo only killed people who wandered across his path after the rabies began to set in, but Christine specifically targets and seeks out people "who have done or intend to do [her new owner] Arnie wrong."[9]

The "good" or "innocent" characters in *Christine* are satellites in the life of Arnie Cunningham. Dennis Guilder, who narrates the first and third sections of the book, is Arnie's best friend from childhood. Leigh Cabot, a new transfer student, started dating Arnie during the first part of the book, but their relationship deteriorated as Arnie's and Christine's grew. Readers fear for Dennis and Leigh because they suspect that Christine is indeed sentient, and these fears are heightened when the couple begins their own relationship. Because Leigh can be seen to be cheating on Arnie, and because Dennis steals his best friend's girl, their position as "innocents" is threatened.

In the middle section of the book, Dennis is literally and figuratively sidelined as the result of a football accident and because Arnie "relinquishes his bond with Dennis"[10] when he gives himself more and more to his car. From late October until just before Christmas, Dennis is stuck in the hospital with both legs in casts. The previous narrator of events is taken out of the middle of the story, and the narration switches to third person to cover the series of deaths for which Christine is responsible. This allows the reader to follow her as she drives herself, slowly tracking down the people who have hurt either her—a group of high school bullies that snuck into the airport long-term parking to beat her into a pile of wreckage—or Arnie.

Readers can thus follow each of these improbable incidents of vehicular manslaughter as they occur. One of the bullies is run over—multiple times—in the middle of the night but, before he dies, he sees that nobody is driving the car. Others, while out with an innocent younger boy who has had nothing to do with Christine or Arnie, find themselves pursued and then run off the road. The last boy to die also notes that no one is driving the car. Another bully, as well as the owner of the garage where Arnie has been keeping Christine and whose illegal operations got Arnie arrested, are killed on Christmas Eve in the middle of such a severe snowstorm that drivers were encouraged to stay home.

Most of the victims—all but the innocent boy who had the bad luck to be with the rest of the gang when Christine came after them—recognize the car and realize *why* it is pursuing them. Christine is not killing willy-nilly but is rather on a "rampage of revenge,"[11] and each of her victims knows full well what it is he must answer for. They recognize their own guilt, and some even attempt to repent in the last minutes of their lives, although mercy is not in Christine's repertoire.

After the first bully is seen meeting his end, however, readers can anticipate that the others will follow. They, unlike the characters in the story, know full well that they are reading a Stephen King book and that something supernatural is afoot concerning the car. Although no full explanation is given, it is also clear that the car, once connected deeply to her previous owner Roland D. LeBay, has now melded in a way with Arnie Cunningham and will work, in her own way, to protect him. The question is not if the other bullies *will* die, but *how* Christine will orchestrate it so that there are no witnesses and the suspicion cannot fall on Arnie.

The logical or realistic approach to the series of murders comes in the form of Detective Rudolph Junkins, who has made the connection between the initial murders and the trashing of Arnie's car. Junkins visits the garage to both speak with Arnie and have a look at Christine to determine that she was not damaged from multiple recent collisions with a human being. Christine's magical odometer runs backward and thus turns back the clock as she speeds away from the murder scenes, repairing the damage before it can be seen. For later murders, Arnie is clearly out of town and, with his only friend still laid up in the hospital, Junkins cannot figure out how Arnie might be managing it.

Garage owner Will Darnell himself is given the role to parallel Sheriff Bannerman, even if his character is solidly on the side of sleaze instead of good. Darnell begins to suspect that something out of the ordinary is occurring in his own garage and, one night, is there to see Christine return without the benefit of a driver. Darnell therefore has dangerous knowledge and readers suspect that something must happen to him even before Arnie gets arrested as part of his illegal activities. It certainly helps Arnie to have Darnell murdered after his own arrest, but Darnell's days were numbered from the time he actually began to suspect that Christine might be more than a car.

The consequences of Darnell's knowledge highlight for the reader the possibilities that face Dennis and Leigh, who have also begun to suspect something about Arnie's car. Aside from Darnell, they are the ones in the best position to see that, "since Christine has been in his life, people have been suffering."[12] Because they are closer to Arnie personally, Dennis and Leigh can see how this threatens not only those who have already died, but those with whom Arnie has a personal relationship, including themselves and Arnie's parents. Dennis even works himself up to asking Arnie what he thinks happened to Darnell and is fed a story about "the Colombians"[13] and a coke deal gone wrong, as though Colombians would have driven a car through a blizzard and into Darnell's house to teach him a lesson.

Even then, Dennis and Leigh's suspicions are not enough to put themselves squarely in Christine's sights, perhaps because they manage to keep their secret longer than Darnell, or perhaps because Christine does not see them as the same sort of threat. Darnell's garage has a car crusher; Dennis has two broken legs, and Leigh does not even have her learners' permit. Whatever the reason, Dennis and Leigh are safe until Arnie discovers them kissing in Dennis's car.

Part of the horror in *Christine* is the fact that Arnie, too, realizes that something must be going on, but he is too trapped to act. Arnie cannot remember doing a lot of the repairs to the car and only has a vague notion that he must have taken her out of the garage, late at night, and simply cruised to let the malfunctioning odometer reverse the damage. When he tries to talk to Leigh, bolts of pain shoot through his back, silencing him above and beyond the impossibility of trying to explain his suspicions of a supernatural occurrence. Arnie becomes less and less himself as the book continues, and clings more and more to the car as he slowly shoves everyone else away. Arnie feels justified in "his refusal to destroy the car that he is almost certain has killed several people"[14] because, if he surrenders Christine, then he has nothing. Besides, the only people who have died are ones who have made Arnie's life more difficult, anyway. No great loss.

But this series of deaths shows exactly what Dennis and Leigh are up against when they are pushed to finally confront Christine head-on. Christine can drive herself and handle herself better than any human driver. Snow is no impediment, and she even forced her way into Darnell's living room to take care of him, so buildings likewise offer little protection. Readers' fear for them is increased not only because they see what the car is capable of, but because they know that Dennis and Leigh cannot turn to others for help in this situation. Because the killer is supernatural, they cannot even warn their families of the danger, much less explain to a wider audience that all these deaths were indeed connected and committed by the same person. Christine was purposeful in her selection of victims, but, not being human, it is difficult to classify her according to human terminology.

The threat in "The Mist" differs from both *Cujo* and *Christine* in that anyone who goes outside any building can fall victim to it, and it does not discriminate while selecting victims. Presented as a written account, *The Mist* presents readers with the point of view of David Drayton as he and his son attempt to survive the various half-seen dangers that descend along with a mysterious fog. There are therefore no scenes to give readers advance knowledge of the threat or to show the various, possibly alien creatures making their kills. What starts as a series of people going out and not returning turns into a series of deaths caused by unearthly, and sometimes unspeakable, creatures.

The danger David and his son face mimics that faced by Donna and Tad Trenton: they are currently trapped somewhere that seems to be safer than going outside, but they cannot stay there forever. Unlike Donna, David has no reason to hope that help will come. Since David is trapped in a grocery store instead of a car, he has longer to think of a plan and more materials at hand to use for survival and defense, but this also gives him more time to observe the creatures' activities and the deaths of other survivors. Because readers are stuck with only David's point of view, they are unable to also go out into the mist and see more exactly what dangers await them. The suspense that builds and readers' concern for David are far more nebulous than in *Christine*, which allows readers to see exactly how the possessed car operates. The mist, by dint of spreading over the land and reaching everywhere, is an unknown and undefinable threat to everyone. While David and a handful of others survive to the end of his narrative, there is no epilogue in which readers can see how David and his son are getting along, like the survivors of *Cujo*, or if the threat simply continues, as in *Christine*.

A TRUE SERIAL MURDERER

In contrast to mindless serial slaughter by a rabid dog, purposeful vehicular manslaughter by a possessed car—each of which increases the tension within the narrative because of knowledge given to the reader when it is not grasped by the protagonists—or a constant hidden threat in the mist, *The Dead Zone* introduces a completely human serial killer. Frank Dodd continues to haunt the town of Castle Rock so that, at the beginning of *Cujo*, he is shown to be the local "monster"[15] or "boogeyman" invoked by parents who want to scare their children into better behavior. Dodd's name is mentioned frequently in King's other novels set in Castle Rock, so that the figure of Frank Dodd is raised to almost mythical proportions.

Generally, a serial killer occupies the center of his own narrative. As already seen, serialization of crime adds to the suspense within a narrative, allowing authors to draw out a story and increase readers' fear for other characters who may not realize the danger. A human serial killer, following the FBI's working knowledge of such very real people, returns to normal life between the murders, thereby going unnoticed by friends and family while the number of victims steadily grows. Castle Rock has lately been faced with several such murders, and Sheriff George Bannerman—still a few years from meeting Cujo and his own end—finally turns to one of the two true central characters in *The Dead Zone*, John Smith, for help.

Smith, recently awakened from a long coma, has resumed consciousness with no small measure of psychic ability. He has used it to keep his physical therapist's house from burning down and shocked the people gathered for a press conference afterward by repeating his psychic feat in front of them. Although Smith would much rather retreat from the headlines and attempt to resume some sort of normal life, he agrees to go with Bannerman to Castle Rock's police station when the latest victim is a child—and Bannerman's own daughter narrowly avoided meeting the same fate.

Dodd, a police officer, is seen and named in the police station. Earlier scenes showing the killer and dipping into his internal monologue do not reveal his name, although they hint at his preference for wearing a raincoat during the crimes and making himself "slick"[16] so that his victims cannot get a grip on him and defend themselves. Dodd delivers his few lines before he leaves the station and, in fact, exits the narrative completely. When Smith and Bannerman next encounter him, he has completed suicide with a sign around his neck that says simply "I CONFESS."[17] This comes less than forty pages after Sheriff Bannerman first contacted Smith to bring him to Castle Rock and identify the killer.

Dodd's appearance in what is really the story of newly psychic John Smith and rising politician Greg Stillson functions as a single touchpoint in the sequence of events that leads to the book's climax. This mimics the way Its series of murders in 1957–1958 is but a small part of Its overall cycle, or how the Outsider's stop in Flint City including all the deaths surrounding the murder of Frankie Peterson was only a single event in the Outsider's true long-term plan. The nameless murderer eventually revealed to be Dodd popped in and out of the still-separate narratives of Stillson and Smith, creating tension for readers and Bannerman prior to Smith's knowledge of the events. All the strange, apparently unrelated scenes in the first part of the book should somehow come together in order to provide narrative satisfaction, so Bannerman's call to Smith after Smith's known psychic events allows readers to anticipate what will happen—if, that is, Smith changes his mind after his initial refusal.

Much of the story of Dodd is taken up with Bannerman's protests that the young man he has treated like a son could not be the monster who has been plaguing Castle Rock with "fetishistic patterns of violation and murder."[18] Once Bannerman contacts John Smith, there are none of the scenes from Dodd's point of view or showing his thoughts. Here the narration follows Smith's personal journey from anger and annoyance at having been tracked down, to his horror at the series of murders, to his terrible vision when he occupies the same bench on the town common that the killer did. Smith echoes some of the nameless killer's previously shown thoughts, focusing on the slick raincoat and the overbearing mother's obsession with sexually transmitted diseases.

Smith's next challenge, however, is convincing Bannerman that his trusted protégé is, in fact, the killer. Bannerman refuses to go to Dodd immediately, instead taking the time to track Dodd's movements against the murder dates and even going so far as to make a call out to Colorado to see if any similar unsolved murders occurred during Dodd's semester-long course there. Bannerman, who had to convince Smith to help him, is now in the position of needing convincing.

When Smith and Bannerman finally go to the Dodd house, their encounter with the overbearing and sickly Henrietta Dodd may be enough for readers to understand that Frank Dodd is, in fact, the killer. Readers, like Smith, have had glimpses inside the killer's head. No further explanation for Dodd's crimes is given and, indeed, he kills himself before he can be questioned, leaving readers "to puzzle out the reason behind his odd crimes for themselves."[19] Although they can flip back through the pages and attempt to make a coherent narrative from the flashbacks and their new knowledge about Dodd, King does not dwell on the serial killer's story itself.

The Dead Zone, then, presents readers not only with a series of murders committed by the same entity, but also a series of deadly events that drives the main character toward the climax. Frank Dodd is dead and out of the story 150 pages before its end, but the identification of the Castle Rock Strangler is a major turning point for John Smith. The newspapers are hounding him again because of his connection to the case and although Smith once again attempts a life of anonymity, this time working as a private tutor, his visions prevent a quiet life from being a reality.

In another previously unrelated, and possibly unremembered, scene, readers followed a lightning rod salesman into a bar and saw an exchange in which the owner refused to purchase his wares. This snippet is left alone and unremarked until, years later, Smith receives a new vision. It is graduation for the boy he was tutoring, and the graduation party, as always, was to be held in that same establishment. Smith receives a vision of the place being struck by lightning and most of the graduating class dying in the resulting fire. His vision scares many of the graduates during a backyard party, and the parents who hired Smith as a tutor agree to shift as much of the celebration as they can to their own house, just to put Smith's mind at ease.

While the Dodd incident served to prove that Smith could indeed have psychic insights into past events, the graduation party cements the idea that his premonitions for the future are also accurate. Lightning does strike, and many of the students who went to the party as usual do indeed die—although far fewer than would have been present without Smith's vision. Again sought by reporters, Smith once more retreats in an attempt to find a normal life.

His own moral compass, however, will not let him rest. Rather than use his psychic abilities as he was shown to prior to his coma, when he won round after round on a wheel of fortune, "Smith applies his powers for the benefit of others."[20] He does not treat his ability lightly, and much of his retreat is to avoid hurting others with his visions, the way the press conference demonstration went so poorly. The problem Smith faces is that he has been following the political career of Greg Stillson, and their paths finally crossed long enough for Smith to shake Stillson's hand . . . and receive a terrifying vision of the future if Stillson became president of the United States.

Dodd and the graduation-night fire have "served to prove that the psychic visions suffered by John Smith are indeed true,"[21] which allows Smith and the readers to shift from wondering if the Stillson future is accurate to asking what he might do about it. Smith compares Stillson with Hitler and begins polling others on what they might do if they were able to transport themselves back to 1933, with the caveat that yes, they would be captured and serve out whatever punishment would be handed out if they chose to murder Hitler.

Readers fear for Smith, who has already lost so much when a car accident and a coma took four and a half years of his life, but they are also unaware of a further motivating factor until after the climax of the narrative is completed. Smith learns that he has a brain tumor and decides that this means he must act sooner rather than later, before his body fails to the point where he could not handle a gun. Smith's plan is to assassinate Stillson during a town hall meeting in New England.

This plan does not come to fruition, but Smith is still shown to have succeeded in his overall goal to keep Stillson from securing the presidency. Although Smith dies—after all, "in King's world, nobody escapes his destiny"[22]—and Stillson lives, a photographer snaps an image of Stillson holding up a small boy as a shield during the shooting. The strange filter that has been hovering over Smith's visions of Stillson is explained by the pattern on the boy's snowsuit. Smith has retained his moral standing and, when readers later learn of his brain tumor, has not lost much of what life he would have had left. Smith used not only his impending personal health deadline, but his past experiences with Frank Dodd and the vision of the graduation party to spur himself on to being the self-sacrificing hero, knowing that few would understand his acts.

King's novella "A Good Marriage" presents readers with a serial killer figure like Frank Dodd in that he is not at the center of the story being told. Instead, as Tony Magistrale explains with an understatement, the story is one in which "a wife must grapple with the sexual maladjustment of her husband."[23] Darcy Anderson is not dealing with her husband of twenty-seven years cheating on her or wanting to experiment in the bedroom, but rather that Bob is in fact the serial killer known as "Beadie." Based on the real-life

BTK killer, Beadie committed a series of murders and sent letters taunting the police, then stopped for over a decade, only to start again. "A Good Marriage" opens with Darcy confronting the fact that Bob has another, secret identity and puts her in the position to decide what to do about it.

Like Frank Dodd, Bob Anderson is not centered as a figure of fascination. The narrative is told from Darcy's point of view and readers are privy to her internal monologue, which functions "as the Greek chorus that guides the reader's response"[24] during both her discovery of the evidence and as Bob is given the chance to explain himself in his own words. Like Dodd, Bob realizes he has been caught, but his response is confrontation rather than suicide. He returns home from a business trip in the middle of the night to explain his actions to his wife and then place their future in her hands.

In this narrative, King does not present readers with glimpses into the crimes as they occur or the killer in action. As soon as the story starts, Beadie has killed his last victim and sent his last taunting letter. King does not allow readers to see inside Bob's head the way he followed the "slick" Castle Rock killer, but Bob is given more than a short, written confession to explain himself. Even then, his defense that all his victims—save a young boy who was apparently collateral damage—were "snoots."[25] Still, Bob's explanations and even his murders are not at the center of the story. "A Good Marriage" is not a serial killer narrative, but a question of what a woman might do if she discovered her husband happens to be one.

The tension in this novella surrounds Darcy's "varying responses to newly found knowledge"[26] as she uncovers Bob's secret and then attempts to sort through all possible responses. Like Donna Trenton, her worries are mostly for her children and how breaking headlines and damning knowledge would affect them as they start their independent lives. Darcy manages to get Bob to promise that his days of murdering and taunting are over, although this is not enough of a guarantee for her. As long as Bob lives, there is the threat that he might once again feel overcome by his urges—she does not quite believe that her husband has a split personality—and kill again.

Unlike Dodd, Bob does not feel the need to complete suicide once he has been discovered. He feels comfortable waiting because he believes his wife has been caught in his trap and will not reveal his identity. Bob also does not believe that Darcy is likewise capable of murder, although she kills not for her own pleasure, but in defense of her children. Darcy manages to make her husband's death look like an accident and to get away with murder so that Bob's secret does not need to surface as justification. Bob's previous murders led, after his wife's long moral struggle, to his own. Although the Beadie case remains unsolved as far as law enforcement is concerned, Darcy and the readers can be comforted in knowing that Bob Anderson is just as dead as Frank Dodd.

"People Are Mortal" 51

SUSPENSE WITHOUT EXPLICIT SERIALITY

The Dead Zone and "A Good Marriage" are not the only of King's works where earlier deaths set up future narrative moves. Others—*Pet Sematary*, *Dreamcatcher*, and *Duma Key*—use early character deaths to foreshadow the extent of the danger facing the main characters. *Pet Sematary* especially deepens the narrative tension by the "repeated warnings"[27] given to Louis Creed and his personal choice to ignore them.

In *Pet Sematary*, death is a central theme. Louis Creed is a physician whose new job on a college campus begins with a student being hit by a car and dying in front of him. His wife Rachel is overly traumatized about death, having lost her older sister to spinal meningitis when they were just children and when Rachel had been left alone to care for her. Their daughter, Ellie, is just starting school and is upset when the neighbor, Jud Crandall, takes the Creeds on a walk to the local pet "sematary" where children have been burying their dead animal companions for generations. When Jud's wife dies, however, Ellie accepts this as a matter of course because Norma was old.

Ellie's big fear—and therefore one of Rachel's as well—is that her cat, Winston Churchill, will die. When Rachel, Ellie, and toddler Gage are out of town for Thanksgiving, Jud finds Church dead on the side of the road, likely hit by a truck. Knowing how much Ellie loves her cat, and with a secret knowledge he burns to share, Jud talks Louis into carrying the cat up to the Pet Semetary and then climbing the deadfall for a mysterious journey beyond. Louis buries Ellie's cat in a patch of strange, stony ground and then, the next day, Church comes back.

Jud's attempts to explain this miraculous occurrence center on ideas of the Micmac (King's spelling) people who used to live in the area. He includes the mention of a Wendigo, suggesting that the Micmacs were forced to engage in cannibalism during a long, hard winter and that they buried the remains of their cannibalized loved ones in the same patch of ground where Louis has just interred Church. Jud's description, though, relies heavily on the popular horror version introduced by Algernon Blackwood in the early twentieth century[28] rather than on Indigenous interpretations. Whether or not he fully believes Jud's explanation, Louis accepts that a version of Church has returned, and that the cat's eventual second—and possibly final—death will not hit Ellie as hard as he and Rachel had feared.

King therefore works during the first part of the book to set up the Creed family as sympathetic and loving, and to introduce the idea of the power of the stony burying ground beyond the deadfall. What Louis undertakes at Jud's urging is seen as an act of love for his daughter, and in fact "Louis does nothing to cause the tragedy that will grip him"[29] and his family during the next part of the book. The road and its dangerous trucks have been central since Jud's warning to the family on the day they moved in, with the danger illustrated by Church's death, and now young Gage Creed runs out into the road in front of a truck and is killed immediately.

The remaining three members of the Creed family find themselves incapable of comforting each other in their grief and instead begin to isolate. The rift increases when Rachel's father blames Louis for Gage's death, beginning a fistfight during the viewing that knocks the small casket off its runners. When Louis plans to have Rachel and Ellie return to Chicago with her parents, readers fully recognize that this is not an attempt to heal familial bonds, but to recreate the situation in November that allowed Louis to learn about the secrets of the burying ground for the first time. When Jud initially explained about the powers of the stony soil, Louis had even asked if anyone had buried a person up there. Jud's answer was too quick to have been honest, and now Jud explains the truth to Louis: yes, and it was awful. Louis should put the idea out of his mind.

This is not, of course, what happens. Louis sees a chance to make his family whole again and gives in to the "Unpardonable Sin"[30] of refusing to accept the limitations of reality. Louis methodically goes about the process of graverobbing, digging up his son in one location so that he can carry him over the deadfall and through the mysterious dangers to inter him in the rocky soil and build a cairn on top of him.

Readers do not entirely know what to expect of Gage's return. Church now smells eternally of graveyard dirt, no longer purrs, and likes killing birds and rodents apparently purely for fun. Jud's story of a young man killed during the war and then buried in the same place does not offer any specific areas of concern for readers or Louis to anticipate. Although Jud was part of a group who had to approach the young man's father and tell him that he had to kill his son again, the resurrected teenager did not seem to be particularly violent. He was an affront to nature, yes, and even Norma had told her husband that something needed to be done, but the story of this young man does not entirely prepare readers for what happens next.

Gage, still restricted by his toddler body but now not merely a toddler in his mind, steals his father's scalpel and uses it to murder first Jud, and then Rachel, who has returned because of Ellie's visions about what is happening to her father. Louis seems to accept the wrongness of his previous actions, because he kills both Church and then Gage, but these events have clearly driven him mad. He reasons, as much as he can, that even Gage spent too long dead before he was reburied. Louis carries Rachel, so recently killed, over the deadfall to bury her there, as well. The book ends with Rachel—or the thing that *was* Rachel—returning, although "[h]er success as a monster is left to the reader's imagination."[31] Audiences must speculate, based on what Jud has told them and what they have seen, what might happen next.

King plays here not only with the horror of death, but with the horror of being unable to accept death. Gage, a small child who has hurt no one and who had his entire life ahead of him—in a particularly poignant scene, Louis has a dream that spells out Gage's path to adulthood before he awakens to the reality of a dead child—is a particularly wrenching loss, made even more so because King based that scene on a similar event with his own son. King, however, managed to grab Owen and the truck sped on by. Gage's death was an accident that could indeed happen to any child, and the horror is embedded in reality. Louis's activities following Gage's burial are therefore perhaps understandable as parents imagine his grief, but Louis is the protagonist of a tragedy. Any and all of his actions, padded with the best of intentions, simply increase the horror.

Not every King protagonist is at the center of a tragedy. In *Dreamcatcher*, he allows his characters a measure of success in that the imagined worst does not, in fact, come to pass. He even allows two of his heroes to live, although they must carry the burden of what this cost them—including the lives of three of their childhood friends. King presents the stakes early on in this novel, not allowing for the longer introduction of his characters as he showed in *Pet Sematary*.

After several short, apparently disconnected scenes reminiscent of the opening of *The Dead Zone*, King settles into the main narrative in November 2001 where four old friends are together in the woods for a week of deer hunting. A stranger, McCarthy, wanders out of the woods near the cabin where they have been staying, meeting first Gary "Jonesy" Jones and Joe "Beaver" Clarendon. Jonesy and Beaver feed McCarthy and listen with incredulity to his tale of being lost in the woods, which includes a mention of the fact that McCarthy was entirely unsure of what he had eaten.

McCarthy's short appearance in the novel begins with noxious belches and farts and ends on the toilet when a strange alien creature, nicknamed a shit weasel but properly called a "byrum," chews its way out of his lower gastrointestinal tract, having already eaten largely of its host's internal organs. The hairless, and apparently limbless, creature is not helpless, despite its recent bloody birth. This creature is quickly shown to be a threat to more than just its host when it uses its teeth to kill Beaver. By the time a third member of their hunting party, Henry Devlin, arrives at the cabin, it has begun laying eggs. Henry, in a state of horror, sets fire to the cabin, killing the weasel and its offspring—and at least proving that fire is up to the task—and burning the bodies of McCarthy and Beaver.

The horror of the byrum, imperfect parasites, has therefore been established, and McCarthy is not the only one so afflicted. Part of Henry's journey included encountering another member of McCarthy's hunting party, and she has been left with Pete Moore. This woman also exhibited many of the symptoms already seen in McCarthy. Readers therefore recognize the danger presented to another member of this childhood quartet before Pete is confronted with a similar situation.

Pete manages to fend off the second byrum without losing his life, but he becomes another warning about the likely future of the human race. The aliens come not just in weasels, but in strange red fungal growth called byrus. Jonesy has inhaled some of this and been taken over by an alien presence who can control the byrus on Pete's body to first cause intense pain and then, once Pete is no longer useful, to kill him. Jonesy is only able to watch this passively from a locked room inside his own mind. Henry, far away from "Typhoid Jonesy" but with the knowledge that at least one alien is likely to escape the hot zone, has the task of not only finding the people in charge of this containment operation, but convincing them that the parasites and the fungus are in fact the least of their worries.

When readers are first introduced to McCarthy, they have no idea what might be causing his strange stomachaches and violent gas attacks. After McCarthy's story unfolds, however, readers can recognize the symptoms when they appear in future characters and more fully anticipate the danger. In the case of the woman Henry and Pete encounter, readers fear for the men, known "good guys," but have little room for hope that the woman might survive. Her fate is sealed, but thin hope remains for the protagonists. Later, when one of the army men sent to contain the invasion and kill all human life in the area starts showing symptoms of his own, such empathy is highly unlikely. The troops led by Abraham Kurtz meant to kill all life within the area surrounding the crashed spaceship, including humans—and some of their own lower-ranking officers. Again, the main concern is not the infected person, but the threat that infection might pose to the protagonists.

Readers' worry is not for Kurtz's men, or even necessarily for the hunters and others who have been corralled and quarantined in Maine. It is important that Henry escapes the paddock full of the others but, even though some of them are children and Kurtz intends to kill them all, a couple hundred people cannot matter when the fate of the world is at stake. When Henry flees with the help of Kurtz's second-in-command, Owen Underhill, he only does so in a way that will give the others a fighting chance—but Underhill rightly points out that Henry's priorities might be skewed. Many of the imprisoned hunters die anyway, via the electric fence or being shot by the soldiers, but some of them live and, more important for the narrative, Henry and Owen are free to pursue Jonesy and his alien parasite.

It takes the characters, and therefore the readers, a while to figure out what, exactly, the alien consciousness in Jonesy's head intends for humanity. Jonesy observes early on that "Mr. Gray" has stolen a truck and killed the driver but allowed his collie to live for reasons that are revealed when the collie farts and releases a very familiar smell. Readers, having seen both McCarthy and the woman die after incubating the byrum, are well aware of what is happening inside the collie. However, since both examples of the alien creature died quickly in the cold air, neither Jonesy nor Henry first understands what Mr. Gray intends.

It would certainly be horrific if what happened to the unfortunate McCarthy occurred on a much wider scale—for example, the population of Boston—and the knowledge of the existence and brutality of the byrum is enough to increase the tension. Mr. Gray wants to spread this disease, and readers can anticipate what this would mean for the human race. His intended method of infection can remain a secret for a while longer, increasing the tension until Henry realizes where their quarry is headed and the final desperate race begins.

But an early death does not have to be directly related to later deaths in order to add to the narrative suspense. In *Dreamcatcher* the entire series of deaths, although enacted by different aliens, is still a series of threats by the same Other. Once McCarthy dies because of the ingested byrus, the fear is that others will die the same way. Early occurrences of death set up the expectation for more deaths that look the same and can therefore be charted, from the swollen stomach, increased instances of belching and flatulence, pain as the creature eats someone from the inside out, and growing telepathy. What has been seen once is anticipated to occur again. *Duma Key*, however, uses death like dominoes not to make readers anticipate another, similar event, but to explore the supernatural power the main character has begun to exhibit.

Since moving to Duma Key, Edgar Freemantle has begun to paint. As the result of an accident on a job site, Edgar has been grievously injured and is living with both brain trauma and the loss of an arm. He uses painting instead of writing, but Edgar is clearly a mirror for King himself after the car accident that nearly killed the author in 1999. For both, creativity is "a road out of misery"[32]—until Edgar realizes that his painting is actually far more than a simple diversion.

The turning point is itself a death. Twelve-year-old Tina Garibaldi has been kidnapped, assaulted, and murdered, and her kidnapper was caught on tape. George "Candy" Brown sits in jail while it seems all of Florida calls for his blood, and the news story is so pervasive that Edgar, who has largely retreated from the outside world, is aware of it. Edgar talks about it with one of his close friends on the key, and the conversation centers not on the horrific details of the child's death, but on the fact that Candy Brown has a good lawyer and might, somehow, manage to get off without a guilty verdict. Even the news that Brown offered a confession of sorts, saying that he got high and may have done an awful thing, is not certain enough for a conviction.

What Edgar does, he does without full understanding. Although his paintings seem to have some sort of power on Duma, he is not aware of the actual extent of his abilities until he creates a rendition of the photograph that has been making its rounds on the news: Tina Garibaldi looking up at Candy Brown as he grabs her wrist. Edgar paints most of this in a sort of trance during a thunderstorm and it is only the next morning, after he has learned of Candy Brown's death, that he really gets a good look at his work. It is heart-wrenchingly true-to-life, except for the fact that Edgar painted a blank where Brown's nose and mouth should have been. The news is that Brown died in his cell, possibly because of sleep apnea, and Edgar cannot help but make the connection: through his painting, he stole Brown's breath.

Any fear that Brown might leave prison and go on to kill other girls is therefore quickly curtailed. Candy Brown is no longer the threat. Even Edgar, who has committed homicide with his paintbrush, is not the threat. Readers fear *for* him, because whatever power Edgar has is not entirely under his control. Between the thunderstorm and the trance, it is understood that Edgar may have been able to tap into something, but not what that something might be, although it seems to be connected to the strange ship Edgar keeps seeing on the Gulf.

Edgar had previously used his powers of creation to spy on his younger daughter's boyfriend, drawing the young man before he ever saw a picture, and also to sketch a mysterious red-robed figure, but each of these instances provided Edgar with information instead of impacting other people and their lives. The power of this painting of Candy Brown, and Brown's death the same night, makes Edgar wonder if he can, perhaps, direct whatever power he now possesses in ways he desires.

What Edgar picks is a way of healing instead of more death. His new friend, Wireman, has a bullet lodged in his brain that is slowly migrating and causing major health issues. It is inoperable, but a man who can stop a killer's breath could surely make a bullet disappear. That, at least, is what Edgar wishes to attempt. He creates a portrait of his friend that is *mostly* painted during times of full consciousness but, again, Edgar feels something else overtake him before the work is done. After another trance and another wild night of painting, Wireman calls with more good news: the sight has returned to his bad eye.

It is a double death that leads to Wireman's healing, and the first has nothing to do with Duma Key or the mysterious figure that fights for control there. Tina Garibaldi was an innocent child, with her death so horrific and her abduction so daring that the news could not help but cover it. Although the power on Duma, later named Perse, reaches out through Edgar to test his abilities with the painting and therefore the death of Candy Brown, there is no indication that Perse first caused Brown to act. Perse simply made do with the stimuli already present in Edgar's world.

And Edgar, who has learned that his creative ability can kill others as well as help to heal himself, does not put down the brushes. Working purely on instinct, he decides to paint Wireman's portrait, which includes a hole cut into the canvas to allow a drawing of Wireman's brain to show through. Although Edgar killed Candy Brown by leaving out some of his facial features, he does not seem worried that this window into Wireman's skull will adversely affect him. Trusting the instinct, not knowing if it comes from the source of his power or not—and not wanting to interrogate whether that source is good or moral—Edgar simply paints. With Wireman, the experiment works. Although he does not have another X-ray to prove that the bullet is gone, his headaches have vanished and the sight has returned to his bad eye.

If Candy Brown had not murdered Tina Garibaldi, Edgar would not have painted the double portrait. If Candy Brown had not died the same night Edgar painted that portrait, Edgar would not have thought to use his skills to save Wireman. The dual deaths serve not to create suspense as to whether someone else might be murdered or die at Edgar's brush, but to add to the questions and concerns surrounding Edgar's strangely powerful paintings. If he can do *this*, without understanding why or how, then are those questions he should answer? Or should he simply accept the power to murder child killers and save his friend and leave well enough alone? Edgar, with a strong push from Perse, chooses to act instead of to question, proving the strength of his power and setting him up both as Perse's tool and as capable of murder.

DEATH AND ANTICIPATION

The deaths described in this chapter are positioned within their narratives as important plot points that must have an impact on future events. The circumstances surrounding the deaths give readers information to guess at what might happen next, and whose life will likely be in danger. This is easiest when all the deaths are committed by a single entity, whether or not the entity has the power to plan ahead to carefully select victims, or is a dog afflicted with rabies and only killing victims of opportunity. The fact of the first deaths establishes the likelihood of subsequent deaths, and the characters' arcs and choices place them in the path of this already established possibility.

Readers who are horror fans in general, or who are King's Constant Readers, may have advance knowledge that the earlier deaths will lead to additional deaths and might therefore be more aware of the connecting threads. Although some of these series might be more obvious—the rabid dog will not be stopped until it dies and two characters are clearly in danger, or Dennis and Leigh give Christine a clear reason to come after them next—not all of King's series of deaths are so clear to new readers. Returning audiences might understand, upon first reading *Pet Sematary*, that Church's death and resurrection will not be the end-all, be-all, or the last time they will see the mysterious burying grounds. These deaths, even without the single-minded intention of a character honestly plotting to commit more, demand more throughout the narrative all the same. Whether or not the characters learn of the deaths as they transpire, the readers can witness them to increase their fear for the main characters and to build suspense through the tension between what the readers know and what the characters know, and when each party knows it.

Even only having the information given to the main characters can build both worry and suspense, such as in "The Mist" or "A Good Marriage." The major threat, whether natural or supernatural, works to "focus our attention onto the tale's real abhorrence: the behavior of human beings who suddenly find themselves confronting adversity and tragedy."[33] Readers hope that characters like David Drayton, Darcy Anderson, and John Smith will make moral decisions when confronted with their individual moments of crisis, and that they will survive their good choices. Because the danger itself comes in the form of a series of deaths, their chances are not high, and the characters themselves already know it. This is especially true in situations where the characters are being driven by the deaths or impending future deaths, as in *Dreamcatcher* and *Duma Key*. They do not have the luxury of taking their time to plot their next move or consult a library or expert for assistance.

These sorts of deaths not only move the plot forward, but also keep the reader interested. Although readers can, and do, anticipate future occurrences based on these early deaths, there are still details that are not completely foreshadowed and outcomes not entirely dictated by these early deaths. Even though Tad Trenton dies, for example, he is not mauled by Cujo the way three other men and even his mother have been. And, even though Church's death in the road may cause savvy readers to suspect that another member of the Creed family will be next, they might have chosen the wrong person as the center of their concerns. Further, even if readers are already aware that Gage is to become the next victim, there is still the question of what a returned human will look like as opposed to a returned cat. The suspense created surrounds not only the next possible death in the form it will take, but also the reactions and consequences of that death.

The deaths in this chapter clearly serve a narrative purpose as they move the story along and introduce ideas of threats and consequences. They help set up the conflicts between what characters want and what they can have, while presenting readers with more information that allows them to fear for the characters and their choices. Even though it is an expectation of the horror genre that the protagonists will make wrong decisions, readers can still hope that their favorites will, somehow, pull through and survive until the end of the book. However, "alive" does not necessarily equate to "emotionally unscathed." The deaths throughout the course of the narrative build on each other, working to increase tension and to foreshadow what comes next. They are specific, important plot points seated throughout the narrative to propel the story on its way.

Not every occasion of multiple death within King is serial death. At times, a single instance can rid the story of many of its main characters. Although King has used things such as bombs to drastically reduce the number of characters within his books on multiple occasions, one of them stands out, not for the number of deaths inflicted, but for the fact that these were driven by the author instead of the plot.

NOTES

1. Magistrale, *Landscape of Fear*, 49.
2. Anthony Magistrale, *The Moral Voyages of Stephen King* (USA: Wildside Press, LLC, this edition 2006), 36.
3. Rebecca Frost, "A Different Breed: Stephen King's Serial Killers," *Stephen King's Contemporary Classics: Reflections on the Modern Master of Horror* (Lanham, MD: Rowman & Littlefield, 2015), 120.
4. Magistrale, *The Moral Voyages of Stephen King*, 96.
5. Carol A. Senf, "*Gerald's Game* and *Dolores Claiborne*: Stephen King and the Evolution of an Authentic Female Narrative Voice," *Imagining the Worst: Stephen King and the Representation of Women* (Westport, CT: Greenwood Press, 1998), 98.
6. Magistrale, *Landscape of Fear*, 31.
7. Pharr, "Partners in the *Danse*," 26.
8. King, *The Stand*, 341.
9. Davis, *Stephen King's America*, 42.
10. Magistrale, *The Moral Voyages of Stephen King*, 54.
11. Magistrale, *Landscape of Fear*, 49.
12. Davis, *Stephen King's America*, 42.
13. Stephen King, *Christine* (New York: Gallery Books, 1983), 412.
14. Magistrale, *The Moral Voyages of Stephen King*, 22.
15. Stephen King, *Cujo* (New York: Gallery Books, 1981), 3.
16. Stephen King, *The Dead Zone* (New York: Signet Books, 1979), 64.
17. King, *The Dead Zone*, 253.
18. Magistrale, *The Moral Voyages of Stephen King*, 14.
19. Frost, "A Different Breed," 120.
20. Magistrale, *The Moral Voyages of Stephen King*, 12.

21. Frost, "A Different Breed," 120.
22. Strengell, *Dissecting Stephen King,* 82.
23. Tony Magistrale, "The Rehabilitation of Stephen King," *The Modern Stephen King Canon: Beyond Horror* (Lanham, MD: Lexington Books, 2019), 13.
24. Frost, "A Different Breed," 127.
25. Stephen King, "A Good Marriage," *Full Dark, No Stars* (New York: Scribner, 2010), 323.
26. Magistrale, "The Rehabilitation of Stephen King." 4
27. Strengell, *Dissecting Stephen King*, 61.
28. Joe Nazare. "The Horror! The Horror? The Appropriation, and Reclamation, of Native American Mythology," *Journal of the Fantastic in the Arts* 11, no. 1 (2000): 30.
29. Leonard Mustazza, "Fear and Pity: Tragic Horror in King's *Pet Sematary*," *The Dark Descent: Essays Defining Stephen King's Horrorscape*, (New York: Greenwood Press, 1992), 80.
30. Magistrale, *Landscape of Fear*, 59.
31. Pharr, "Partners in the *Danse*," 27.
32. Pharr, "Partners in the *Danse*," 27.
33. Magistrale, *Stephen King: The Second Decade*, 89.

Chapter Four

"I Saved My Book by Blowing Approximately Half Its Major Characters to Smithereens"

To Narrow the Focus

This chapter sits separately from all the others. The purpose of these deaths is not integral to the plot itself. They do affect the narrative, although they were not written because of demands of the plot. They were not planned from the beginning to propel the main characters onto their final confrontations, although they do assist in this way. These deaths are different because they were done not for plot purposes, but to make the author's life easier.

In *On Writing*, King candidly admits to having gotten stuck well into his longest book. Although *The Stand* begins with him killing off more than 90 percent of the people in the world, his cast of characters was still overpopulated. He needed a solution that would allow him as the author to push the story forward and get him over the hump that, he admitted, was indeed writer's block. The idea that King opted for was "one quick, hard slash of the Gordian knot."[1] He needed to decrease his cast of characters back down to a manageable number and so, instead of plotting a second draft that did not bring so many disparate stories together, he decided that his solution was a bomb.

Once the idea hit, King recalls that he spent a couple of days getting his notes in order and figuring out the rest of the plot—including who would place the bomb, and why—before quickly finishing the rest of the draft. At least one of the victim characters, Nick Andros, had been a major player since the beginning of the book, with his whole life story being told and his movements followed since before the plague struck, but he had to die so that King could keep composing.

Readers who encounter *The Stand* without having the knowledge shared in *On Writing* will likely interpret the bomb in Boulder by considering its function from within the closed world of the narrative, treating it as an example of suspense. Although Boulder is supposed to be the location where all the "good" post-plague people have gone, readers are already aware that at least two people in the Boulder Free Zone do not fit this description. Harold Lauder has been nursing his hate since the woman he was obsessed with fell in love with another man, and Nadine Cross is meant to be Randall Flagg's bride.

The reveal of the bomb is a slow one. At one point Harold is seen modifying walkie-talkies based on an old science project in which one can be used to ring a bell at a distance. Other characters see the remnants of this build but cannot attach any specific meaning to it. Nadine is later seen out and about with a bag of groceries, knocking on the door of the house at which the Free Zone committee will next meet. She has the bomb in that bag, and readers see her place it in a closet near the main meeting room. Although Nadine hesitates, caught in last-minute doubt, all fates are sealed when Flagg takes over and forces her to leave the bomb where it was placed.

Although both Harold and Nadine have been positioned to be aligned more with Flagg than with anyone in Boulder, neither has done anything up to that point to actually threaten the lives of anyone else. Nadine has in fact stopped the small boy she was traveling with from attacking fellow survivor Larry Underwood while he slept, and made the statement that she knew would come back to haunt her: that she defined the biggest sin in this post-plague world as murder.[2] Readers have seen Nadine struggle with her emotions and her relationship to others, and Harold is full of anger directed specifically at two Free Zone leaders, but there is nothing to explicitly indicate that Harold or Nadine would willingly participate in mass murder. Despite her conversation with Flagg, when it comes time to actually set off the bomb, Nadine wavers. She is sick with what they have done, while Harold only calmly and coldly declares that they must move on.

It should be noted that this differs from other mass murders within King's works, such as the fire that rages at the end of *Under the Dome*. This is not to say that none of the other instances of mass death in King's works were also meant to serve this purpose and this purpose only—to counter writer's block—but that these other narratives worked to plant the seeds of this kind of destruction from an early part of the plot. The meth lab, explosives, and paranoid character are already in place far in advance of the events that killed nearly an entire town. Since this explosion is the climax of *Under the Dome*, unlike the bomb in Boulder which is only used to keep the story moving along, it seems more logical that this mass death was planned from the beginning. In *The Stand*, however, Harold only begins to create the bomb after King has written himself into this corner and then assured himself that the bomb will be his way out.

When King talks about writing, either as himself or through one of his author characters, it seems that he cannot conceive of meticulously plotting out an entire book and then having it conclude exactly the way he expected when he set out to write it. As Paul Sheldon explains in *Misery*, "Having a novel end exactly the way you thought it would when you started out would be like shooting a Titan missile halfway around the world and having the payload drop through a basketball hoop."[3] Generally, it seems King ends up close to where he thought the book would go, but he also does not plot every single element in the story. This is how he can end up the way he did in *The Stand*, uncertain how to proceed and in need of something drastic to keep going. It is entirely possible that such plot points within his other works were created in this way—as life preservers thrown to a drowning narrative—but this is the one instance in which King has shared with his readers that it was true. It is therefore set apart from these other examples because the deaths function to serve the author himself, outside of the narrative, and not solely for a purpose within the plot.

There are, of course, deaths in Kings works that serve an internal purpose of driving the plot forward, and these are the subject of the next chapter. These are, presumably, not surprise deaths to the author himself but plot points he has planned to urge his main characters onto action. All too frequently, King's characters find themselves at some sort of slump amid their troubles, caught in a personal version of the horse latitudes and in need of some external, and often extreme, motivation in order to keep moving.

NOTES

1. Stephen King, *On Writing* (New York: Pocket Books, 2000), 204.
2. King, *The Stand*, 840.
3. Stephen King, *Misery* (New York: Scribner, 1987), 279.

Chapter Five

"Question: Death, Where Is Thy Sting? Answer: Every-Fucking-Where"

To Urge the Characters on to Action

It is not infrequent in King's works that characters need some sort of push to action. They are caught up in a situation that seems either overwhelming or outright impossible and, as a result, withdraw into themselves or slip into stunned indecision. The threat, however, refuses to go away simply because the protagonist is unsure how to confront it. In many cases, King uses death to shock his characters out of this fugue and urge them on to the offensive.

Some series of murders occur when the antagonist intends to drive the protagonist onto a specific action. George Stark in *The Dark Half* and Norman Daniels in *Rose Madder* each mark their journey toward the protagonist with a series of murders. Readers, as well as main characters Thaddeus Beaumont and Rose McClendon, realize "that nothing this strange happens just by chance"[1] and grasp both what the antagonist wants and how dangerous he is. Their battle is not simply against Stark and Norman, no matter how many people are killed, but against the skepticism and dismissal of others who either do not believe in the man's existence, or in the very real level of danger he presents.

Other antagonists isolate the protagonist before enacting the crucial murders, giving them fewer resources in their responses, but also fewer others to convince of the true danger. The climax of *Duma Key* comes after Perse has either killed or attempted to kill Edgar's closest friends; Charlie only uses her pyrokinesis against The Shop in *Firestarter* after her father has been killed; and Paul Sheldon's time line is drastically shortened in *Misery* once his captor murders the state trooper sent looking for him. While Edgar has two friends with him on his small island, cut off from the rest of the world, Charlie and Paul are alone, and finally convinced of how dire their situations are.

At other times the death that motivates the protagonist into action is a suicide, whether or not the character who completed suicide meant it as motivation. *Cell* and *11/22/63* both have characters who kill themselves specifically as part of a plot to motivate the protagonist into action, and hopefully victory. *Needful Things* and *The Tommyknockers* contain suicides that function more like the murders in *Duma Key*, *Firestarter*, and *Misery*, drawing the protagonist out of his fugue state and forcing him to act even though the character had not specifically intended it. These are all situations in which the protagonist has been ineffectual or inactive up until that point and is specifically driven on to a course of action because of the suicide.

Finally, it is also possible for King's antagonists to accidentally self-motivate through murder. Brady Hartsfield is a paragon of self-restraint in *Mr. Mercedes*, as long as his plans are working. "His moments of being out of control are rare,"[2] which explains why he has been able to commit mass murder without being caught, but as the narrative unfolds, Hartsfield begins to unravel. When his mother eats poisoned meat Brady had prepared for other purposes, he first realizes he cannot call an ambulance for her and then is forced into action, quickly changing his long-standing plans and ultimately setting the stage for his own downfall.

Whether or not these deaths spur the protagonists onto the action that the killer intended is largely a function of the intention of the murderer. If the deaths were caused by the antagonists who wish the protagonists to act a certain way, then the plan will fail as the protagonist first sees through it and acts to counter it. Suicides, on the other hand, work to push the protagonists in the right direction, especially when the character completed suicide with good intentions. Even here the complexity is evident, since outcomes, even following motivational deaths, are not necessarily predictable.

DEATH AS INTERNALLY LOGICAL MOTIVATION

The character of George Stark—still meant to be merely a fiction rather than a real person in the world of *The Dark Half*—rises from his fictional grave with a single-minded purpose: to convince author Thaddeus Beaumont to write his next book and therefore honestly bring him to life. Stark was Beaumont's pen name for his more violent novels, and Thad had created an elaborate backstory for his alter ego. Everything that Beaumont described, and all that he knows about Stark, comes true, including Stark's penchant for violence. The newly resurrected Stark realizes that only one of them can exist, so Thad will have to die to allow him to live. Stark, being Stark, decides to convince Thad to go along with this idea through murder.

The "death" of Beaumont's pseudonym occurred because of a "Creepazoid"[3] fan who made the connection between Beaumont and Stark and who then attempted to blackmail Beaumont so that the secret could remain. However, Beaumont, his wife, his agent, and his editor all agreed that the best course of action would be for the author to come clean on his own. The announcement, published in *People*, featured a photo of the Beaumonts shaking hands over Stark's "grave." This setup not only gave the physical Stark a place from which to emerge, but also added two names to his hit list: the journalist and the photographer responsible for the article. By working his way through the people associated with his death and therefore his current strange half-life, Stark hopes to convince Thad to agree to start the next book and transfer both his talent and his life force.

Readers who know they are holding a Stephen King story in their hands are much more likely to believe this series of events than the characters within the narrative, especially since readers are allowed to "watch everything happen."[4] This begins with the landlady's discovery of the blackmailer's murdered and mutilated body, although Stark's later crimes are shown unfolding as they happen. Readers, and the very practical Sheriff Alan Pangborn, are never fully given an explanation as to how Stark could actually exist—the handwave explanation involves a brain tumor Thad had removed as a child that was shown to have been tissue from a twin he absorbed in utero—but readers at least know that he *does* exist. Thad and Liz Beaumont are also quickly convinced of both Stark's reality and his mission. They understand the reason Stark is murdering these specific people, and so they know that the Beaumonts, especially Liz and the couple's infant twins, are in danger of being next.

Stark murders these people to send a message to Thad about what must be done to prevent further homicides. If Thad does not want to be responsible, as Stark puts it, for the torture and deaths of his own babies, then he must comply with Stark's wishes. Stark uses not only the murders themselves but his understanding of Thad's psychology to manipulate him into, at the very least, appearing to agree to his terms, but he is not the only character to go on a violent spree in pursuit of his ambitions. Norman Daniels, of *Rose Madder*, has his own goal in mind: to track down his runaway wife, Rosie McClendon, and make her sorry for leaving him and making him a laughingstock among his coworkers. While Stark manages to operate under police protection in that law enforcement, Alan Pangborn among them, believes that somehow Thad had to have been the murderer and Stark does not exist, Norman is one of the brothers in blue himself and happens to work with men just as violent as he is.

For Norman, the main conflict of *Rose Madder* is that his wife has stolen his bank card and left him. It is not the fact that he abused her for over a decade, or even that his anger has caused him to commit murder in the past. Professionally, Norman Daniels is doing better than ever, recently recognized by the city and promoted in his job as detective. Before taking up his new position, though, Norman wants time off so he can track down his "Rambling Rosie." He follows in her footsteps, taking the same bus his wife did weeks earlier and tracking her down through those who helped her establish her new, Norman-free life.

The setup is similar to the Stark-Beaumont narrative in that Rosie knows full well that Norman is after her, but has difficulty explaining the situation to others, in part because she does not trust policeman. She believes that all of them will be like Norman, and will band together to protect him. Norman slowly tracks down the people who have helped Rosie since her move, working his way closer and closer to her. Because readers know his intent, Norman's path is clear, and we fear for both Rosie and her new boyfriend, who seems to be a good man.

These are not strangers Norman kills, or characters who really only come into the story for their own death scenes the way many of Stark's victims do, but characters readers are meant to like because they have been kind to Rosie. The suspense is increased because none of these people are deserving of death, unlike perhaps *The Dark Half*'s Creepazoid. All of Norman's victims are in his sights because they have helped his abused wife find her new life, away from him. Norman is angry because his coworkers are laughing at him, which is not the same as Stark being angry that these people—completely unknowingly—killed him.

Norman, like Stark, is foiled in the end despite his willingness to disregard human life—and even his own future, beyond his final encounter with Rosie. Also like Stark, there is no body left behind for rational members of law enforcement to see, process, and use in their creation of a sensible explanation for the events. What Norman's murder spree does accomplish, however, is to push Rosie toward a final solution in the problem of her abusive husband. She left him, and gave up his bank card after a single withdrawal, and took a bus to a city far away from home, but Norman was not content to let her go. He decided that the proper response was a series of murders, and his own murder was the only way to stop him.

The character choreographing these deaths does not need to be a man and does not need to have a close personal relationship with the protagonist. In *Duma Key*, recently relocated and newly artistic Edgar Freemantle discovers that the power behind his paintings, if not the talent itself, comes from the mysterious Perse. Although he suspects that there is something special about

Duma from his first night on the island, it takes Edgar and his friends time to piece together the facts of Perse's existence and the extent of her powers.

This uncovering happens in a series of acts both murderous—Edgar stops the breath of a child murderer through his painting—and healing: Edgar removes a bullet from his friend's brain. The one survivor of Perse's previous activities on the island, Elizabeth Eastlake, has dementia and is unable to warn Edgar. He has to learn Elizabeth's horrific childhood story through newspaper articles and supernatural encounters that lean to the side of good, and what they show him is horrific. Although Elizabeth used to have five older sisters and a nanny, only two of her sisters remained alive at the end of her own final battle with Perse.

Perse used those deaths to try to scare a young Elizabeth into compliance, and she uses her powers to attack Edgar's friends and family, as well. Two of his friends die before Edgar figures out what is happening, and he believes he has acted to prevent any more, making the next death all the more horrific: one of Edgar's friends from Florida murders his favorite daughter before completing suicide. These deaths again move closer to the central character, the same way Stark's murders became more and more personal to Thad Beaumont. Perse, who is inhuman and therefore unlikely to understand human emotions and motivations, believed that Edgar would see her power and choose to flee Duma instead of confronting her. If he did persist, she believed the Edgar who comes to the far side of the key would be ill-informed and have his mind deadened by grief, thereby making him far less than a worthy opponent. Had Perse not sent one of her minions after Ilse, she might have succeeded in press-ganging Edgar and his friends to her ship of the dead. Having lost his favorite child—and therefore perhaps having nothing left to lose—Edgar is committed to his quest and his mission, and the details surrounding Ilse's murder even mean that Perse has helped Edgar understand exactly what it is he must do.

Because these examples are set up as the narrative's antagonist committing murder to drive the protagonist, they all fail. The murders are indeed committed, and those characters remain dead, but the antagonist does not manage to get what he or she wants in the end. The main characters refuse to allow themselves to be driven in such a way and instead resolve to follow a path that aligns with their own morals and free will. They, at least, know that they are fighting against the aims of one specific Other and can therefore act and react against the Other's desires. Here, the ones enacting the deaths are themselves still alive and must be faced, although this is not always the case.

PLOT-DRIVEN MOTIVATIONAL DEATHS

Although the foregoing examples are those in which characters kill other characters with the express purpose of forcing the main character to act, not every instigating death is so planned. At times characters die with a far different intent, and yet the main character is spurred on to action because of it all the same.

In *Firestarter*, young Charlie McGee is forced into stasis when members of The Shop finally catch up to her and her father, Andy. Her mother, Vicky, was already dead at the start of the narrative, leaving Charlie with no one in the world but her father. Now captured and separated from Andy, Charlie is caught alone and being pressured to demonstrate her pyrokinesis for the Shop. Vicky and Andy "fire-trained" their young daughter to keep her from burning herself, and Charlie vowed never to start fires again after a previous incident with Shop agents meant she killed some of them and brought harm to the good people protecting them.

Although only seven and eight years old throughout the course of the story, Charlie stands by her convictions. She spends months of her imprisonment quietly refusing to use her pyrokinesis in spite of the various overt and veiled threats directed at her. The Shop, however, "engage[s] in psychic blackmail"[5] with their young hostage, introducing a janitor/spy named John Rainbird to first win over Charlie's trust and then convince her to start participating in demonstrations in exchange for her own demands. Readers, allowed to see Rainbird's thoughts, know to fear for the child long before the book's violent climax.

The problem is that "Charlie is too young to understand that adults wish to manipulate her,"[6] at least beyond the clearly identified Shop agents. She adopts Rainbird, in his disguise as orderly, as her new father figure, since she is not allowed to be in contact with Andy. This means that both Rainbird and Andy die in front of Charlie on the same day, right after Andy revealed Rainbird's treachery to his daughter. She lost two father figures in quick succession, events that The Shop had neither planned for nor foreseen.

Charlie had shown earlier in the novel that she could be convinced to use her powers to help her daddy, or to protect Andy from armed Shop agents, despite the "fire training" she was given as a much younger girl. During her time imprisoned at The Shop, the memory and thoughts of Andy helped Charlie put the brakes on her powers and thereby finesse her control of her pyrokinesis. Without the encouragement from Rainbird to give in to the requests for demonstrations, she would not have been able to bring herself to practice. Even then, Charlie would likely not have decided to use her ability against the Shop all on her own. With the revelation of Rainbird's betrayal followed by Andy's death, Charlie had no reason to hold back any longer and used her newly honed powers to destroy The Shop compound.

Andy McGee's death was, from the perspective of The Shop, only a matter of time, although its actual occurrence had consequences that were not entirely foreseen. In contrast, in *Misery* a young state trooper named Duane Kushner was not expecting to go to his death in the course of a routine missing person inquiry, but at least one other character had planned ahead for the eventuality. Annie Wilkes knew that, eventually, people would come looking for her pet author, and she proved incredibly resourceful in the wake of Kushner's surprise arrival.

Like Charlie McGee, prisoner Paul Sheldon spent months in stasis doing what he could to please his captor. Annie single-mindedly focused on getting Paul to complete her desired manuscript, and her home's relative isolation worked in their favor as far as time. It was only after Paul's abandoned car was discovered that people began looking for him in that part of the country. Duane Kushner was the unlucky trooper who was assigned Annie's house for initial queries. When he saw and recognized Paul, Annie murdered the young man to keep her pet writer a secret for a while longer.

Paul, like Charlie, is confronted with his caretaker suddenly showing violent tendencies in real time. Although he knew that Annie had murdered in the past, thanks to the scrapbook she meticulously kept, and although Paul knew that Annie could be scary and threatening, up to and including forced amputations, he had not seen her murder anyone. Not just the bloody event itself, but the careful and methodical way Annie plans the aftermath, cues Paul in to how little time the two of them have left before he is discovered. He knows that Annie would rather opt for murder-suicide than get caught and so, after so many long weeks of passive compliance, he begins to take steps and make a plan to save himself, finally spurred on to action in the real world instead of just in the book Annie demands. Annie's reaction to the murder of Duane Kushner allows Paul not only to plan her own demise, but also gives him access to the lighter fluid that becomes instrumental in his plan. Without Kushner's murder, Paul could not have killed Annie.

In each of these cases, the main character was spurred on to action because of a death outside their control that helped outline exactly how dire their situation was. Again, because the murders were committed by the antagonist, the reactions were not, in fact, what the murderers intended. To triumph, the protagonists had to respond to these deaths in a way that helped spur them on to their own success, rather than continuing the course of inaction that would have likely let the antagonist win.

SUICIDE AS MOTIVATION

Although some of King's characters commit murder in their attempts to lead the main characters into action—and the previous examples generally show cases in which the main character subverts the expected reactions when murder is committed by an antagonist—there are two narratives in which King's characters complete suicide to purposefully guide the protagonists' movements. They see no other course of action to bring about the events that they, personally, desire, and they can only hope that the main character will properly interpret the event.

In *Cell*, surviving "normal" people find themselves battling altered humans—"Phoners"—who have the ability to read minds. Main character Clay encounters minor character Ray only briefly before Ray does the inexplicable: hands Clay a cell phone—the author of all the chaos and misery within the book—and complete suicide with a cryptic comment about how he hopes Clay will know the proper moment to use it. Even after Clay explains this to the surviving group members, none of them know what to make of it, especially because the survivors are being herded into a dead zone for their impending execution.

Even though he is barely in the book at all, Ray is the real hero of *Cell*. Without letting the other members of the group know what he was up to, so that they could not give it away to the Phoners, he loaded the group's bus with explosives and wired it up to a cell phone. The surviving members realize that, if Clay uses his phone to dial the number Ray gave him, the bomb will go off. Since it is nighttime, most of the Phoners have laid down to rest, congregating a large number of them in a small area. If the group can manage to get the bus closer to the flock, then a single phone call will hopefully kill enough of them that they cannot come together again—and, thanks to the planned fair, the area temporarily has cell service so that those involved with setting things up could keep in touch with each other.

Ray's sudden suicide creates a high level of tension in the narrative because of the many points of conflicting information: that Ray is not the sort of person to complete suicide; that cell phones will not be useful in Kashwak; and that the surviving members of the group must decide on a plan and act on it before morning. If they cannot figure out Ray's plan with enough time to put it into action, it seems that the rest of them will be executed as they have foreseen in their dreams. Fortunately Clay is able to clear his thoughts enough to puzzle it out so that the group can enact Ray's plan and save themselves.

Less confusing is the suicide of Al Templeton in *11/22/63*. Al, like Ray, is only in a small part of the book, but Al appears in the beginning. He is the one to tell the main character, Jake Epping, about the time travel portal hidden in the pantry of his diner. Al oversees Jake's first two trips back in time—the initial one to inform him what the portal does, and the second one for Jake to prove to himself how and if the past can be changed—but then kills himself after sending Jake home, ostensibly to think things over. What Al wants is clear: Jake needs to take the portal back to 1958 and live in the past for long enough to determine that Lee Harvey Oswald was the sole assassin of JFK. By killing Oswald before the infamous date, Jake should prevent Kennedy's assassination and therefore change the course of history.

Unlike Ray, Al has left Jake with a full road map and a complete understanding of the task at hand. Al attempted living in the past himself and was foiled by lung cancer, so his own future is distinctly shortened no matter what time period he chooses and he cannot survive long enough to complete his mission. Both before and during his life in the late 1950s and early 1960s, Al amassed a lot of information about the time period, from the outcomes of sporting events—so good bets could finance the endeavor—to information about Oswald. Jake is therefore given far more than a single item before Al's suicide, and he knows exactly why Al did it. At the end of the month, the diner will be towed, and both Al and Jake suspect that the time travel portal will not survive the move. Al's death gives Jake a much shorter amount of time in which to mull over his choices.

Jake can act more quickly and decisively than Clay and his friends, having full understanding of what is expected of him. Although things do not go as smoothly as Al's notebook suggests, Jake still has more guidance than a single cell phone and a piece of paper with a number on it. Jake, too, does not have anyone else in whom to confide or with whom to brainstorm. Alone, he plunges back into 1958 to save Kennedy and change the course of history.

SUICIDE WITH UNINTENTIONAL CONSEQUENCES

Suicide, like murder, can also have unintended consequences within King's works. The two previous examples of suicide were cases in which the character who died had a very clear idea of what should happen after his death. In each of the foregoing narratives, the main character complied and carried out the dead character's wishes just as that character intended. However, it is also possible for a suicide to have unintended consequences that still lead to acts of heroism by a main character who has previously been spinning his metaphorical wheels.

In *Needful Things*, the character who completes suicide is not doing so with the intention of spurring someone else onto action. Young Brian Rusk, only eleven years old, was the first customer in Castle Rock's newest shop. He purchased a special baseball card from the owner for the price of a few cents and pranks to be played on his neighbors. It is through Brian's eyes that we first meet the character of Leland Gaunt and begin to suspect that he is something other than human. Since he is only a child, however, Brian finds himself agreeing to Mr. Gaunt's suggested price and then, when he finds himself in over his head, withdrawing from his family and friends.

The issue begins when Brian realizes he cannot share his purchase with anyone else, considering the usual cost of his card, and he starts obsessing over it. When he sees a newspaper report that the woman upon whom he played his pranks was half of a double murder, his guilt increases. Unable to talk to his parents about it—his mother has made her own obsessive purchase and his father is largely absent—Brian completes suicide in front of his younger brother, Sean. Hospitalized for shock, Sean is nevertheless able to relate this story to the town's sheriff, Alan Pangborn, and thereby allow Alan to put enough pieces together to confront Gaunt in the book's climax.

It is Brian's suicide that puts Alan at Sean's bedside and perhaps only shock that allows the eight-year-old boy to speak of these things. Alan personally knows at least two other people who have made purchases at Needful Things, and that one of them—his girlfriend, Polly Chalmers—has been acting strangely ever since. Even though Alan is presented as a man who has encountered the supernatural before, specifically in *The Dark Half* with Thad Beaumont and George Stark, he does not immediately come to the conclusion that something similar might be happening again. *The Dark Half* was the narrative in which Alan had to be dragged, kicking and screaming, into admitting the existence of the supernatural, but Alan is now distracted. His wife and younger son were killed in a car accident a year and a half previously, and certain members of the town were already unraveling—and demanding Alan's attention—prior to meeting Leland Gaunt. It takes Brian's suicide, and this conversation with Sean, to let Alan see what is really happening.

In *The Tommyknockers*, it is also a suicide that leads a main character on to action. While Brian Rusk intended to kill himself, it is unclear whether Ruth McCausland went about creating her signal knowing or only suspecting that it would end in her death. Trapped in her own town, surrounded by people "Becoming" alien as a result of a flying saucer's excavation, Ruth was herself initially immune to the changes and the groupthink. Unable to physically leave the village, she rigged a device to set off in the town's clock tower, which ended up taking off like a rocket and killing her in the process. The explosion in the tower acted on Jim Gardener the way Rainbird and Andy McGee's deaths acted on Charlie McGee, or how Duane Kushner's death acted on Paul Sheldon: Gard realizes that he cannot continue his current passive participation and that he must act. Further, Ruth's funeral allows two other men the chance to investigate Haven and create ripples of their own.

"*Question: Death, Where Is Thy Sting? Answer: Every-Fucking-Where*" 75

Tony Magistrale notes the emphasis of this narrative on both group identity and mental fusion. He goes so far as to describe the Havenites as "the walking dead who have sacrificed their reason, vision, and morality"[7] for the sake of belonging to a larger group. It is of course easier to give in and be told what to do, and so many residents of Haven show not even a token sign of resistance. Gard's drinking is his attempt to anesthetize his morality and his own conscience so that he, too, can join the ranks of the walking dead. Total mental fusion is beyond him, at least until the very end of the book, due to the metal plate in his head, but Gard has always wanted to be part of the solution. He yearns to rise up and fight back against something, to make a difference and leave his own mark on the world. Gard allows his friendship with Bobbi as well as Bobbi's own rationalizations to lull him into participating without the benefit of also Becoming. It is Ruth's resistance to the idea of Becoming, and her large and violent response that can be seen so far away, that starts to break down Gard's own status as the walking dead.

Even though Brian Rusk did not intend to save the town with his suicide, and Ruth hoped that her own message—and accidental suicide—would lead to salvation from outside the town rather than inside it, each of them sent a message that was heard by perhaps the only character who could act and attempt to save the day. Prior to these events, Alan Pangborn had not even realized who the true adversary was, and Gard had been doing nothing but working alongside the Tommyknockers and maintaining his drunken state to keep from thinking about it. The two men, both protagonists, were spurred on to action by the suicide of others.

ACCIDENTAL SELF-MOTIVATION

It is also entirely possible for one of King's characters to accidentally cause a death and therefore push himself into action sooner than he may have liked. Brady Hartsfield, the main antagonist of the Bill Hodges trilogy and the murderer initially only known as Mr. Mercedes, would like to add to his current death toll. Specifically, he would like to murder the detective who could not solve his case. At the start of *Mr. Mercedes*, the first book in the trilogy, Bill Hodges is depressed, and it seems as though Brady might be able to push him into suicide. Unfortunately for Brady, Hodges takes the anonymous note and communications as a new challenge and finds himself invigorated.

Instead of inspiring Hodges's suicide, Brady attempts to take the detective's death into his own hands. His bomb kills not Hodges but another character and, although this is frustrating to Brady, it is not overly worrisome. When a second slip results in Brady accidentally poisoning his own mother instead of the intended dog, Brady ends up hurting not Hodges by proxy, but himself, directly.

To save his mother, Brady would have to let others know what was happening, and he would be discovered to have poisoned some hamburger meat. Thus far, to the outside world, he is only a figure of "bland anonymity,"[8] just some guy still living at home and working two jobs to make ends meet, but this would change all of that. If Brady were discovered to have purchased the poison, what other questionable transactions might they find? In this moment, he makes the decision to sacrifice his mother to his greater cause.

Although Deborah's death cannot move up Brady's final act indiscriminately, since he chooses a specific venue on a particular date, the presence of her dead body does spur him on to leaving home perhaps sooner than he had originally planned. By the time Bill and his assistants focus on the name Brady Hartsfield and track down his address, Brady has already left the house and begun his final preparations for his suicide bombing. Here the antagonist played his own role of accidental motivator, although, like many of King's antagonists, his own plan does not fully come to fruition. Because he is the bad guy, his best-laid plans are not allowed to succeed, even if he manages to cause deaths along the way to his defeat.

ONE FINAL PUSH

The foregoing examples create a curious mix of death as motivation. When antagonists attempt to use murder to spur the protagonists on to their own preferred action, the protagonists do indeed act, but not in the way the antagonists plan. When George Stark, Norman Daniels, and Perse "kill people we like,"[9] readers feel the increased suspense and tension. They know that the antagonist is not only capable of murder, but counting on committing more in order to get what they want, even if the protagonists do not already realize it. Readers hope that the protagonists catch on in time not only to save themselves, but also to prevent themselves from being driven to act instead of choosing how to act. Characters like Charlie McGee in *Firestarter* and Paul Sheldon in *Misery* are in more danger of being driven, because the deaths occur much closer to the narrative's climax when the protagonists are already in a heightened state of tension.

When secondary characters who are still coded as "good" characters complete suicide to encourage the main characters to follow a specific plan, their deaths become meaningful when the main characters do so. Ray Huizenga in *Cell* and Al Templeton in *11/22/63* have specific goals in mind and use their suicides to push the protagonist into actions that should save them. However, in other examples, a suicide that does not carry this intent still manages to pull the main character out of a rut so that he can complete the narrative with his own heroic action. Alan Pangborn is largely reactive until Brian Rusk's suicide in *Needful Things* pushes him to be proactive, the same way Gard passively goes along with the Tommyknockers until Ruth McCausland's death. Neither Brian nor Ruth specifically meant to motivate Alan or Gard, the way Ray and Al clearly intended to push the protagonists of their own narratives into action, but their deaths had that effect all the same.

And finally, an antagonist more inept than others might accidentally commit murder of his own loved one and therefore push himself onto his final action, even though, being the antagonist and now a man who has committed matricide, he cannot be allowed to carry out his final plan. When Brady Hartsfield accidentally poisons perhaps the only person who actually cares about him, it creates a moment of crisis for the character. However, "King's readers' sympathies lie firmly with Hartsfield's victims"[10] even in this emotionally charged moment. Brady is suffering the loss of his mother, yes, but he is the one to cause her death, the way he has already callously caused so many others.

All these deaths are necessary in their narratives not in and of themselves but because of the actions and reactions they inspire. Although readers can largely see how the situation is unfolding, and how things will continue to spiral downwards without intervention, the main characters often find themselves uncertain of how to act. As a reaction to the doubt, they frequently do nothing, or find themselves chasing down red herrings or inconsequential matters as a form of distraction. They are therefore in need of a drastic event to provide the metaphorical slap necessary to break their stupor.

These deaths end up either serving the purpose of the protagonists or backfiring against the antagonists. The protagonists themselves do not directly cause the deaths, but only benefit from learning about them, even if they were not meant to. Suicides, like homicides perpetuated by the antagonists, can be necessary calls to action for protagonists who have frozen. Even when intended to be dreadful, horrific experiences, deaths can turn into the protagonists' cause to finally act and attempt heroics.

This basic setup, though, is called into question in King's first novel, where the vast majority of deaths that occur are caused by the protagonist and title character in response to acts of violence that have been done to her. Here the line between "main character" and "antagonist" is blurred. Readers might end up empathizing more with the character meant to be demonized within the narrative than with the survivors. Although Carrie was the first, and played a major role into bringing the term "horror" into common usage,[11] she is only one of King's characters to kill others as an act of revenge.

NOTES

1. Russell, *Stephen King: A Critical Companion*, 83.
2. Rebecca Frost, "Razors, Bumper Stickers, and Wheelchairs: Male Violence and Madness in *Rose Madder* and *Mr. Mercedes*," *The Modern Stephen King Canon: Beyond Horror* (Lanham, MD: Lexington Books, 2019), 87.
3. Stephen King, *The Dark Half* (New York: Signet Books, 1989), 30.
4. Russell, *Stephen King: A Critical Companion*, 93.
5. Magistrale, *Landscape of Fear*, 34.
6. Davis, *Stephen King's America*, 59.
7. Magistrale, *Stephen King: The Second Decade*, 83.
8. Phillip L. Simpson, "From the Meat World to Cyberspace," 118.
9. Russell, *Stephen King: A Critical Companion*, 147.
10. Hayley Mitchell Haugen, "Horrific Sympathies: The Comingling of Violence and Mental Illness in Stephen King's *Mr. Mercedes*," *The Modern Stephen King Canon: Beyond Horror* (Lanham, MD: Lexington Books, 2019), 101.
11. Helen Marshall, "A Snapshot of an Age: The Publication History of *Carrie*," *Journal of Popular Culture* 53, no. 2 (2020): 289.

Chapter Six

"More Than Any of Us Probably Know, She Hurt"

As Revenge

Frequently the cause of murder within King's narratives is shown to come from an internal compulsion, especially in the case of serial murder. The innate makeup of the character, whether human or inhuman, means that a certain level of personal satisfaction can only be obtained when that character kills others. It can be to literally feed and provide sustenance for a longer life, or it can be in response to some inner need of a maladjusted character who was apparently unable to find emotional fulfillment through interpersonal relationships. But, sometimes, it is other people who drive characters to commit murder, not out of personal gratification, but as acts of revenge.

These characters can present explicable motives in order to justify their acts of murder. They are not meant to be the inhuman Other but rather relatable characters whose humanity is bound up in their reasons for murder. King plays with both human and nonhuman murderers within his books, at times blurring the lines by adding human serial killers who are still not meant to be entirely empathetic. In his very first book, however, King presents readers with the title character, who is superhuman but also sympathetic. Although Carrie discovers that she has telekinetic powers, and although she uses those powers to commit mass murder—what Heidi Strengell describes as "overreacts when taking a moral stand"[1]—she is still presented as an unpopular high school girl and not always as a monster. The overreaction is there, but so is the injustice. King takes the time to develop her in his narrative so that readers can see where she is coming from and can hope alongside her that perhaps the Cinderella moment of prom night will last. The real enemies within *Carrie* are the fully human, including Carrie's high school classmates and her own mother, but they have still managed to persecute her.

King's characters suffer from all kinds of abuse, including emotional, physical, and sexual. Not all these characters respond with violence to their mistreatment—frequently they are shown to accept it as a matter of course—but some of his characters are pushed into situations where they honestly contemplate homicide as the proper reaction to what they are facing. Characters like Dolores Claiborne are "situated at crisis points where they must either rise above their oppression or capitulate to it entirely,"[2] and Dolores is one character who chooses action over inaction. Dolores, like Tess in "Big Driver," is pushed to the breaking point not because she herself is threatened, but because others are. They act not on behalf of themselves, but on behalf of other women who may face sexual abuse and death if the perpetrator is allowed to live.

The character enacting revenge does not have to be a woman or girl. In *Cell*, preteen Jordan is the one to seek revenge against the group of zombie-like Phoners who forced his mentor and father figure to complete suicide. The threat here is much wider: not simply to women who might cross the antagonists' path, but presumably the entire world. Further, revenge is not solely the domain of the protagonist. In "1922," the narrator's murdered wife "does not rest"[3] and exacts her revenge by either driving the main character mad, or by actually returning from the grave to murder him.

All these vengeful characters share a similar trait in the fact that the murders they commit, and the way they commit them, are reactions to the treatment they have been receiving. They are looking for some way to take back control of their own situations and to use the powers given to them to make amends for the ways in which life has wronged them. Even then, their success is not always guaranteed. There are still consequences for taking lives, even when the situation demands it.

SOCIAL ABUSE

As seen in King's first published novel, *Carrie*, the author accepts the idea that perhaps at least some of his characters may be driven to kill by the actions of others. The book opens with one of myriad incidences of bullying of the main character, Carrie White. This one takes place in the girls' shower after gym class and is triggered by the arrival of Carrie's first menstrual period. Here, King already sets up two of the antagonists in the story: Carrie's fellow classmates, especially the popular girls, and her own mother, who did not properly prepare her for this time. Carrie is, then, isolated and left to fend for herself on all fronts.

The fact that Carrie herself possesses telekinetic powers sets her apart from many of the supernatural or nonhuman figures within King's works. She is the title character, a point-of-view character, and one who invites readers to see themselves in her. Carrie is allowed to tell much of her own story, and to invite the reader in, so that "she demands the reader's sympathy"[4] even when the narrative positions her as its monster. Although Carrie is a threat to Chamberlain, Maine, the town itself first failed her when it could not protect her from her mother and refused to take her in and accept her as one of them.

The isolation began before Carrie's birth, and the teasing started on the first day of kindergarten and continues up to her final night. For King, there is a "social cause behind Carrie's actions"[5] on prom night, making her both monstrous and explicable. She did not explode out of nothing or even on the basis of a single horrific incident. Carrie's history is one of abuse by both her mother and her peers, with her teachers either siding with her fellow students or simply being ineffectual at stopping their reactions. Even her Cinderella-like transformation to prom queen is nothing more than another prank orchestrated by one of the schools' popular girls, meant to humiliate Carrie once again before graduation.

Even though the teenager then goes on a rampage, killing most of the prom attendees before seeking out others in the town, "King considers *Carrie* a story about a girl who does a terrible thing but she was justified because she has been driven mad by all the teasing."[6] Within the vast majority of King's works, a humanlike figure who exhibits inhuman powers and kills so-called normal people is considered to be the enemy. These monsters, taking the form of vampires, killer clowns, and Outsiders, to name but a few, are generally not even the main characters in their own story, even if their names do make up the title. Their differences make them monstrous and therefore not sympathetic. However, in Carrie's case, King has followed her from being a bullied girl to someone with power at her fingertips. Carrie is simply another victim of bullies in high school, but she has powers that none of her classmates could imagine, and she can use them to strike back. She is therefore able to turn a teenager's emotional outburst into an act of monstrosity, killing most of the prom attendees before taking her outburst out on the town, including her own mother.

Carrie's rage, and therefore her revenge, is targeted widely, because the attacks on her came from so many directions. Although she dies as a result of this exertion, she leaves one unlikely survivor: Sue Snell, who asked her boyfriend, Tommy, to take Carrie to prom in the first place as a sort of apology for how Sue had treated Carrie. This decision on both Sue and Tommy's part is confusing to survivors and outsiders, although Carrie used her powers to look into Sue's head and determine her motives. Carrie apparently understood what Sue meant to do, since she does not kill Sue. Carrie does not, then, enact revenge against Sue—unless leaving her alive to face all the questions in the aftermath qualifies.

Chapter Six

SEXUAL ABUSE

The questions in the aftermath are the main focus of *Dolores Claiborne*. While *Carrie* intersperses third-person narratives of the present moment with snippets from books, newspapers, and the White Commission proceedings, *Dolores Claiborne* is made up almost entirely of the transcript of Dolores's police interview. The questions asked by the other people in the room—the two male officers and the female transcriptionist—are not included in the written text. Readers have to infer the interruptions and the questions from the way Dolores pauses, addresses the others, or repeats something. Only the epilogue is not told in Dolores's voice, instead coming from a newspaper clipping, giving Dolores full control over "both the events of her story and the manner in which these events are told."[7]

Dolores is being questioned because of the death of Vera Donovan, her employer, but the story entwines with that of her husband's death from decades prior. Vera was a widow whose cheating husband died in a car crash that was not in fact an accident; Dolores herself became a widow and only now reveals that her husband's fall down a well happened after the couple's daughter revealed that her father was sexually abusing her. Vera's two children died not long after their father did, although she continually lied to Dolores and told her that they were alive and thriving. One of Dolores's sons is dead, but her other two children are estranged, likely because they always suspected their mother of murder but had never confirmed it.

Although officially cleared of suspicion in Joe's death during the inquest, Dolores admits that her neighbors have never actually believed she was innocent. Public opinion held that Dolores murdered Joe because he beat her, which was only comforting to Dolores because it meant their daughter's secret was safe. During her long interrogation, Dolores reveals that Joe not only sexually abused Selena, but that he cleared out all three kids' college accounts, leaving Dolores with no money. Since she could not get her children away from Joe, she had to find a way to remove Joe from the equation. Given this fuller explanation, as far as Dolores, and readers, "can see, Joe has no redeeming qualities,"[8] and his murder seems justifiable.

Dolores, like Carrie, did not act straightaway to defend herself. She spent most of her marriage being physically abused by Joe, and it was her choice to finally stand up to Joe that created the initial divide between Dolores and Selena, giving Joe the chance to pursue his own daughter. With this knowledge well in hand, Dolores realizes that any action she takes must be final and very carefully planned so as to leave her children out of it as much as possible. This includes lying to her own children as well as to the coroner after Joe's body is finally discovered.

Dolores has therefore spent decades going under the suspicion that she killed her husband, which is why so many people find it easy to believe that she must have killed Vera, too. And, although she has spent those long decades denying what happened to Joe, in the face of an accusation of a murder she did not commit, Dolores comes up with the truth. She is allowed to speak largely without interruption, and apparently she is believed, because the end result is not in fact interesting. She finishes her tale, and the main part of the narrative ends, but the newspaper clipping included as epilogue indicates that Selena will be returning to the island for Thanksgiving dinner with her mother. Had Dolores been arrested, she would not be preparing for the visit or cooking the turkey.

Unlike Carrie, Dolores is alive to face the consequences of her revenge, and her children are likewise hostages to her future. Carrie's fate was death, caused both by the injuries inflicted by her mother and the overuse of her own powers. Dolores ended up living on an island where many people suspected that she had murdered Joe but were unable to prove it. Although they also thought they knew that Joe had abused her, even after she had put a stop to that, they would not have accepted murder as a proper consequence. Dolores had to hold her tongue about the true reasons behind Joe's murder to do what she could to save Selena. While Selena was worried that her mother might have murdered her father, she was even more concerned that others would find out what her father had done to her. Dolores therefore chose the lesser of two evils, although the price she paid was still very high.

In the end, however, readers learn that Selena will be returning to the island for the first time in decades. It is unclear whether Dolores has confessed to her daughter, and also whether this means Selena has given up her dependence on alcohol, but it seems to be an uplifting end to the story. Dolores refused to let Joe trap Selena in a life of incest and paid her own price with her children as a result of it in a way that perhaps only Vera could have understood. Aside from that one day, Vera and Dolores never spoke of it. They lived out the end of Vera's life together trapped by the choices they had made and the consequences that came from them, but Dolores at least had two children still left alive who could make amends.

Tess of "Big Driver" has no children, and the abuse she sets out to avenge is her own. After giving an author talk and taking the librarian's suggested shortcut home, Tess is raped and left for dead. She realizes that the librarian had procured her as the next victim for her own son and decides not to involve the police. Instead Tess, author of cozy mysteries and now a diligent student of revenge films, takes her gun and kills all three members of the family who happen to be involved in serial rape and murder.

For Tess, it is both personal and much closer to the present. Dolores tells her interrogators of something that happened decades ago, based on concrete fears. Dolores knew exactly who Joe would threaten if he continued to live with the family, while Tess had no idea who the next victim might be. She simply had to remind herself that there *would* be more victims if she did nothing, since she had been shoved into a pipe where other bodies were already hidden. Tess, like Dolores, wanted to protect the privacy of a sexual assault victim and take care of the abusers herself. Tess was simply both victim and avenger in one.

Because of the condensed time line of Tess's story, readers are left to wonder whether she was able to get away with three murders. Unlike Dolores, she had little to connect her to the victims, which might work in her favor. However, Tess's triple murder takes place in the twenty-first century and involved a gun, both points that might make her easier to track down and connect to the crime. While Dolores had to spend decades living on an island with close neighbors who suspected her of murder and treated her coldly for it, Tess should at least be able to avoid public conviction if she escapes legal prosecution.

Dolores, Carrie, and Tess all found themselves in situations where their revenge was of the sort that calls for legal prosecution. While each was only reacting to the previous actions of others, their responses included murder, and specifically the murder of recognizable human beings. In *Cell*, at least, although the characters must live with the consequences of their behavior, they could do so knowing that the creatures they killed were no longer human.

EMOTIONAL ABUSE

Although the final bombing of the so-called Phoners at the end of *Cell* has been discussed in chapter 5 in terms of a character's death spurring the main character onto action, it also needs to be covered here. Once the remaining group of "Normies" realizes that Ray's suicide and the cell phone he gave Clay were to protect the secret of the bomb aboard the bus, they need to hatch a plan for how best to use it. Only one of them, twelve-year-old Jordan, is small enough to be able to escape out of the window of their prison, so he is the one tasked with moving the bus to a better location before they set off the bomb.

Because the narrative is told from Clay's point of view, this scene is one of extended suspense. The other survivors quickly lose sight of Jordan as he goes to find the bus, although they can see that a number of the Phoners are up and around, even though it is nighttime and they should all be rebooting. They worry that one of the Phoners will grab Jordan; that Jordan might not be able to start or steer the bus; and that Jordan will not be able to reach a safe place before they set off the bomb. When they see that the bus begins to move, the mood first lifts, but quickly deflates when Jordan in fact drives the bus over the supine bodies of the Phoners so he can leave it in the middle of the flock.

This is far more dangerous than the plan they had discussed with Jordan before he left. They worry that the bus might tip or otherwise get damaged as he attempts to drive it over the bodies and are especially concerned because Jordan must make his way out of the flock on foot. The boy quickly trips over a body and has to crawl for a while before he gets up again. Then, away from the sleeping flock, he nearly gets caught by some of the wandering Phoners. Once he finally makes it back to the safety of the building where the others are being held, Jordan breathlessly explains his reasoning for the risks he took: "I did it . . . for the Head."[9]

This statement turns an act of desperation, meant to save the lives of the few who were still surviving, into one of personally motivated revenge. Each protagonist has lost someone since the events of the novel began. Jordan even witnessed the death of teenage Alice Maxwell, whom Jordan revered. Alice, however, was killed by two Normal people who were then themselves killed by the Phoners, so perhaps revenge there had already been enacted. Charles Ardai, headmaster of the prep school Jordan attended, had been forced to complete suicide by the leader of the Phoner flock. That leader was at the center of this sleeping mass, and so Jordan steeled himself to take the risk and place the bus where it would cause the most damage.

This small group of people had been brought together because they had already destroyed large flocks of Phoners. The group Jordan and point-of-view character Clay had been part of had previously driven gas tankers into the middle of a flock and exploded them with a machine gun. This mass murder led to retaliation from the Phoners, including the forced suicide of the Head, who was too feeble to join the others on their forced march. Now, at the climax of the narrative, Jordan finds himself in the position to set off yet another bomb and destroy another flock. Because the Phoners retaliated against Jordan's group by killing the Head, Jordan in turn responded by risking his own life to get this bomb where it would do the most damage.

At the end of the novel, it is not entirely clear what the ultimate consequences for this action will be. After the bomb has gone off, Clay sees the sweatshirt worn by the leader of the Phoners, now bloodied and no longer around the body, thereby allowing readers to assume that Jordan's actions meant his one main foe has indeed been killed. However, Jordan and Clay once again part ways as Clay continues on his own personal mission. Readers do not know how successful Clay's quest is, nor the long-term outcomes for the surviving Normies. However, readers do know that the amazing destruction of this main flock was really caused by the murder of one old man.

Chapter Six

SUPERNATURAL REVENGE

Within King's works, it is also possible for characters to seek revenge for their own murders. As discussed in chapter 1, Sara Tidwell of *Bag of Bones* induces the descendants of her rapist murderers to kill their own children, gradually ending their family lines. George Stark, as seen in chapter 5, existed solely as a pseudonym until he was killed off and "buried" for a photoshoot. Rising from that grave, he began a murder spree dedicated to giving himself a real life. Neither Sara nor George was allowed to triumph, and their final intended victims lived. Arlette James of "1922" is a different story.

"1922" is a written confession from Wilfred James that begins with an explanation of why and how he decided to kill his own wife in the year of the novella's title. He involved his teenage son, Hank, in the murder, a decision the Wilf of 1930 sorely regrets. Wilf had decided to murder his wife so he could keep both his farm and his son but, after committing and even getting away with uxoricide, he loses Hank, his farm, and apparently his sanity.

The explanation for Wilf's troubles could be mundane and natural. When teenage Hank loses his mother, he seeks comfort in his girlfriend and then pursues her when she is sent to a home for unwed mothers. After a number of successful robberies to fund their flight, the girlfriend is shot and killed, and Hank completes suicide rather than live without her. The story is tragic, but not supernatural, and Wilf's loss of his farm can be explained by the Great Depression. However, suffering a fever from a near-fatal infection, Wilf claims that he saw Arlette come to him and tell him how Hank's story would turn out weeks before the final, fatal scenes happened.

Wilf's vision then, and his impression that Arlette is coming as soon as he finishes writing his confession, could still be explained away by his fever and his guilt. Those who find Wilf after an apparent suicide are quick to identify it as just that, although they are confused about his method of death. The implication is that no one else believes that it was Arlette who came back from the grave to get her revenge—and indeed, since Wilf's written confession was torn up, no one believes she would have any reason to need to get revenge—but Wilf was certainly convinced. Whether she was a continued hallucination as a result of his guilt, or truly a psychic ghost, Wilf attributes the downslide of his life to his own choice of murder and the insistent way he involved his son. He believes that all these bad things happened for a reason, and that Arlette's vengeful spirit is that reason, making it real for him if for no one else.

PAIN AND MOTIVATION

In three of these cases, those of the children and that of Tess in "Big Driver," the personal consequences for these revenge murders are not explored. Carrie dies, leaving the survivors with no one on whom to fix the blame. The others, including outsiders such as the White Commission, search for explanations and someone to hold accountable in the face of Carrie's own death. Although "the White (male) Commission will eventually have to acknowledge its own responsibility in the creation of Carrie,"[10] they attempt to pin guilt on survivor Sue Snell, fixating on another female teenager who, readers are convinced, only meant well in her actions. Sue was truly penitent after being swept up in the communal teasing of Carrie White, to the point where even Carrie herself, with full access to Sue's thoughts and memories, allowed her to live. Carrie cannot be questioned, confronted, or held responsible for her actions, and neither can her telekinetic abilities be studied. After a lifetime of taking abuse, and a single night of finally exploding, Carrie leaves the town to pull itself back together as well as it can without being able to fix any blame.

Jordan is not a point-of-view character in *Cell*. That role falls to Clay, who parts from Jordan shortly after the bomb's explosion. Clay hopes to find the boy and reunite with him later, but Jordan's personal reactions to what he has done, especially after he has had time to rest and fully absorb everything that has happened in the past few weeks, are not explored here. Jordan's act is heroic, and was possibly an unnecessary risk, but Jordan and his psyche are not Clay's primary concern. Clay is more interested in the possibility of saving his own son, and so he leaves Jordan and their other friends to continue on his own personal quest.

Granted, it is highly unlikely that Jordan will face legal persecution, considering the drastically altered world of Phoners and Normies, but it has also been made clear throughout the book that Normals who destroy large flocks of Phoners can be persecuted by surviving flocks. Clay's small group believes that Jordan has just helped them wipe out the largest flock in the area, and that they will not encounter any other coordinated groups, but that is not a certainty. They already know that Phoners can get into their dreams, and it is likely that Jordan will have nightmares enough without any outside interference. The full consequences of Jordan's actions, although he lives through them, are not explored.

"Big Driver" ends with Tess apparently wrapping up her own version of the movies she watched to prepare for her spree: "wronged women who act on their own to gain often violent, bloody closure."[11] Whether Tess truly gains some measure of closure is not shown. Although she seems to have taken care of all loose ends that would tie her to a triple murder, the Tess at the end of the narrative will still have to wait and see if the police come knocking at her door. If she is connected to the murders, the crime committed against her will also be brought to light, an event that Tess literally killed to keep from coming to pass. Her success, and her safety, is implied, but not certain.

Two of these characters have lived for years—or even decades—with the secret knowledge of being a murderer. Dolores Claiborne has had to put up with the suspicions of her fellow islanders, as well as those of her own children, and all of this has taken its toll. She was intimately aware of the psyche of her murder victim, and the fact that she could not trust him to keep his promise to stop abusing their daughter. She knew full well that the only possible course of action to save her daughter and to retrieve the college money she had worked personally so hard to save was to kill Joe. Dolores is therefore also the only one of these characters to plan her revenge in cold blood and to have time to fully think all of this through. Carrie responded to one final outrage at what was meant to be her moment of triumph; Jordan was working under a tight deadline between the group's discovery of the bomb in the bus and the knowledge that, come sunrise, they would all be ritualistically executed; and Tess felt pressured to act quickly both to cover up the fact that her murder had failed and also to prevent any other women from suffering. Although Dolores acted rather quickly to inform Joe that she knew what he was doing and that he needed to keep his hands off their daughter, she had plenty of time between discovering what he had been up to and the day of the eclipse in order to fully plan out how she meant his murder to go.

Joe's murder, of course, did not unfold exactly according to that plan. Although she believed any love she had for the man was long gone, Dolores is still plagued with guilt and convinced that he will somehow get out of the well and come back to kill her. One of these visions means that she gets up out of bed in time to stop him from actually emerging from the well but, even after she is fully convinced that he has died down there, she still remains jumpy. Even with all her planning, many things go awry, from losing her slip on the path to the well, to forgetting to put on jeans for the event and scratching her legs up, to the amount of time it took before searchers finally found him. Dolores was therefore in full suspense with her listeners, and therefore her readers, as she waited to see exactly how much of this would be uncovered. What her listeners and readers know that Dolores on the day of the eclipse did not was that she did in fact get away with it, and so the suspense is of a different kind: we are not waiting to hear what it was that undid her careful plans, but to hear how, exactly, she managed despite all of these difficulties.

The answer, it turns out, is rather poorly. Readers learn that Selena moved off the island as soon as she could, and that she rarely visits and is frequently drunk during her phone calls with her mother. Dolores's younger son was killed in Vietnam shortly after he arrived there. And, although her middle child uses photographs of her home on many of his campaign materials, he has also largely left Little Tall behind. Even when a character commits murder for what may seem to be the best of reasons, the consequences are steep, although not always death for the seeker of revenge him- or herself.

Dolores, though, has coped with her secret far better than Wilfred James of "1922." He also murdered his spouse, but Wilf involved his only child in that murder and damned him, as well. By the end of that terrible year, Wilf has lost not only his wife, but his son, potential daughter-in-law, future grandchild, and the farm he literally killed to keep. Although Wilf might argue to himself that mariticide was in itself an act of revenge against a wife who refused to submit to her husband, the real revenge comes in Wilf's own death, although his secret remains a secret. Wilf was not tortured socially by friends and neighbors who knew he was responsible for Arlette's death, but rather by "the reoccurring apparition of Arlette in the house [which] transgresses boundaries of real and surreal."[12] While Wilf's death is real, the cause—possibly his own guilt, possibly the ghost of his murdered wife—might not be.

Although some of his characters can choose to commit murder and not thereafter face their own deaths, certain choices within King's works are the equivalent of agreeing to one's own death sentence. While Carrie killed in defense of herself, and Dolores, Tess, and Jordan chose their own actions to protect others, it is possible for King's characters to choose paths for their own personal gain that involve the sacrifice of their fellow humans. These characters are far more likely to meet their own deaths in the course of the narrative.

NOTES

1. Strengell, *Dissecting Stephen King*, 198.
2. Magistrale, *Stephen King: America's Storyteller*, 133.
3. Alexandra Reuber, "In Search of the Lost Object in a Bad Place: Stephen King's Contemporary Gothic," *Stephen King's Contemporary Classics: Reflections on the Modern Master of Horror* (Lanham, MD: Rowman & Littlefield, 2015), 111.
4. Davis, *Stephen King's America*, 61.
5. Douglas Keesey, "Patriarchal Mediations of *Carrie*: The Book, the Movie, and the Musical," *Imagining the Worst: Stephen King and the Representation of Women* (Westport, CT: Greenwood Press, 1998), 37.
6. Strengell, *Dissecting Stephen King*, 161.
7. Magistrale, *Stephen King: America's Storyteller*, 135.
8. Russell, *Stephen King: A Critical Companion*, 144.
9. King, *Cell*, 419.

10. Keesey, "Patriarchal Mediations of *Carrie*," 37.
11. Frost, "A Different Breed," 122.
12. Reuber, "In Search of the Lost Object in a Bad Place," 110.

Chapter Seven

"What If He Has a Helper?"
As Renfield

The characters in the previous chapter sought revenge specifically on people or groups who had personally harmed them. For Carrie White and Dolores Claiborne, the abuse had been going on for years by the time they acted. Carrie needed the flash point of one final, terrible prank at prom to encourage her to finally use her newly discovered powers, and although Dolores had already stood up for herself against her husband without having to escalate to murder, her discovery of her husband's sexual abuse of their daughter was enough to convince her it was necessary. The events of *Cell* and "Big Driver" happen much more quickly but are no less traumatic. Preteen Jordan had clung to the only other surviving member from his private school, the Head, and formed a close bond. After the older man was murdered by the Phoners, when Jordan was given the opportunity to enact revenge, he took it, and then in a way that surprised his other group mates with its brutality. Tess, on the other hand, was brutally attacked and left for dead, with no knowledge of when the people responsible might act again and murder another woman.

Carrie was not allowed to survive, but Dolores, Jordan, and Tess make it to the end of their narratives alive. Even after Dolores confessed to being a murderer, and even when Jordan's travel mates knew what he had done, they were each forgiven. Their punishment was having to live with their actions. However, they had done nothing that was considered a threat to their community, and so any possible illegality of their actions was overlooked. They acted in defense of others—a statement that cannot be made of either Wilf or Arlette James of "1922"—while the subjects of this chapter acted for their own personal gain.

Like so many movie monsters of King's childhood, King writes his own supernatural creatures with weaknesses. Even Superman has his kryptonite, and a vampire comes with multiple mythical deterrents: garlic, wild roses, and a wooden stake through the heart, just to name a few. Because they are limited to moving around in the dark, or only able to harm children because of their faith in the monster, King's characters need to find a way to compensate for their weaknesses. They, like Stoker's Dracula, call upon other humans to help them in their fight against the heroes. Although the monsters have incredible abilities, even a single human helper can compensate for their weaknesses.

The problem with becoming a Renfield, however, comes in the fact that the man or woman who does so pledges an alliance to the monster and takes a stand against fellow human beings. Frequently the monster quite literally feeds on humans and therefore the Renfield is offering up the lives of people that should be recognizable as the self, and not dehumanized enough to become mere sustenance. It is known, however, that the monster is dangerous before the Renfield even agrees to the task, and the people chosen to assist the monster are themselves frequently already violent. They do not necessarily need convincing that other people are less worthy than they are, and they have already made their choice in their hearts before they make it in the narrative.

The terms of assistance might be unclear, such as in *'Salem's Lot* where the partnership predates the narrative's opening. Other supernatural creatures seduce the borderline unstable, as in It's use of Henry Bowers; drive someone—or an entire town—toward the edge of insanity, such as the way the Tommyknockers create "a demand for conformity so rigid and relentless that it crosses over into the realm of madness"[1]; or force the undead to come to their aid. Still other Renfields might not even realize that they are serving the Other, whether that power is located in the Overlook Hotel or behind a pet sematary. As Tony Magistrale observes, "one's humanity—or one's soul—is dreadfully easy to lose."[2] The protagonists may not even realize the loss but, once gone, it is irretrievable.

Because of the range of monsters King has written, there are also a variety of ways in which the Renfield is selected, presented, and then disposed of. This assortment means that very little is common to all of them, except for the fact that, if the monster is to be defeated, then his Renfield needs to go first. There is no redemption for the Renfield in these works, likely because, even before the monster has chosen him, he has already shown an apathy toward his fellow human beings. These are not good men who have been tainted and could be rehabilitated, but already bad men who were given the opportunity to be so much worse in service to a monster.

INDIVIDUALS AS RENFIELD

The most obvious Renfield comes in the character of R. T. Straker in King's *'Salem's Lot*. The book is itself King's retelling of the Dracula story, set in a small Maine town instead of in Transylvania, and allows King "to explore the darkest corners of the human condition."[3] In the introduction to the book, he outlines all the similarities between his text and Stoker's. Although King's version is narrative instead of epistolary, he includes a number of the same plot elements, and Renfield is one of them.

Even supernatural killers have weaknesses. The vampire in 'Salem's Lot, Kurt Barlow, seems to have a number of the classic flaws. He does not go out during the daytime; he and his vampire children must be invited inside a house; he can be repelled by a cross, if the wielder has true faith; and he sleeps in a coffin or similar small space. The effectiveness of other vampire repellents such as garlic is not shown, and there are no plot points involving whether these vampires reflect in a mirror, but a wooden stake to the heart still proves deadly. Granted, a wooden stake to a mortal man's heart would do the same, but it seems to be the only way to get rid of the vampire.

As King's plucky band of vampire hunters concludes early on, Barlow is therefore vulnerable during the daytime. If they can find either him or the vampires he has created in the town, they can stake them easily if the sun is out. Straker, on the other hand, has been seen around town during daylight hours. Although he may not be entirely human, Straker is not confined to the night. When two members of the main group approach Barlow's house during the daytime, it is Straker who catches them. Although Susan Norton is turned into a vampire, young Mark Petrie both escapes and relieves Barlow of his helper.

The loss of Straker is what ultimately leads to Barlow's demise. Without Straker to protect the house during the day, the vampire hunters can return to destroy Barlow's coffin, putting him on the run. Barlow further fuels Ben Mears's anger by forcing him to stake Susan, making the grudge between them personal. Forced to quickly find a new safe place to spend his days, and now without active protection during daylight hours, Barlow had to rely on the passive methods that killed Jimmy Cody but could not, in the end, protect him.

Straker not only had to die for the book's heroes to confront the vampire, but because any ally of evil cannot be allowed to endure. Although he himself was not a vampire, as shown by the fact that he could appear in sunlight, clearly Barlow had offered him something in exchange for his service. His superhuman strength and his use of a very old bill mark Straker as being different, a man perhaps out of his time. Straker is not perfectly camouflaged, but, compared to the vampires, he has the simple power of being able to go out in the daytime. As seen when he confronts Susan and Mark, he is willing to sacrifice fellow human beings to his master in exchange for whatever he gets out of the deal. Straker has been a faithful servant for a long time, and, had he lived, he would have presumably continued to be one.

Because Straker's death precedes his master's, the narrative presents readers with Barlow alone and without his servant, but we do not see the servant without the master. Straker, unlike the original Renfield, does not have a change of heart or any hope of redemption. The book provides no background on why Straker may have agreed to this arrangement, or how he might have been convinced to take up the position in the first place. There is no indication that Straker had to be blackmailed into it, and likewise no explanation that clarifies Straker's complete willingness to participate. It is also unclear what, exactly, Straker gets from the deal, aside from his own continued life. Whatever arrangement Straker and Barlow have struck has long been in existence in its current form, and by now is simply a matter of course.

However, it quickly becomes clear that Barlow does indeed depend a lot upon Straker. Once Mark kills Straker, to avoid either death or transformation into a vampire, Barlow unravels quickly. Mark acts not only as "the connection with childhood Ben needs"[4] to properly accept and confront the vampire, but as the one who provides the turning point in the battle against Barlow. The modern vampire cannot survive alone. He needs a man who can deal with real estate and delivery of his own self inside a coffin, so that the vampire is never touched by a beam of sunlight. Men can no longer do business purely by letter, and so he needs a partner to be the literal face of their operation. It is only through Straker that Barlow was able to get a position in the town and therefore a place in which to hide and from which to create more vampires. Once Straker has died, Barlow has lost a large amount of protection.

In *It,* the supernatural monster is not as easily categorized as a vampire. Although It can indeed present as one, It is, in fact, a shape-shifter, able to adapt to the fears of Its prey. Because It is seen terrorizing children of the late 1950s, It frequently takes on the form of the monsters from schlock horror films: a vampire, a mummy, a werewolf, a thing from the Black Lagoon, and so on. Throughout the book, It, the children, and the reader learn that Its forms also come with constrictions. In 1958, when confronted by a band of children, It took on Its werewolf form and was grievously injured by a silver slug. Because werewolves can be killed by silver, when It became one, the silver harmed It.

It, however, never works alone.

As the children quickly discover, all of Derry seems to rally around and support It. The town is allowed to grow and prosper beyond many in the region as long as Derry continues to provide It with Its preferred meals. Once every twenty-seven years or so, It awakes from Its slumber in order to feed on children and their fears. Its meals are not merely the fright It gives Its victims, but their actual bodies, since children are discovered with bite marks and missing body parts. The town therefore sacrifices "a part of its future"[5] to maintain prosperity in the present.

What It requires from most of the town is inaction and compliance. No matter what he might say or think, the police chief must be inept in his attempts to track down and identify the child killer who was on the loose. Despite the curfew and scheduled adult supervision, children must still be allowed out alone, including at night. Even when others witness impending violence, they either dismiss it or simply get up and go inside so they do not have to witness. The entire town of Derry exists in order to help It survive, and its residents risk "becoming the victim of a monster . . . or *becoming* a monster."[6]

The adults of Derry cannot see It and would not believe in It even if the children attempted to explain. The Losers Club, eleven years old in 1958, returns to Derry in 1985 to confront It again, making them part of only a small number of grown-ups who can see and believe in It. Other adults who have seen the clown have done so generally in the middle of violent acts and have dismissed It as being a man who did not wish to be identified. The grown-up Losers, however, still see It in different guises drawn from their childhood and recognize It in all of them. It believes that, because they are now adults, they will not be able to perform the act of belief that led them to nearly destroying It previously. However, It does not want to simply depend on their age for Its own safety. It, like the vampire Kurt Barlow, has a human helper.

Henry Bowers, schoolyard bully in 1958 and psychiatric ward escapee in 1985, is even given an explanation for his role in the violence. It tells him "I can take care of them if they only half-believe, . . . but you're alive, Henry. You can get them if they believe, half-believe, or don't believe at all."[7] Like Straker's ability to move about in the daylight, Henry's humanity is in fact an advantage over Its fantastic abilities. Henry's knife can harm the Losers' physical bodies in a very mundane and human way. They do not need to be subjected to visions or hallucinations for Henry to kill them, and they are not even aware that Henry is coming.

Henry's role is in fact much like Straker's. Straker's job was to protect his master and to prevent anyone from harming him in his own home while he slept. Although It is currently in Its active stage, instead of hibernating, It hopes that Henry will be able to kill the Losers before they descend into the sewers once again. If Henry can stop that, then It does not have to worry about facing them at all. It believes that, should Henry manage to kill even one of them, the remaining Losers will not be able to face It.

Henry is not Its only individually selected Renfield. In 1985, It also relies on two of the Losers' spouses, one of whom has drawn direct comparisons to Henry in the text. If the Losers cannot be prevented from coming down to the sewers, It might be able to distract them and keep them from banding together in order to defeat It. Therefore, It uses Bev's abusive husband Tom to kidnap Bill's wife, hoping to distract the leader of the Losers and fragment the group.

Unlike Henry, who needs to stay alive as long as possible to help It, Tom can die as soon as his task his finished. As a Renfield, he is expendable.

Both Henry and Tom die, and their deaths do not save It from Its own fate. The narrative ends with Bill crushing Its beating heart between his palms, witnessing Its death in a way that he did not in 1958. Rather than assuming that Its physical form is retreating to die, Bill and Richie have followed It deeper into Its lair in order to actively kill It. Even though Eddie dies, he first contributes in a major way to Its own death, and Bill can ignore his wife's unconscious body long enough in order to crush Its heart. The distractions It hopes to offer, and the multiple deaths It hopes to enact, did not happen.

In the case of both Henry and Tom, It was able to play on the anger and resentment the men already felt toward their shared targets. It did not need to convince either of them that the Losers were "deserving" of these actions, and each character was already a well of anger. Tom thought he could track down his wayward wife—and perhaps her lover—to teach her a lesson, and Henry believed that he could finally get rid of the misfit kids who ended up haunting him his entire life. Although It was able to provide assistance in this shared goal, It did not, in the end, offer much in the way of protection. The men were tools that had outlived their use.

The preference of shape shifting supernatural creatures to use human help surfaces again in 2018's *The Outsider*. This character is in many ways far weaker than either Barlow or It, because the Outsider is merely human in physicality. The Outsider's one ability comes in the fact that it can take a DNA sample from any person and then clone that person exactly. The Outsider then commits a murder in the guise of another person, leaving plenty of evidence behind, and feasts on the emotional reactions of the community. Although the full number of the Outsider's victims is not shown in the book, the murders that can be traced back to the Outsider are of children, both gruesome and sexually graphic. Like It, the Outsider is theorized to feed on the child's fear prior to the child's death, as well as the resulting community reaction and response.

The Outsider, however, prefers to work alone. It does not have the ability to create another, the way Barlow created Straker, and does not have Its ability to ensnare an entire town in exchange for prosperity. The Outsider, unlike It, is not sedentary, but travels around to commit its murders. Unlike Barlow, the Outsider also does not need a companion to secure a home or a business as an explanation for its presence. Because the Outsider takes on the face and identity of someone who is already a local, it is much more discreet than Barlow, and does not need to stay as long. According to the book, the Outsider does not even usually linger in public spaces after it has committed the crime. The fact that it followed its most recently framed victim to the courthouse, and was present on the day Terry Maitland was shot, is one of the things that works against it. Because of the discrepancy between his memory and the filmed footage, Detective Ralph Anderson finds himself at the center of a group of people looking for the full explanation of what happened in their town.

The Outsider, weak because of the physical change it is undergoing, chooses one of Ralph's fellow detectives as its Renfield. It touches Jack Hoskins and infects him not only with poison, but with the idea that he has advanced skin cancer, preying on Jack's own fears. Too scared to go to the doctor, Jack agrees to do what the apparition orders, believing it can heal him of the cancer. He beats the others to the Outsider's lair and waits outside with his rifle, ready to kill anyone who tries to enter. Rather like Jimmy Cody, Hoskins is too fixated on the supernatural elements of the situation to account for more mundane threats and dies from a rattlesnake bite before he can kill all of the intruders.

Straker and Bowers are both brought down by the group on the side of "good." The main characters in King's ka-tet are personally responsible for stopping their Renfield, and, in these cases, stopping him through death. Both Barlow and It have offered their assistants something that they could not otherwise get. Although it is not entirely clear what all Straker has received, Henry Bowers is given the chance to not only murder his father, but to seek revenge on the kids who have been standing up to him all summer. In contrast, the Outsider can only offer Jack something after it has already inflicted him with the threat. The Outsider could not tempt Jack with a long life, or power, so it had to first curse him and then offer him the remedy.

Straker, Henry, and Jack all knew for certain that they were working for some sort of entity that was not human, and that it was harmful. Straker and Henry willingly entered into their contracts because the destruction was apparently a mutual desire. While Jack would not have minded hurting Ralph, the full extent of Jack's actions in defense of the Outsider came from fear that the injury to the back of his neck would develop into full-blown skin cancer. Jack was not working to have something beyond what he already possessed, but to rid himself of something that the Outsider had given him.

The Outsider, it seems, chose wisely when it picked Jack Hoskins, because Jack bought into the scenario completely. He did not question whether the threat of skin cancer was real, even though everyone he asked to look at his neck told him that it was a bad sunburn. Jack accepted the Outsider's existence and its power mainly because of his own fear of the shadowy figure, and the Outsider was able to play on his already present fear of skin cancer. Like the two supernatural creatures before it, the Outsider was able to choose an assistant who was himself an outsider and therefore willing to harm the same people the Outsider wished to hurt.

As skilled as he was, however, Jack Hoskins still ended up only being mortal. Although he managed to kill some of the group that would come after the Outsider, and wound one more, Jack was unable to prevent both Ralph and Holly from going into the cave and having their final confrontation with the Outsider. Jack's death, with his duties unfulfilled, occurs in the same way that Straker's and Henry Bowers's did: in service to his supernatural master and as a prelude to his master's own death. Once Jack dies, there is no one to protect the Outsider, especially since Ralph is willing to die if it means the Outsider goes with him.

USING MORE THAN ONE RENFIELD

Other supernatural creatures in King choose to rely on more than one Renfield in their pursuit of their goals. As seen above, the death of the Renfield can very quickly lead to the death of the master, who is now unprotected by his human supporters. These Renfields therefore play crucial roles in the plots of their supernatural masters, even though those masters look down upon them as being equal to their prey. Other supernatural forces choose to distribute the task of the Renfield to prolong their own lives and make it harder for the side of "good" to rid them of their assistants.

In *The Tommyknockers*, the supernatural force is literally alien, although it, like Barlow, is no longer alive. All the power comes from an inanimate object that Bobbi Anderson discovers buried in her backyard: a spaceship that is itself entirely passive. It cannot move from town to town or stalk its prey, and it is entirely dependent on Bobbi to first stumble over it and then dig it up. The ship itself is absolutely enormous and buried completely in the earth until the day that Bobbi trips over the barest amount of its leading edge.

The effects of the buried spaceship have long been felt in that part of Maine, but they were more subtle as long as the ship was covered. Compasses have frequently failed to work in the nearby woods, and lost hunters have emerged after days of wandering, somehow missing some of their teeth. These effects have been largely downplayed, and seasoned hunters at times laughed out of town, until the day that Bobbi stumbles over the ship. Bobbi becomes the ship's first Renfield, although the entire town of Haven quickly joins her.

As the ship's surface hits the air and oxidizes, those who breathe it undergo physical and mental changes that make them something other than human. Their understanding comes through telepathy, and part of Becoming a Tommyknocker is a period of manic invention. Many of these devices are used during the book's climax as weapons to keep outsiders from entering Haven and discovering the ship. The sole member of Haven to attempt to resist what is happening, Ruth McCausland, has already been discussed in chapter 5. However, the rest of Haven—even those who helped the ship—meets the same end.

The town unites to protect the ship not only because it is their agent of change, but because they need the air it produces. When the sole outstanding human in the town flies the ship away to save the world, the remaining Havenites slowly suffocate on Earth's atmosphere. Had they not died on their own, the surviving citizens of Haven would have lived out the rest of their lives as guests of the American government, if not sacrificed in the name of science. They would not have been allowed to live even if they had endured the loss of the ship and its supply of their air. Once the alien thing supporting their Becoming was gone, and their existence was known to the wider world, they could not be allowed to live, because they had Become inhuman and horrifically Other.

In *Duma Key*, the supernatural threat, like the Tommyknockers' ship, has been buried for quite some time. Here, instead of a flying saucer encased in earth, there is a small china figure which has been sunk into fresh water. The exact origins of the china figure and the sentience that inherits it is never fully explained, and the main characters are only able to uncover a few things about it. It is not human; it uses humans with artistic talent; the art that is created turns out to be dangerous; and fresh water is the only way to "*Drown her back to sleep*."[8] The figure—perhaps a goddess, perhaps something unnamable—wants her victims to join her ship of the dead and can control the earthly remains of those she has already killed.

Called Perse, the figure is so shrouded in mystery that it is difficult to determine what, exactly, she actually wants from main character Edgar Freemantle. She stokes his artistic creativity and imbues his paintings with a dangerous power that Edgar understands too late. Those who buy Edgar's surreal paintings and sketches find themselves under Perse's control, even far away from Duma Key. While one of Perse's intended Renfields completes suicide before he can murder Edgar's ex-wife, another murders Edgar's favorite daughter. Perse cannot kill Edgar himself because he is the conduit for her power, so she works on hurting him emotionally.

All of this is meant to protect a relatively defenseless Perse from Edgar and his friends. Like vampires, Perse's assistants—her slaves on her ship of the dead, including Elizabeth Eastlake's twin sisters and brother-in-law—can only rise after sunset. Perse herself, or at least the little china figure, is also shown to be able to come alive at that time, but, much like the Tommyknocker ship, she was unable to free herself from her prison without outside influence. Also like the ship, she could neither be destroyed nor killed, but rather removed from her original location and sent somewhere to greatly decrease her chances of enslaving or harming anyone in the future.

Perse might be neutralized, but it is entirely unknown whether she can actually be killed. Edgar and his friends trap Perse in multiple layers of fresh water and silver, since both work to neutralize her power and influence. By interring Perse in a much larger body of fresh water, and by then using the last of his powers—which he somehow still possesses despite this neutralization—to destroy Duma Key with an out-of-season hurricane, Edgar hopes to put off Perse's return for longer than a few decades this time. But the threat, like some of the vampires Barlow created in *'Salem's Lot*, still remains. It is entirely possible that Perse might literally resurface in a King novel in the future.

A Renfield can be resurrected from a past King work and not just from the grave. In *Needful Things*, although newly arrived supernatural shopkeeper Leland Gaunt makes use of the entire town of Castle Rock to do his murderous bidding, he specifically advertises for, and finds, a shop assistant in the character of Ace Merrill. Ace, like Henry Bowers, was the town terror in his younger years, as was documented in other works by King. From his first appearance in the novella "The Body" to a mention in the short story "Nona," Ace has been seen to be a bully who relies on a close-knit gang to do his bidding, generally in violence against younger children. At the start of *Needful Things*, Ace has been out of town for a while, with part of that time being spent in prison, but it just so happens that he feels the desire to return to Castle Rock on the same day that Gaunt posts his "help wanted" sign in the window.

Like so many other citizens of the Rock, Ace sees something in Gaunt's shop that he feels he must have, and this desire opens him up to be "motivated by an evil power"[9]—although it seems that Ace does not need much convincing in that aspect. He is already a bitter outcast before allying himself with Gaunt, already prone to violence and enemies with Sheriff Alan Pangborn. While readers might feel sympathy for some of Gaunt's patrons, Ace is not one of them.

For the grand finale, Ace is joined by another outcast. Second Selectman Danforth Keaton does not fall into the same young hoodlum category as Ace, but from the beginning of the book he is shown to have a persecution complex. His paranoia stems from the fact that he has embezzled town funds to pay for his gambling addiction and is about to be found out. Both Ace and Keaton have little to lose by supporting Gaunt and apparently much to gain through Gaunt's ability to "turn human magic into the supernatural."[10] Childhood beliefs in buried treasure and games seem to be the answers to these Renfields' problems. Unfortunately for them, their alliance with Gaunt results not in riches, but in their own deaths.

Unlike in some of these other examples, however, the death of the supernatural's assistants did not then lead to the death of the original threat.

Although Gaunt has been prevented from taking the town's souls with him, he was still able to leave Castle Rock. The story ends almost exactly as it began: with a member of a small town greeting the reader and welcoming him back, outlining all the town's various interpersonal issues that have either sprung up or continued since the last visit, and pondering the name of a new, soon-to-be-open store.

The problem with Ace Merrill and Danforth Keaton is the same as all the human helpers who have gone before them: they have betrayed their own kind in alliance with evil. These two have very clear reasons for doing so, both of them caught up with the idea of money, but having an understandable motive does not save them from death. Ace and Keaton are clearly not very good people even before their encounter with Gaunt. Readers are not set up to cheer for either Ace or Keaton. Their alliances lie with the story's heroes: both those who had made purchases from Gaunt and ended up fighting back against him, and Alan Pangborn, the only one to confront Gaunt not to have bought anything from him. Even the most innocent and unknowing of Gaunt's helpers, Brian Rusk, does not escape his fate. Between Brian's suicide, a double murder, and the fantastically violent final night of Castle Rock's existence, much of the town is dead. Even people who had no dealings with Gaunt are killed in the end.

Ace and Keaton, however, have at least bought and paid for their deaths. They, like Straker, or Bobbi Anderson, or so many of the others, willingly allied themselves with "satanic visitor"[11] Gaunt, either because his superhuman nature fascinated or scared them. Gaunt convinced them that he would be a powerful ally, even if they questioned whether they really should accept his help. By only looking out for themselves, these men made the wrong decision and are destroyed along with the town.

THE UNWITTING RENFIELDS

Most of these previous examples involve a supernatural threat communicating directly with human helpers and asking, usually in English, for assistance. The exception here has been in *The Tommyknockers* where Bobbi Anderson and the entire town of Haven simply did as they were moved to once the alien ship was being uncovered. Even then, the group telepathy that formed meant that they all had some sort of understanding of what was happening, even if that knowledge was skewed falsely toward the positive. Bobbi and her fellow "shed people," who were Becoming faster than the others, soothed their worries and made sure that the people of Haven were leaning into their newfound powers and knowledge, instead of resisting it. The Havenites all understood that *something* was happening, even if they could not properly name it, and, giving in to groupthink, willingly embraced the changes. However, not every instance in which a human helper assists a supernatural evil is entirely conscious or voluntary.

In *The Shining*, Jack Torrance spends much of his time believing that *he* is the special one chosen by the Overlook Hotel for further greatness. When he discovers a scrapbook about the history of the hotel, he believes this is a sign that a higher power wants "to involve him personally to make him an intimate and integral part of the Overlook's ongoing history."[12] Jack views himself as a failure in most aspects of his life, but he believes writing the definitive book about the Overlook will help him succeed in many of them.

Jack was already possessed of his own demons by the time he encountered the novel's evil, a trait shared by Danforth Keaton. Jack, like so many other Renfields, is given a tragic backstory to explain why, perhaps, he might be so open to suggestions from the supernatural. The hotel is able to prey on these weaknesses and smooth things over whenever Jack starts to suspect that his son is in fact the special one. However, when the hotel itself fails to capture Danny, it relegates that responsibility to Jack. Unlike so many of these other Renfields, Jack does not calmly surrender to his task. In the final, crucial moment, Jack shifts from assisting the hotel to fighting it just long enough for Danny to escape with his life.

Perhaps the least likely to be categorized as a Renfield is the character of Jud Crandall from *Pet Sematary*, but his actions still fit the description. The cemetery itself—or rather, what King calls "the Micmac burying grounds"— has both power and constraints. Any living creature buried in this mysterious, rocky soil rises again as a facsimile of its old self, whether it was a dog, cat, bull, or human being. But the land itself cannot travel or spread its own story, and those who do tell it "make it somehow, somewhere, new in effect"[13] as they share it and expand the circle of the burying grounds' power. This is not a Leland Gaunt who goes from town to town to spread his power, but a place that is both hidden and protected. The first step in reaching the special place—climbing an old deadfall that threatens to collapse and break someone's leg—would not be attempted without a guide who knew the secret of crossing it. The entire path up to the strange burying grounds is dangerous and unmarked, so, if the power that inhabits the soil wishes to continue bringing creatures back to a so-called life, it needs people to share its story.

Like the Overlook Hotel, it is difficult to tell exactly how far the power of the burying ground stretches. Tony Magistrale suggests that the incidents leading up to the Torrance family's arrival at the Overlook Hotel may have in fact been caused by the hotel,[14] and it is possible that the deadly road running near the pet sematary may have been created as a means of feeding the burying grounds. When the road kills the Creed family's pet cat, Jud reveals the secrets of the burying ground to patriarch Louis. The stony soil appears to be hungry, because the road next takes toddler Gage. Knowing how to resurrect the dead, grieving Louis refuses to listen to Jud's warning about what the ground does to people and buries his son there anyway. Like Jack Torrance, Jud at least attempts to undo the damage he has begun. When he suspects that Louis has not listened to his warning, he attempts to sit up and keep watch, either for Louis or a returned zombie-like Gage. It seems that the burying grounds' power is strong, since Jud first falls asleep and then is murdered by the returned toddler creature.

Even though Jud has died, he served his purpose. He passed on the message of the soil's secrets, and even the imperfect resurrections of the past cannot stop its hold. In fact, no one within the book attempts to destroy the burying grounds. In this case, the main character only wishes to use it, and use it again, until he gets it right. Its Renfield is not killed defending it, but because Jud came to his senses and began arguing against it. Jud, like Jack Torrance, realizes he has made a mistake and ends up paying for it. Unlike the Overlook Hotel, however, there is no damage whatsoever done to the Micmac burying grounds. Unless he is murdered by his newly returned wife, Louis will be able to perform Jed's duty of passing on the knowledge of the burying grounds in his own time.

A CHOSEN FATE

There are few decisions a King character can make that will automatically translate into a death sentence. With King's wide cast of characters, it is entirely possible for two of them to have rather parallel storylines and choices and yet one, being labeled "good," will have a very different ending than the one who is "bad." Mistakes made early on in a narrative do not necessarily translate directly to a character's end, and redemption is nearly always possible. Even a Renfield might be able to find it deep within himself to fight at the very last minute, allowing the main characters to escape, but what the Renfield cannot fight is his own death.

Choosing the self far above and beyond other human beings is a death sentence in King's world. Such a selfish person cannot be allowed to live, even if he remains human, and all monsters must be killed to resolve the narrative tension. The surviving members of the story must find it within themselves to pick up and carry on in spite of the damage done but should not lament the passing of the monster and its attendant power.

In some versions, the narrative's main threat enlists not only singular members like Straker or Henry Bowers, but the entire town. Tony Magistrale observes that "King wishes us to view Derry's citizenry in league with the monster,"[15] meaning the Losers have to fight against not only It, but all of

Derry, including their parents. When 'salem's Lot, Derry, Haven, or Castle Rock falls under the spell of a supernatural influence, that influence also causes them to draw together to support it and stand against outside interference. Even Duma Key finds itself under Perse's spell, even if she has more control over the undead than the living. Although each of these threats is supernatural, they must enlist others in their quest because they "cannot be effective without their help."[16] Mortals are necessary to assist in bringing about the downfall of mortals.

Single people apparently cannot stand up to the temptation or threats of these supernatural creatures. Detective Hoskins and Jack Torrance both find their weaknesses preyed upon, be it by the Outsider or by the Overlook Hotel. Each character is already desperate, and their current condition adds to their dire situation. Hoskins is an alcoholic who believes he has been given skin cancer, and "Jack's inability to put his son's welfare in front of his own job"[17] is a result of his own perception of his various failures: as a writer, a teacher, a husband, and a father. Each man believes that he needs to appease the power in order to have not just a return to his normal life, but an increase in success. Jud Crandall seems to be the outlier here, because the burying grounds have nothing to promise him, although its risen undead can certainly threaten him. He is simply ensnared by the marvel of a place that seems to have power over death.

The death of the Renfield is a requirement because such selfish people cannot be allowed to move forward into the narrative's brave new world. Recovery from the trauma of the narrative can only occur after the complete elimination of the threats, cauterizing the wound and preventing the spread of infection. Any human who has thrown his lot in with the monster can never be trusted because he has chosen himself over a sense of community, and that is an unpardonable sin.

A Renfield chooses his fate without fully understanding that he has selected death. He believes that his decision puts him in a position of power and favor, and that he will personally gain something because of it. He cannot look for the value of anyone but himself and would certainly never sacrifice anything he has for the greater good. This stands in direct contrast with the subject of the next chapter: characters who knowingly and heroically go to their own deaths in support of a future that they, themselves, will never see.

NOTES

1. Magistrale, *Stephen King: America's Storyteller*, 69.
2. Magistrale, *Landscape of Fear*, 62.

3. Hoppenstand, *Critical Insights: Stephen King* (Pasadena, California: Salem Press, 2011), 4.
4. Davis, *Stephen King's America*, 65.
5. Magistrale, *Stephen King: The Second Decade*, 45.
6. Erin Mercer, "The Difference Between World and Want: Adulthood and the Horrors of History in Stephen King's *IT*," *Journal of Popular Culture* 52, no. 2 (2019): 322–23. Italics in original.
7. King, *It* (New York: Scribner, 1986), 590.
8. King, *Duma Key*, 508. Italics in original.
9. Russell, *Stephen King: A Critical Companion*, 111.
10. Russell, *Stephen King: A Critical Companion*, 126.
11. Russell, *Revisiting Stephen King: A Critical Companion*, 68.
12. Magistrale, *Stephen King: America's Storyteller*, 112.
13. Sternberg, "Telling in Time," 524.
14. Magistrale, *The Moral Voyages of Stephen King*, 16.
15. Magistrale, *Stephen King: America's Storyteller*, 64.
16. Russell, *Stephen King: A Critical Companion*, 125.
17. Magistrale, *Stephen King: America's Storyteller*, 98.

Chapter Eight
"I Want to Die Well"
As Heroic Sacrifice

Just as it is possible for King's characters to choose themselves above anyone else, and therefore start on the path to their own deaths as the monster's accomplice, it is also possible for characters to die in the name of good, as they act in support of other people. Sometimes characters who are simply going about their business in their fight against evil meet their deaths along the way, as required by generic convention. Matt Burke and Jimmy Cody do not live to see the end of *'Salem's Lot*; Sheriff Bannerman becomes Cujo's last mauling victim; Eddie Kaspbrak dies fighting It to save his friends; and Howie Gold and Alec Pelly are killed before the final confrontation with the Outsider. Only Eddie truly knew the depth of the danger he was walking into.

At other times, this decision is entirely conscious as a character knowingly faces death, realizing that his or her death is a step in the right direction for the community as a whole. These are instances in which "individual will proves to be a viable element of salvation"[1] because the willing sacrifices do indeed improve the general situation. Both the spies and the remaining Free Zone Committee Members in *The Stand* choose to obey the wishes of the Committee and Mother Abigail, knowing that they will almost certainly die and never see the result of their sacrifices. John Smith of *The Dead Zone* knows he will likely be demonized after his death as the greater public would not even believe the threat. Duddits in *Dreamcatcher* and Nick Hopewell in "The Langoliers" have a short amount of time in which to make their decisions, but they both know that the choice they make will lead to their deaths.

Finally, there are the characters who rise up at the very end of their lives and perhaps even go against their previous characterization to sacrifice themselves for the good of others. Jack Torrance resists the Overlook long enough to save his son, Gard manages to make it to the Tommyknocker ship to get it away from Earth, Johnny Marinville accepts the suicide mission to once again trap the evil god Tak menacing our world, and young Avery Dixon hatches his own plan to save his friends while preventing them from reading it in his mind. Even Ralph Roberts of *Insomnia* forgot that he had made a deal to save someone's life by giving his. All of these characters are plagued with "the doubts that are reportedly common among those who are facing death,"[2] and while Ralph might be reassured by the supernatural beings he sees while dying, Tak especially makes use of these apparent human failings, although in the end humanity is stronger than these fears.

Readers who are familiar with horror and who are, after all, cognizant of the fact that they are reading a book, will likely recognize this first kind of impending death while the protagonists themselves will not. Using foreshadowing and suspense, King sets up the fear that one of the beloved "good" characters will soon die, even if the protagonists themselves have no such intuition. These deaths feel entirely unfair, because it seems that the characters have not done anything wrong—and were in fact intent on the business of doing everything right. They are forced to suffer and die, and not to see the end of their efforts, even though readers have more pages left in the book. These deaths, however, are demanded by the narrative because success against such an evil, especially a supernatural evil with inhuman powers, comes at a price.

UNSUSPECTING SACRIFICES

As readers who understand that they are engaging with a narrative, King's audience members may often suspect that death is coming when his characters do not. For example, although the characters in *'Salem's Lot* compare themselves to Bram Stoker's fearless vampire hunters, even going so far as to relate Matt Burke to Van Helsing, they do not honestly believe that any of them are true parallels to the characters in *Dracula*. Granted, King does not make a one-to-one analogy of his characters—for example, there is no surviving female to truly be Mina Harker's double—but he does acknowledge that the Dracula storyline, and the characters themselves, were major influences on his own tale. Even then, King plays with the expected narrative, introducing failures of faith that "would not happen in Dracula."[3]

Defeating a supernatural monster demands sacrifice. A creature that can be easily overcome without the threat of human death does not deserve the title—it is merely an annoyance. Many of King's characters are spurred on to action because their foe is indeed deadly and is at least suspected of having already killed people. Readers, who are not confined to a single point of view within these books, can be far more certain much more quickly than the characters. King allows his readers to witness horrific acts, at times doling out this information piecemeal, so that readers can feel the suspense while watching the human characters determine what, exactly, it is that they face. For King, unbelief is often a death sentence.

The small band of vampire hunters in *Salem's Lot* decreases quickly. Initially, the residents who not only admit that vampires are present but who are willing to confront them consist of Ben Mears, Matt Burke, Dr. Jimmy Cody, and twelve-year-old Mark Petrie. Ben's girlfriend, Susan Norton, shows the most resistance to belief, possibly as an attempt to subvert the usual argument that women are more emotional and men more likely to stick to science. Susan's belief waffles—and perhaps never entirely solidifies—so that her only dynamic change in the book is from human to vampire. She functions as a test for Ben's faith and his strength.

Matt Burke's death is more in alignment with Joseph Campbell's idea of the hero's journey and the loss of the mentor than with Matt's position as a double of Van Helsing. Matt is the first adult believer and the one who, from his hospital bed, begins researching vampire mythology. He later addresses Mark as being "a scholar"[4] due to Mark's own knowledge of horror films, but Matt is the one positioned as the sensible leader of the group even though he cannot physically join in on the hunt. Matt never faces down the head vampire and his death is caused by a heart attack instead of by a vampire directly. Although his death is a blow because it removes the group's mentor, it does not in and of itself increase animosity or hatred toward the vampires. The death that does this is Jimmy Cody's.

As a fully engaged and supportive member of the group, Jimmy's death by booby trap is surprising and brutal. In a story where "[f]ew escape, and even fewer triumph,"[5] Jimmy had the faith that should have helped him live until the end of the book. Instead he is blindsided by an inability to anticipate trouble, a major element in the narrative's demands for one final sacrifice before victory. Jimmy assimilated the vampiric threat more easily than survivor Ben Mears, but that belief was not enough to save him. Neither Jimmy nor readers anticipated his end, and the suddenness and brutality of his death strengthens the survivors' resolve.

In *Cujo*, readers are fully aware of the situation that awaits Sheriff George Bannerman as he drives out to Joe Camber's place. Because of King's choice of narrative point of view, readers know that Cujo, the enormous Saint Bernard, had encountered a rabid bat without his owners realizing it. The suspense therefore starts early in the novel as readers wait for any of the Cambers to notice that there is something wrong with their dog, and then worry as the story centers on Donna Trenton, her four-year-old son Tad, and their troublesome car. Prior to Donna's arrival at the Cambers', the only two men to realize that Cujo has gone rabid were immediately killed by the dog and are therefore in no position to warn anyone. Because readers have more information than any single character, they can anticipate the scene before it occurs: Donna and Tad, trapped in a car that will not start, sitting in the Cambers' dooryard as Cujo circles them.

While Bannerman might have emerged the hero in another type of story, he had the misfortune of being a character created by Stephen King. He is sacrificed to Cujo to move the story forward, again in multiple ways. Donna has been dreaming of help coming, since she has no weapons and her long confinement in the car has weakened her. She has held on to the hope that someone else—one of Camber's friends or even the mailman—would stop by, see them, and come to the rescue. The arrival of a man not only in uniform and a squad car, but carrying a gun, followed quickly by his death, shows Donna that she must act herself if she has any hope of saving her son.

Donna does finally emerge from the car and face the rabid dog, although not in time to save her son. But Cujo's death is the climax of the narrative, and Tad's is part of the falling action. Heidi Strengell acknowledges that "King has never been comfortable with the child's death in the closing pages of *Cujo*,"[6] and the text does not linger on it. While Bannerman could spur Donna to act, and finally called the cavalry to the Camber place, Tad's death is not a spark. The narrative moves on to summary and epilogue. Had Bannerman arrived earlier, or had he remembered to call in, Tad might have lived, but the dead man cannot be blamed. While Jimmy Cody knew that he was approaching the place where a vampire was sleeping, Bannerman had absolutely no idea of what he would be facing that day.

As lone men charging ahead toward their destinies, Jimmy Cody and George Bannerman felt a sense of danger, but also believed that they had the situation handled. They did not go already concerned for their lives. The adult Losers in *It* in 1985 come home to Derry with enough restored memories to make every last one of them terrified, and yet all but one returned anyway. While Jimmy and Bannerman rather haphazardly encountered deaths because of their destiny, Eddie Kaspbrak stood up to many of his own fears to face It head-on.

Again, in the tradition of Dracula, it seems that any group going to fight a monster cannot defeat it with every member still alive. At least one person involved must die during the final confrontation, and in *It*, that person is Eddie. Adult Eddie must battle his own fears in many ways, including going against the wishes of his wife in order to return to Derry in the first place. Afraid of sickness and pain, physically small and generally seen as weak, Eddie has his arm broken and yet still beats It back. Paralleling his own heroic actions as a child twenty-seven years earlier, Eddie is able to face It in Its true form—as opposed to one of Its disguises—and to once again use his inhaler to harm It. Eddie's inhaler, and asthma, are defining features of his character, and generally seen as markers of his weakness. By using his inhaler against the child-killing monster, Eddie shows the strength of his imagination and his courage.

In neither confrontation, 1958 or 1985, does Eddie get to duel with It during the mysterious Ritual of Chüd. However, in 1985 he can bring himself to approach It during the ritual to distract It long enough for Ben and Richie to succeed. Instead of imagining his inhaler to be full of battery acid,[7] as he did in 1958, Eddie summons up all his childhood belief in its contents as medicine.[8] By shooting this medicine—and his belief—down Its throat, Eddie both harms It and allows It the opportunity to bite off his arm. Eddie, like It, dies in the sewers under Derry.

Fighting a similar sort of shape-shifting child killer in *The Outsider*, another group makes the journey for their final confrontation. Like the Losers, they are composed of multiple men and one woman, and they are similarly very much aware of the danger, but go anyway. Of this group, only one has knowingly faced a supernatural threat before, but, as a requirement of the quest, all have agreed to believe in the mysterious "Outsider" just for this day. Unfortunately, two members—Howie Gold and Alec Pelly—find themselves in a similar situation to Jimmy Cody. Their deaths are not caused by the mysterious creature, but by a mundane trap the creature has laid. Rather than a static pitfall of kitchen knives on the cellar floor, the Outsider has contracted a sharpshooter who kills Howie and Alec before the rest of the group understands what is happening.

The difficult part of Howie's and Alec's deaths, like Eddie's, is that these characters seem to have done nothing wrong. They each chose to go along on this dangerous trip to clear a wrongly accused man's name when neither played a role in Terry's arrest or his death. In *The Outsider*, the group that has gone to face the creature is led by those "guilty" people: Detective Ralph Anderson expedited the case that resulted in the murder of the wrongly accused man, and now that man's wife and children are unable to continue their normal lives. One of the other men assisted Ralph on the case. Howie and Alec, however, were on the innocent man's side the entire time and therefore had nothing to atone for, but they died anyway. They made the journey and risked so much when even the district attorney, just as guilty as Ralph, could not bring himself to do so. This unexpected firefight, the deaths of two group members, and the injury of a third were meant to stop the remaining two from actually confronting the Outsider, but instead Ralph and Holly chose not to let Howie and Alec die in vain.

Many of these sacrificial deaths come directly prior to the final confrontation between the threat and the remaining heroes. They are largely bound up in the death of the Renfield character, and therefore also predict the death of the supernatural evil. There is no victory for the side of "good" without also death and sacrifice made by people whose ends might seem senseless or unjust. Part of the horror, then, comes in the fact that being a good person does not always pay off in King's books. It is possible to be morally good, intelligent, and even a reader favorite, and yet still to die before the end, suddenly and perhaps without knowing whether the greater goal will be met.

KNOWINGLY MOVING TOWARD DEATH

It is easier for characters to see that their own lives might have to be sacrificed when they also have some sort of overarching narrative to apply to their lives. This is why there are so many willing sacrifices within *The Stand*. *The Stand* is not made up of individual characters all fighting each other, only looking out for themselves, but rather exists in a post-plague world where people are divided into two sides, each with its higher cause. The "good" side lives in Boulder and follows the teachings and inclinations of Mother Abigail. Mother Abigail herself says she listens to God, and, as many of the characters point out, she means the God who sacrificed His own Son. The "bad" side has gathered in Las Vegas around someone calling himself Randall Flagg.

The survival of the Boulder Free Zone is dependent on "people giv[ing] of themselves for what they believe,"[9] with a heavy Christian influence. This means that four leaders of the Free Zone are instructed by God, through Mother Abigail, to walk to Vegas unarmed. She cannot tell them for sure what will happen, but the men know they are walking to their deaths. Although Stu Redman bucks the odds and readers' expectations by eventually returning to Boulder, Glen Bateman, Larry Underwood, and Ralph Brentner all die in Vegas. Glen dies first, shot in his cell with only Randall Flagg and his right-hand man to witness it. Heidi Strengell argues that the "true conclusion of the novel"[10] happens here, right before Glen's death and during his outburst of laughter when he first encounters Flagg. When finally confronted with the Dark Man, the bogeyman of nightmares and the subject of so much discussion back in Boulder, Glen could only laugh. Such ridicule could not be allowed to stand although, for Strengell, victory has already been won through the recognition that Flagg was not in fact the boogeyman the Free Zone had feared. Larry and Ralph die in an atomic blast that takes out all of Vegas, securing the safety of the Free Zone in a much more dramatic end.

Although Glen, Larry, and Ralph are the sacrifice at the climax of the novel, and their actions most directly lead to the continued safety of Boulder, there were two others sent West willing to die for the Free Zone who did indeed already give their lives for it. Back before the bombing in Boulder, when the Free Zone committee still numbered seven, Nick suggested that they should send spies into the West to see what Flagg was doing. Because of both the time of year and what they already knew about the Dark Man, the committee knew that whomever they picked had very little chance of returning alive, or quickly. Of the three sent West, only one returns to Bolder.

Judge Farris, the oldest spy, does not make it to Boulder, but his death does not go as Flagg had instructed. It is one indication that Flagg's hold over his people is not complete. The second spy, Dayna Jurgens, goes unnoticed in Vegas for quite some time before she is brought to Flagg. Rather than let herself be tortured and reveal the name of the third spy, Dayna completes a quick and brutal suicide, "the first indication that Flagg's indomitable will, particularly over women, is not so indomitable."[11] Dayna not only protected the third spy and the Free Zone, but caused rumbles in Vegas because it was Flagg himself she had defied. The threat, and loss of control, was moving closer to the center of Flagg's domain.

The Judge and Dayna, like Glen, Larry, and Ralph, willingly went toward Vegas fully anticipating they would die. Unlike Stu and the third spy, Tom, who had the same expectations, all of them did in fact die. They were willing to sacrifice their lives for the greater cause of the Boulder Free Zone and Mother Abigail's God, rather than selfishly clinging to whatever little they could claim for themselves. Each of them had to trust that their death would indeed mean something for the greater good, but they were also able to rely on Mother Abigail and her interpretation of God's word to reassure themselves that they were, in fact, surrendering their lives for a good cause.

Johnny Smith of *The Dead Zone* faces similar concerns about his own impending death. While the characters in *The Stand* had Mother Abigail and her God to guide them, Smith only has himself and his visions. Throughout the book, and as discussed previously in chapter 5, Smith faces multiple situations in which his psychic ability allows him to save people and to prove to himself that what he envisions is true. The vast majority of these instances happen quickly: when he sees that his physical therapist's house is catching fire, the flames have only begun, and she is able to call the fire department. When Smith sees a restaurant similarly in flames, the dreaded lightning strike happens that very night. What has been bothering Smith is a vision showing him something that may or may not happen much further in the future: whether a politician will honestly turn out to be as horrible as Smith has foreseen.

The difficulty is that, if Smith is to act, it will be long before the general public realizes that Greg Stillson is anything but their personal savior. Cursed with psychic powers, Smith spends the book using them "for the benefit of others"[12] rather than for personal gain. Killing Stillson before he can be elected to the presidency would indeed benefit others, if Smith's vision is true, but Smith has already experienced negative reactions to his abilities even when he was proven to have been right. Because of current public opinion about Stillson, Smith even refrains from overtly discussing his decision with anyone else. When he decides to attempt an assassination, he tells no one his plans, only sending letters to his loved ones that will be read long after his own death.

Smith, unlike Larry, Ralph, and Glen, acted alone. He was not able to make his final journey to what he knew must be his death in the presence of friends, or even with anyone else knowing what was about to happen. Although the judge and Dayna Jurgens were also alone, sent as spies into the West, they at least had the comfort of the handful of others who knew about the spies' existence. Smith, through his experiences with his other visions and people's reactions to him because of them, took no one into his confidence and went to his death knowing that the world would think poorly of him. His few letters reassure his loved ones that he knew what he was doing and that his act was indeed heroic.

The character of Douglas Clavell, nicknamed Duddits, can similarly commit to an act of heroism at the end of his life, although he does not leave behind a letter in order to explain this to his mother. Duddits spends much of *Dreamcatcher* as a shared memory between his four childhood friends, only belatedly joining the action. When adult Duddits enters the story, he is not only living with Down syndrome but is in the final stage of leukemia. Leaving the house at all would be dangerous to his health, but Duddits insists on not only going out in a snowstorm, but also heading off in pursuit of an alien entity intent on infecting the Earth, while his companions are hunted by a deranged army official. Both Duddits and his mother know that, if he leaves with Henry Devlin and Owen Underhill, he will die. Duddits goes all the same, knowing he is *"Their dreamcatcher"*[13]: the connection his old friends need in order to triumph over the extraterrestrial threat.

Duddits's and Henry's new companion, Owen Underhill, also dies during this final encounter. He was not as deeply connected as Duddits and his four childhood friends, but Underhill was driven by a personal sense of guilt from a shameful boyhood memory. While Duddits's sacrifice was born of love for his friends, Underhill's was a means of personal redemption. Due to his individual choices throughout the novel, Underhill knew that he would die soon, but he wanted to make sure his death was meaningful and for the right cause.

Nick Hopewell of "The Langoliers" finds himself in a similar position to Owen Underhill, not having as much time to anticipate his own death as the spies and chosen men in *The Stand* but also having elements of his past that compel him to make amends. While Owen is not able to apologize to the people he directly hurt in the past, Nick has enough reassurance that the other members of his group will survive his death so that one can pass on a message to his father. Because "The Langoliers" "uses devices derived from the thriller genre,"[14] Nick is hinted to have been a spy or assassin for the

British government, making his own past regrets more serious than those of his companions.

"The Langoliers" centers around a limited cast of ten people, those who were asleep when their red-eye flight passed through a strange rip in the fabric of time. After battling each other and the new world that awaits them when they land, they return to the air seeking to fly back through the same portal. At the last minute they realize that they can only survive the passage if they are asleep or unconscious. Because the plane is low on fuel, they have to make a quick decision. Nick volunteers to be the one in the cockpit in charge of lowering the cabin pressure so the others pass out before steering the plane into the phenomenon and restoring cabin pressure at the last minute, allowing them to wake up after the danger has passed. This is especially traumatic because Nick and another of the survivors have expressed interest in pursuing a relationship once they have returned to their own world. Nick makes his sacrifice in large part for her, so that she and the others can confront their past regrets, make amends, and live fulfilled lives. Although the survivors only met recently, they have shared enough in their struggles that Nick is willing to make this sacrifice for them.

SACRIFICE AS A FINAL, DESPERATE ACT

Just like in *Dreamcatcher*, the sacrificial deaths in *The Stand* feel rather nebulous and disconnected from the cause. Each of the characters must venture far from home and from the people they intend to save, dying by the side of the road, or in a penthouse suite, or in a jail cell, or on display, and none of these situations lend comfort that what they are doing is indeed for the greater good. They die in a strange place, and alone, and can only hope that their intentions will be fulfilled. It is easier for other characters to go to their own deaths when the choice is more immediate—that is, they do not have to first travel across the country to meet it—and when they are in the presence of those they are saving.

There are multiple examples in which a character has been swept along by a force stronger than he is for much of the novel but who, in the end, manages to find a way to fight back and save others. The amount of success they experience differs, depending on what characters can be saved. When given the chance and forced to act, each chose to give his own life to save others.

Jack Torrance spends most of *The Shining* allowing himself to believe that whatever haunts the Overlook Hotel has chosen him, specifically, because he is special. The hotel has lulled him into actions that put his entire family, but especially his son, in danger. While Jack might be seen as helpless in the face of a greater power, Tony Magistrale argues that Jack is still "responsible for his own doom"[15] because, any time he was given the opportunity to change things, he made a poor decision. As the character in a story modeled on Shakespearean tragedy, Jack's future has "already been decided."[16] He will die before the story ends, but Jack makes one final—or perhaps one singular—heroic effort to ensure that he will not kill Danny before he does. Since he has allowed himself to be dragged so deeply into the Overlook's desires, there is no other way out for Jack.

Jim Gardner in *The Tommyknockers* finds himself in a position unenviably similar to that of Jack Torrance. Gard is also an alcoholic, although he has not taken the pledge and continues to drink while he is kept in isolation. After waking up from his latest alcoholic bender, Gard meant to kill himself and therefore cure his alcoholism that way, but he first gives in to the strong feeling that his only friend in the world, Bobbi Anderson, is in trouble. Gard therefore goes into isolation not seeking out employment and his last gasp at being the responsible head of a household, but in an attempt to rescue the only person who has yet to fully turn her back on him.

Gard's purpose and motive, like Jack's, tend to shift and mutate depending on the moment. Gard is driven not only by his concern for Bobbi, but by his own personal beliefs, specifically about nuclear power. Before this latest extensive bender, Gard was shown having his usual argument about nuclear power during what was supposed to have been a casual cocktail party. While attempting to make his points, buoyed by far too many drinks, Gard not only created a spectacle instead of a rhetorical argument, but also happened to cause his host to have a heart attack that proved fatal. Gard, like Jack Torrance, is at his lowest ebb at the start of the story before he encounters the supernatural. And Gard, like Jack, goes into seclusion with the only human being who still thinks he might be able to make something of himself.

Instead of being stuck in a hotel and isolated from the rest of the world, Gard finds himself trapped in the town of Haven. There are more characters who know what is going on than in *The Shining*, but, in Gard's case, this means there are more people who will prevent him from doing anything to stop it. Residents of Haven prove their dedication to the uncovering of the alien spaceship when they kill one of their own beloved citizens, and the only thing keeping them from killing Gard is the fact that Bobbi is still mostly human. Gard knows, however, that this protection cannot last, and so he attempts to gird himself for his final moments when a confrontation will be necessary. He, unlike Jack, realizes that such a moment is coming.

While the solution to the problem of the possessed Overlook Hotel involved exploding it, Gard cannot do such damage to the Tommyknockers' spaceship. Throughout the book, Gard and his various coworkers have been using dynamite to loosen the rock holding the ship in place, showing exactly how indestructible this material is. But the ship, unlike the hotel, is meant to move and can therefore be taken away. Gard, who has at least been able to form some semblance of a plan, has also been expecting this attack. He knows that, after they reach the hatch of the ship, the citizens of Haven will not have any need for him, and Bobbi will no longer be able to protect him. He cannot fully anticipate what Bobbi will do, or when his own barriers against the others' telepathy will fail, but Gard is first able to arm himself and then kill Bobbi—or at least what Bobbi has Become—before the others can come to her aid.

Even then, Gard acts heroically "more by accident than by design"[17] when he manages to beat the Havenites to the ship and to send it off into deep space, where it will harm no one but him. In this shambling, painful quest, Gard is aided not only by two other prisoners of the Tommyknockers, but also somehow by the spirit of his now-dead friend. All of Haven turns its attention to Gard's dash for the ship, but the fire his temporary allies helped Gard set prevents them from stopping him. The unchecked flames, along with the sight of the enormous spaceship rising into the air, also turn all eyes to Haven. The town that has very carefully isolated itself against outsiders suddenly becomes front-page news as firefighters, policemen, journalists, and gawkers all flock across the town line and find themselves confronted with the side effects that "mimic radiation poisoning."[18] Not only is there a raging fire that needs to be contained, but there are also strange physical reactions that must be investigated.

Unlike Jack Torrance, Gard was correct in believing that he was the "special" one the others were after. Jack was fooled and lulled into believing the Overlook wanted him instead of his son Danny, but in Haven, Gard was unique. The metal plate in his head, the result of a skiing accident from when he was a teenager, protected him against Becoming a Tommyknocker alongside the rest of the town. While the metal plate meant that he was able to work close to the ship day after day without any major side effects, it also prevented him from joining the group mind and participating in groupthink. Gard remained an individual until the end, which allowed him to perform a series of desperate heroic acts in his final moments.

Gard therefore spent most of the book, and most of his time in Haven, preparing himself to make this final sacrifice. Although he was not generally a heroic man, and had done many bad things in his past, not unlike Owen Underhill, Gard was able to pull himself together in the end and give his life to save the world. In this way, he parallels Johnny Marinville of *Desperation*.

Marinville is another author in isolation, this time trapped in the small town of Desperation, Nevada, with a handful of strangers. There is a recently released power residing in Desperation, much like the Tommyknocker ship in Haven, and Tak, like the Tommyknockers, takes over and ruins the bodies of the people it inhabits. The dwindling group of human survivors must first define Tak before they can figure out how to defeat it, a role that largely falls on the shoulders of young, newly Christian David Carver.

Because this is a world where "faith is in short supply,"[19] David must first overcome the adults' resistance to his beliefs. Gradually, through repeated miracles, he convinces all but Marinville. David knows how to defeat Tak, but "King's God requires human assistance"[20] and Marinville is one of the humans He has chosen. During the final encounter, one of the remaining people must die. God has chosen Marinville but, like Jack Torrance, David wants to be the chosen one. In order to comply with God's will—and in an act that once again emphasizes the novel's repeated "notion of God's cruelty"[21]—Marinville has to both admit that God has commanded him and defy David's spoken wishes in front of the group, making himself the one to die for the others.

Also, like Jack Torrance, Marinville is forced to act in the moment and in defense of a child. Because of Tak's increasing power and anger, there is no time for the author to stop, think, or possibly reconsider. At the end of his life, Marinville's one goal is to send David Carver up and out of the mine, hopefully to safety, while he himself descends to its depths in order to set off the charge that will end his own life and, hopefully, once again trap the evil entity. He, like Gard, is a rather accidental hero, although David Carver would argue that God drew him to the town of Desperation so that he could perform this final act. Even so, there seems to be very little honorable about what Marinville does in his service to God. The fact that his first action is to once again set himself against David means the work is difficult and very much unglamorous. However, Marinville goes to his death willingly and laughing, knowing that he has at least saved the people Tak had been unable to kill.

Marinville and Gard were in the same position of knowing that, unless they could escape, they would die. Although readers may have known or suspected this about Jack Torrance, Jack himself believed that the Overlook Hotel had chosen him and would keep him safe. Avery Dixon, of *The Institute*, knew that his position was more like Marinville's and Gard's. Throughout all the decades of its existence, only one child ever escaped the clutches of the Institute, and it was not young Avery. In fact, his friend Luke's escape made things worse for Avery, who was tortured for information before prematurely being sent to the "Back Half" of the Institute, where the children's life expectancy drops considerably.

All the young "residents" of the Institute have been kidnapped from their families and isolated in a compound in the middle of the Maine woods. Their access to outside news, including the internet, is limited, although the grapevine within the Institute provides them with a surprising amount of information about their current predicament. The director of the Institute tells them, one and all, that they will have their minds wiped and then be returned to their families once their duty to their country is complete. The children themselves, even in Front Half, share the knowledge that this is a lie. Here in Front Half, the children chosen for their telepathic or telekinetic talents are given tests and experimental treatments to improve their abilities for the work they will be asked to do in Back Half and then in the Back Half of Back Half. Although none of the children encountered in Front Half have ever seen the rest of the facility, they are aware that they will be used, and used up, eventually dying and never returning to their families.

Avery, like the others, first resists this information and then comes to accept it as true. As soon as he woke up at the Institute, in the bedroom oddly decorated to look very much like his own room at home, his days were numbered. The children taken by the Institute, supposedly to protect their country, will all die. Sometimes even the tests and experiments performed in Front Half will cause their deaths, as seen earlier in the narrative, but especially once Avery is taken to Back Half, he knows that he cannot expect to survive. The way the Institute uses the children first causes massive, constant headaches and then turns them into "gorks"[22] who cannot even care for themselves. Avery thus finds himself in a position similar to Gard or Marinville: if he stays, he will die, but the chances of ever leaving alive are minuscule.

Due to the strength of his own naturally occurring power, combined with the torture and experiments inflicted upon him in Front Half, Avery discovers that the chances of escape are actually greater than he thought. By working together with his friends on the inside and Luke on the outside, Avery finds himself in a position to help a number of the children escape and to bring an end to the Institute itself, but there is a cost. First, the amount of energy necessary to do what Avery has in mind is immense. He ends up drawing upon not only his friends, the ones strong enough to then escape, and the "gorks" who form the Matrix-like battery pack for the Institute's dealings, but also upon any of the children still left in Front Half. The only survivors of this attack are the ones Avery shoos out of his mental and physical circle. All the children who remain end up dying.

Like Duddits, Avery does his best to conceal his knowledge of his impending death from his loved ones. Also, like Duddits, many of Avery's loved ones can read his mind. He therefore focuses on the children's common image of a gigantic phone and the repeated mantra of "You're my friends."[23] This prevents the others from fully reading his thoughts and intentions, while providing both them and the readers with suspicions of what is to come. If Avery thought that all of them could escape and walk away, then he would have nothing to hide.

Avery is acting to save other children, the way Jack triumphed long enough to save Danny's life or how Marinville went against David's wishes one last time to both fulfill God's desires and to spare the boy. Although he is the youngest in the group, Avery is also the most powerful. He seems to be the only one who fully understands what must happen in order to save even some of them, much less the only one who was capable of doing it. Although Avery and the others have talked and thought about escape their entire tenure at the Institute, it is only in these final hours that Avery sees how it can happen, and that it is indeed possible.

Avery fully accepts responsibility and, in his refusal to let his friends see his plans, also denies them the chance to talk him out of it. When Avery tells the others to leave the joined circle, they go. They are prevented from either waiting for him or going back to get him because, now in a much smaller group, they do not have the power to get through the locked door. Avery achieved the apparently impossible by helping them escape from the room in which they had been trapped, and the fact that he is now using their combined power to destroy the building itself means the survivors are forced to run for their lives. Readers, if not the other characters, are able to see the pure motivation behind Avery's actions through his final thought: "I loved having friends."[24] His sacrifice, like Jack Torrance's, was selflessly given for the people he was saving as he put them above himself.

Although Jack, Gard, Marinville, and Avery willingly gave their lives to benefit other characters, none of them was entirely sure that the sacrifice would be worth it. Jack, for example, realized that the Overlook Hotel was about to explode, and he had also already injured Wendy, who may or may not have been able to rescue Danny in time. Further, without the hotel building as protection, Danny would have been stranded in the middle of winter, after dark, in the mountains of Colorado. Although Jack could ensure that he would not personally be used to murder his son in that moment, he could not be certain that Danny would survive the night. Similarly, although Gard was able to remove the Tommyknocker ship from Earth, he was not aware of what all the consequences would be when Haven was finally invaded. Marinville could tell David Carver and the others to go, but he could not both physically restrain David and run to destroy the pit. And although Avery could be sure that his friends got out of the locked room, he did not have the reassurance that they would escape the building in time, or that their lives afterward would be free.

Avery and Jack are not the only King characters who give their lives to save children. Ralph Roberts, in *Insomnia*, made the same sacrifice, and was perhaps comforted by the fact that the act had indeed been bargained for. In the midst of the book's main conflict, Ralph is given a vision of someone dying. The image is apparently clear to him, but hidden from readers as King gives "only ... partial information, failing to provide fuller explanation until later in the novel."[25] This act of authorial concealment continues during a scene where Ralph makes a bargain with the novel's higher powers. Although readers can assume it has something to do with the death he has foreseen, the scene is presented from the point of view of a character too far away to hear what is being said, aside from the fact that Ralph's proposal is accepted.

Ralph then forgets the bargain until shortly before it is to be enacted, although this still gives him more lead time to think about his impending death than other characters. Jack and Avery acted in the desperation of a moment and could not be entirely sure that their own deaths would save the intended children. Ralph at least has the benefit of knowing that a higher power has agreed to his deal, and that the person he chooses to die to protect will indeed be saved.

Since *Insomnia* is directly connected to King's epic *Dark Tower* series, the author "suggests that both his characters and the reader have roles to play by participating in the realization of some cosmic plan."[26] Therefore Ralph's life, and his death, truly serve a purpose, and he can meet the little doctors at the end of his life and greet them as old friends. Ralph, and readers, can draw more comfort from his death because of the circumstances surrounding it and the reassurance for both character and reader that his death was necessary and good.

FALLEN HEROES

These deaths—the deaths on the side of "good"—are generally seen as the cost of success. Heroes cannot be heroes without risk and, although it is possible for King's heroes to live, many of them do so with a healthy dose of survivor's guilt thrown in. These heroic deaths largely occur at the end of the story, just before the final confrontation, and this position within the narrative generally prevents King's characters from having the chance to fully explore their feelings or even be shown to mourn the loss. The surviving characters are usually in a position where they must act immediately following the deaths, and any epilogue that comes along only returns to their emotions months later, after the time of greatest grief and mourning has passed.

The epilogues, set at such a distance from the main body of the narrative, allow the readers to see that the heroic deaths did indeed have an impact. They were purposeful, and these characters did not die in vain. Many of them are remembered as heroes, if only by the few survivors who know what actually happened, and some are publicly recognized as such. Attempts to make sense of the events of the narrative include attempts to make sense of these deaths, and to make the knowledge of these deaths more bearable for the survivors.

This distance allows the characters to have more perspective, and to put them more in line with the reader. While the reader has been aware this entire time of consuming a narrative, real life—which the characters believe themselves to be living—does not occur in a narrative structure. Humans impose narrative on their lives in the telling and retelling, adding beginnings, middles, and ends where they do not in fact exist, and making connections to introduce the idea of cause and effect.[27] Having had the time to process the traumatic events of their pasts, the surviving characters are able to make their arguments concerning the deaths of their friends, and to reassure themselves that those deaths were not in vain.

Readers can see, then, that the surviving vampire hunters return to 'salem's Lot with a new plan for eradication, although the success—or rather failure—of this mission is not revealed within the book itself. Although Sheriff Bannerman does not know that Donna Trenton lives, or that young Tad dies, readers have a glimpse into the future where Donna and her husband attempt to collect their lives and continue on. Eddie's death is similar to those in *'Salem's Lot*, because the Constant Reader receives clues that It still somehow survives, but the novel itself ends on a happy note. Although bad dreams haunt the survivors of *The Outsider*'s final showdown, that creature has been thoroughly destroyed, and one of the survivors is prepped to confront another Outsider in the future.

Those who sacrifice themselves in the name of the Boulder Free Zone, like Ralph Roberts in *Insomnia*, at least have in-world reassurance that their deaths will be worthwhile. John Smith can be reasonably certain that his actions will serve the greater good, due to his psychic abilities and the numerous ways he has tested them throughout the book, and Nick Hopewell of "The Langoliers" likewise has the benefit of knowing what happened the last time this plane passed through a strange rip in reality. Duddits of *Dreamcatcher*, though, is not even fully appreciated during his lifetime, and the epilogue months later is necessary to ascribe full meaning to his character. "Only the survivors see"[28] how completely he bound them together, but even then, they flounder at language and grasping the entire significance of their old friend.

Those who give their lives at the last minute are a mix between truly selfless characters and those who have managed to finally rise up against who they have been for the entire book and make a better choice. Jack Torrance, Jim Gardener, and Johnny Marinville all fall into the second category, becoming heroes more by chance and pressures from those around them than by internal motivation. Avery Dixon, on the other hand, decides on a selfless course of action to save his friends since he can see no other way of helping them.

The deaths of heroes are not the only deaths likely to occur at the climax of the narrative. Others—at times many others—will fall during the final confrontation. It is necessary for the book to complete the restoration ritual and return life to the normal, expected order the characters experienced in the beginning. This means getting rid of the threat, but it can also mean more than simply the death of a single antagonist. At times, restoration itself comes covered in literary blood.

NOTES

1. Tom Newhouse "A Blind Date with Disaster: Adolescent Revolt in the Fiction of Stephen King," *Critical Insights: Stephen King* (Pasadena, California: Salem Press, 2011), 272.
2. Patrick McAleer, "The Fallen King(dom): Surviving Ruin and Decay from *The Stand* to *Cell*," *Stephen King's Modern Macabre: Essays on the Later Works* (Jefferson, NC: McFarland & Company, Inc., 2014), 176.
3. Russell, *Stephen King: A Critical Companion*, 43.
4. King, *'Salem's Lot* (New York: Pocket Books, 1975), 475.
5. Reino, *Stephen King: The First Decade*, 56.
6. Strengell, *Dissecting Stephen King,* 252.
7. King, *It,* 983.
8. King, *It*, 1023.
9. Magistrale, *The Moral Voyages of Stephen King,* 72
10. Strengell, *Dissecting Stephen King*, 149
11. Magistrale, *Stephen King: America's Storyteller,* 78.
12. Magistrale, *The Moral Voyages of Stephen King,* 12.
13. King, *Dreamcatcher*, 790. Italics in original.
14. Sears, *Stephen King's Gothic*, 136.
15. Magistrale, *Stephen King: America's Storyteller,* 107.
16. Strengell, *Dissecting Stephen King,* 97.
17. Magistrale, *Stephen King: The Second Decade,* 84.
18. Strengell, *Dissecting Stephen King,* 239.
19. Patrick McAleer, "The Fallen King(dom)," 175.
20. Strengell, *Dissecting Stephen King*, 236.
21. Strengell, *Dissecting Stephen King*, 193.
22. Stephen King, *The Institute* (New York: Scribner, 2019), 369.
23. King, *The Institute*, 507.
24. King, *The Institute*, 520.
25. Russell, *Stephen King: A Critical Companion,* 129
26. Strengell, *Dissecting Stephen King: From the Gothic to Literary Naturalism.* 231
27. Jerome Bruner, "Life as Narrative," *Social Research* 54, no. 1 (1987): 12.
28. Russell, *Revisiting Stephen King*, 151.

Chapter Nine

"It Could Destroy Everything"
To Restore Order

To make for an interesting and entertaining read, books must first start with an everyday situation—everyday for the world of the narrative, if not for us—before introducing a disruption. The protagonists must then define and confront whatever has unsettled their everyday lives to restore balance and equilibrium. In horror, this frequently means getting rid of the disruption and returning, as much as possible, to that ordinary, mundane life that was so rudely interrupted. Characters who may have previously wished for adventure quickly discover that they would, in fact, prefer what they always already had.

The characters within Stephen King do not always want every single facet of their old lives back, but they certainly want to return to most of it. Whether the intrusion has been alien, supernatural, or rabid, they want to restore order and go back to life as they knew it because they believe that, before, things made sense. Actions have known consequences and people are kept within both the laws of the country and those of physics. It is comforting to return to "normal" at the end of these narratives. Leaving them open for question might threaten a reader's idea of their own safety.

Frequently, the main threat against the characters can infect others around it. This could be in an actual physical way, as vampires turn normal humans into more vampires, or through ideas and madness. It is therefore not enough to eliminate patient zero, since others have already become infected. Many roots of the tree therefore must be destroyed in order to be sure that the trunk will topple. All of the Tommyknockers from Haven, vampires in 'salem's Lot, members of the True Knot, and employees of the Institute need to be destroyed in order to ensure that a new threat does not arise from any survivors. While the aliens do all die, the vampires live on in their infected town. Whether or not the surviving few from the True or the Institute gather new members and begin their evil deeds again has not yet been answered within King's works, although both of these are open for a recurrence.

In these mass cases, it becomes perhaps easier to overlook the deaths of possible innocents because they die alongside the positively threatening. Individual instances are best, because readers and characters alike have seen the danger and the threat inherent in that single person, and they understand that, should that person live, he will only continue causing harm and pain. The mass deaths, which might include children, are both more easily dismissed because the victims do not need to be dealt with on an individual basis, and harder to swallow, especially when readers know that children are involved. If the children are themselves no longer human, and if they can infect others, then at least their deaths can be justified.

It is easier, too, to see death as the sole final recourse against a character when that character has lost all reason. Ed Deepneau, George Stark, and "Zak McCool" are just three of King's characters shown to have little response to reason. Each one sets about his task with a singlemindedness that does not consider the cost of life, either others' or his own. This is explored at more length with the character of Brady Hartsfield through the Bill Hodges trilogy and distilled again in two novellas. While not given as much room to demonstrate their mental condition and drive as characters in King's novels, Mort Rainey and Todd Bowden quickly slip into their violent delusions. Whether or not they can be rehabilitated is a moot point, since each is killed in the middle of attempting to take more lives. Todd especially deteriorates quickly, not following the "gradual moral and physical disintegration"[1] of characters in longer pieces. While novellas do not have as much room to explore the permanence of these mental states, they can still portray the violent depths.

There are, however, cases in which the restoration of the "normal" comes at a high, disturbing price. In these instances, individual children whose names and lives are known to the reader must die for some sort of greater good. It is never their own choice or their own sacrifice, and this can make the deaths seem far less "fair." When lives and deaths do not appear to balance, the restoration of the narrative's normal world seems to be unjust. While readers are then given more insight into the event, the deaths of Seth and Audrey in *The Regulators* seems unfair at the time it occurs and to the other survivors of Poplar Street. Their neighbors are not allowed to see the more hopeful ending.

This may be more uplifting, however, than John Coffey's death in *The Green Mile*. While Seth and Audrey continue to exist in a life after death, Coffey has no such resurrection. Although he was used by the death-row prison guards "to counteract the evil"[2] of a previously botched execution by using his powers for good, there seems to be no good in his own death, even though he asked for it. In this he at least has more free will than the Dunning family in *11/22/63*, whose deaths began the protagonist on his time-traveling adventure in the first place. None of these deaths seems fair or to even approach a happy ending.

These stand in contrasts to the short stories and novellas in which death seems to be the only way to stop the bad things from continuing to happen. Whether it is a nameless bad little kid, a librarian and her two truck driver sons, or a husband with a secret serial killer identity, in these cases the perpetrators are already shown to be serial killers—and then serial killers of women. Even the bad little kid, a supernatural serial killer instead of one bound by human definition, only causes women and girls to die.[3] Because these characters cannot be rehabilitated any more than George Stark could be, they have to die in order to protect future women from suffering the same violent fates. The standout example in this section is that of the astronaut Arthur from "I Am the Doorway," whose body has been overtaken by a malicious alien presence. Arthur's death is a suicide after the presence has once again returned and his previous attempt to halt it has been shown to be unreliable.

All of these deaths are meant, or hoped, to be the final end to a continuing threat. Something absolutely terrible has gone wrong, and the order of the world cannot be restored through any other means. At times the cost seems too high, while at others the deaths are of the no-longer-human, or of the human monster, and therefore less emotionally fraught. Each of the deaths in this chapter is meant to end the chaos or continued threat of violence and restore the world to its previous level of order.

THE MAIN THREAT AND THE INFECTED MASSES

In *The Tommyknockers*, Gard dies removing an alien spaceship from the town of Haven. This is a dramatic event, and a heroic undertaking for a not-so-heroic character, but it is not the end. While the ship has at least left Earth and no longer has influence, much of its work has already been done. The citizens of Haven are no longer human.

Although some of them have begun to undergo more drastic physical changes, all the remaining survivors are linked together telepathically in ways that no humans should be. Much criticism has been leveled at these changed people. Tony Magistrale calls them "the walking dead who have sacrificed their reason, vision, and morality for inclusion in the group identity."[4] Heidi Strengell blames the transformation on the townspeople's "reluctance to shoulder responsibility"[5] for any of their actions. It seems that the people of Haven were not necessarily *good* people before, and have become worse, and less human, as the narrative progresses. When outsiders finally enter Haven, they discover what the Havenites have been hiding, and must now decide what to do with the beings they have encountered.

King makes it relatively easy on these newcomers. Although they must first fight their way into Haven through the bad air created by the Tommyknocker ship, and although they encounter some very strange weapons created by the citizens of Haven, they do not face off against hale and hearty pseudo-aliens. Humans do not have to confront other humans, and, had they chosen to simply cordon off the area instead of killing the people they found, those in Haven would have died anyway. Because Gard has taken the ship, the Havenites have lost their life support system.

Previous scenes showing both outsiders coming into Haven and two Havenites attempting to leave town for an extended time dramatically illustrate what happens to each group in the wrong atmosphere. Aside from the extreme physical alterations, citizens of Haven also underwent a drastic community change "that signifies a breakdown in their communication skills, the inability to tolerate divergent thought, and their incapacity to function in a social context."[6] They no longer look human, and they no longer *are* human. Even if the issue of air could be resolved, they could not have been reintegrated into society and rehumanized.

The remaining vampires in *'Salem's Lot* are in a similar position. Survivor Ben Mears, along with young Mark Petrie, managed to kill Kurt Barlow, the original vampire who first came to the Lot and created the others, but the pair was not able to rid the village of all its vampires before they left. The fact that Ben keeps his scrapbook of articles, and that he seeks out the Maine newspaper even as they live in Mexico, shows that he understands their work is not done. It seems that Barlow was not the only one capable of creating vampires, and so even a single vampire left in the Lot will continue to feed and to produce more.

It is not entirely clear how much of a threat the Tommyknockers will remain to others once the ship has gone. Directly after the incident, when the air in Haven was still inimical to humans, the Havenites were also in possession of several inventions that could be used to hurt anyone trying to enter. These gadgets were all produced thanks to the effects the ship had on their creativity, and all the items were powered by a combination of batteries and the Havenites themselves. It seems that most of these devices needed a living being on the other end for both power and direction, and it is unclear if the telepathic abilities of these former people would still be strong after the ship was gone. The police, though, were aware of what was happening in Haven to a greater extent than in 'salem's Lot, and the survivors found themselves guests of the government. What happened in Haven was so spectacular that it could not be hidden.

Ben and Mark face a different prospect in that, if things must be seen to be believed, they would have to drag people into town during daylight and show them a hidden, sleeping vampire. The heroes are not assisted by such a spectacle as an incredibly large flying saucer and an accompanying forest fire—although fire does factor into their plans. Working alone, the two of them eventually return to Maine after some months away and decide to set a wildfire that mimics one from Ben's youth. Their plan, as discussed at the end of the novel, is to burn the Lot to the ground and therefore remove many of the vampires' hiding places. Then, as Ben proposes, it would be much easier for the two of them to track down and stake any survivors.

Unlike the Tommyknockers, the vampires show no signs of decaying or dying out on their own. They are not necessarily any more intelligent than the Tommyknockers—who, after all, fixated so completely on batteries that they forgot they could buy a converter and use power from wall outlets[7]—but they manage to find food and shelter all the same. Ben's newspaper articles show that something strange is indeed going on in the town, but that most people dismiss it as a wild dog pack or individual cases of delusion. The wider world remains unconvinced of what is happening within the town, and thus the threat is allowed to remain.

Vampires also feed on people, turning them into vampires as well who must then find more victims. With the Tommyknocker ship gone, it seems highly unlikely that any more of them would be made, but, given a single surviving vampire, no one will be safe. Therefore, Ben convinces Mark that they have to return and finish the job. The short story "One for the Road," however, reveals that they were not successful. Those who live in the areas surrounding the Lot have begun carrying religious symbols with them, and, although they do not talk about it, they avoid going anywhere near the town after dark. Unlike the Tommyknockers, the vampires have survived and continue to prey on the unwary who cross their paths.

The main enemy in *Doctor Sleep* consists of a slightly different form of vampire. The True Knot, led by Rose the Hat, is a close-knit band of wandering inhumans who are not immortal but have very long lives all the same. They feed not on blood but on what they call "steam" and what King's Constant Reader would know as the shining. This does not make them any less destructive, however, since this steam is only released at death and can be purified and made all the more delicious through torture. Further, the True feed largely on children.

Unlike the vampires of the Lot, the True must travel to find their preferred victims. The vampires remain largely stationary, dining first on friends and neighbors and then on unwary through-travelers, but the True lives on the road in expensive Winnebagos and are willing to go great distances for their next meal. They are also on the lookout for anyone who has the sort of talents that might help the group—not the shining, which is their veal, but other abilities that could help such a long-lived group of people survive and thrive unnoticed. Like the vampires, the True were all once human beings, and an early incident shows that membership is indeed apparently an offer instead of a command, albeit a loaded one. Newest member Snakebite Andi agrees to join the True because her other option is to be stripped of her power and left alone. Rose also fails to fully inform Andi of what her choice means for her future, forcing her to take steam without explaining how it was acquired. However, once Andi becomes a member, her fate is bound up with that of the others. They must stick together to find their next victim and continue their long, long lives.

As such, every member of the True Knot is guilty of murder, even those who seem to be small children themselves. They live not only off the death of human children, but also off the torture that prolongs their deaths. The True are presented as "automatic monsters who deserve to die for what they practice and believe."[8] The narrative cannot end, and order cannot be restored, until Rose is dead and any surviving members have scattered. This is a personal mission for the main characters, since Rose has set her sights on young Abra as her next source of sustenance, and Abra has a close relationship with the now-adult Dan Torrance. These two each shine and therefore have a deeper personal connection to the chosen victims of the True. Although their heroic group expands beyond one adult and one teenager, they face the same difficulty as Ben and Mark: no one will ever believe them.

Dan and Abra do not need to destroy every last member of the True during their final showdown. Unlike the vampires, one single person is not capable of finding prey all on their own. The True have survived this long only by working together and relying on each other's strengths to compensate for their weaknesses. A vampire could presumably grab any human being and feed, but the source of the True's power, energy, and youth is rare and getting rarer. This is why Rose fixated so much on Abra in the first place, because the girl might have been able to offer an almost never-ending source of steam. Whether or not Abra would have ever agreed to it or submitted to it without heavy drugs is not a concern for Rose, which is another indication that she is truly monstrous and both she and her worldview must be destroyed.

Although it seems that Rose's following is the only such group left in the country, there is no mention of whether there might be others throughout the world. Members need to be brought in by those who already know the secrets of taking steam. Without the True's supply of steam, no new members can be inducted, and the current members would age and die. By removing the source of their power, the way Gard removed the Tommyknocker ship, it might be possible to simply wait out the unnatural ends of these once-human creatures. Dan and especially Abra, with their Torrance family anger issues, are not content with anything but the direct, confirmable destruction of the True, especially Rose. Unlike Ben and Mark, they need to stick around and ensure that the job is done. Even though the True were really only a threat to such a small amount of the population, they were monsters who could not be allowed to live if order were to be restored.

DESTROYING AN INSTITUTION

A slightly different example in which a large number of people have to die in order for things to be set right again happens at the end of *The Institute*. This situation has a key difference from the previous examples in that the enemy is made up of people who are purely human, without any special abilities, and many of the characters on the side of "good" are naturally telepathic or telekinetic. Although a number of children do die in the final confrontation, the main goal is the death of the Institute itself.

Much like the True Knot, the Institute seeks out and kidnaps children with special abilities. In this novel, they specifically look for children who are telepathic or telekinetic, tracking them since birth and determining the proper time to kidnap them and murder their families. None of the adults at the Institute have any sixth sense, but all of them willingly participate in this brutal process that ends with the children's dehumanization and deaths. Unlike many of King's novels in which the supernatural is itself the enemy and the humans must triumph, success and restoration in the *Institute* means destroying the organizational structure, freeing as many talented children as possible, and protecting future children from kidnapping and death.

The children at the Institute are operating largely under the same circumstances as Gard when he faces the Tommyknockers: they can witness what is happening around them and to them, but they do not have any larger narrative with which to explain what they see. Readers are given more scenes and therefore more explanation in both *'Salem's Lot* and *Doctor Sleep* so that they understand before the main characters do why the vampires and the True Knot are killing people. Both groups are set up as needing to enact their violence for their own survival, and readers fear that the main characters will not fully understand this threat in time to save themselves. With *The Tommyknockers* and *The Institute*, however, the true end goal of the antagonists is kept hidden.

Gard dies without any such explanation, perhaps because there is none, but at least some of the children who survive that night at the Institute are granted a backstory of sorts months after the event. The man who shows up to confront them—and who really seems to wish to speak only to the adult who is taking care of them—is identifiable to readers as the one to whom director Mrs. Sigsby once reported. They understand that, while Mrs. Sigsby oversaw that specific installation, this man was in charge of her, making him dangerous for any of the survivors. He must work to convince the others that he knows what he is talking about, and that he speaks the truth. While the survivors, especially child genius Luke Ellis, believe part of what he is saying, they do not fully buy his entire explanation and his attempt to make the children feel guilty for saving their own lives.

Although it is unclear why any alien race like the Tommyknockers would send out a ship to mutate living creatures on another planet, the lisping man explains that the children at the Institute are used to kill very specific people because normal methods of assassination are deemed inappropriate. Apparently there exists another, much nicer, Institute on neutral ground, filled not with telekinetic or telepathic children but with adults capable of precognition. They, much like Johnny Smith of *The Dead Zone*, identify future threats to global peace so that those people can be eliminated and nuclear war can be avoided. This man argues that the Institute, while killing children, in fact worked to save the world.

Although he has not come to kill the survivors, this man hopes to inflict them with such guilt that their lives will be miserable from this point on. He wants to blame the children for acting to save themselves and their friends in the face of a situation they did not entirely understand, although this lack of comprehension was really the fault of the adults who refused to enlighten them. He wishes to guilt the children for not simply lying down and allowing themselves to be sacrifice to the greater good—in this case world peace rather than the continued existence of vampires or the True Knot, but the general concept is still the same. There is something bigger and greater out there than a mere human life, and so these mortals should simply accept their fates.

Part of what the lisping man tells them in an attempt to add to their guilt is in fact encouraging to the children: that uprisings have happened at other Institutes around the world following the one that Luke and his friends instigated. What the children did that night did not simply end there, in Maine, and shut down only one of the many Institutes. The children, linked up to so many like them in other countries, inspired them to seek their own freedom and began a domino effect, the way Gard removing the alien spaceship and Dan and Abra's relentless pursuit of Rose meant that the others could not survive. Here the antagonist took the form of a group that needed to be dispersed if not destroyed completely.

STOPPING MADNESS BEFORE IT SPREADS FURTHER

Not every antagonist within King takes the form of a group. When the antagonist is an individual who has come into the lives of the protagonists and caused a disruption, their deaths are more likely bought and paid for on a personal level. These are characters who will not be swayed by the law or morality, and the only way to stop them is through their deaths.

In *Insomnia*, although the larger threat is not human and is only dictating the actions of a human being, the danger is personified in the character of Ed Deepneau. Ed's mental state is first questioned in the book's prologue. Although Ed is not present for much of the narrative, his deterioration is steadily tracked through secondhand conversations and news reports. The main threat of the book intertwines with threats against Ed's abused wife and baby daughter before Ed himself emerges as the singular issue in the form of a kamikaze pilot intent on flying a small plane, rigged with a bomb, into a packed Civic Center.

Ed's madness is not something that naturally developed. Although he may have been unstable prior to the events of the book, it is his interactions with a character from another level of existence that push him over the edge. The book's heroes have their own interactions in the short term and begin to feel some strange effects, supporting the idea that Ed's exposure must have been more prolonged and damaging. The beings interacting with the main characters want to protect them, but the one interacting with Ed just needed him long enough to use him and dispose of him. Ed, like the Tommyknockers, seems beyond all hope of rehabilitation.

George Stark in *The Dark Half* was not a normal man who has been driven crazy by his interactions with other beings. In fact, just what he *is* is never entirely clarified. He originated as the pen name of human author Thaddeus Beaumont and somehow gained a physical body. Stark's purpose entails saving his own life, such as it is, although his process involves murder. He must convince Thad to give up his own life in order to keep on living—and, as Thad suspects, keep on murdering even after his original purpose has been fulfilled.

Although most of the murders Stark commits are clearly directed toward intimidating Thad to give in, there is still proof that he is "purely concentrated evil"[9] and cannot be trusted. Stark's very first murder was entirely unnecessary. There is absolutely no indication that he will stop killing just because Thad gives him his life. Healing Stark, and making him a permanent fixture in reality, would simply lead to more murders.

The difficulty here is that Stark is not, in fact, a man. There is no handy label to affix to him, such as "vampire," with its accompanying weaknesses. From readers' first encounter with Stark, they realize that Stark might be superhuman. It is possible that he was only able to commit so many murders because no one expected to see him—after all, a pseudonym coming to life is very difficult to believe—but his utter lack of compassion for people, who are Other to him, functions very nearly as a supernatural ability as far as murder is concerned. Perhaps if Stark were to complete his task and become fully human, at the expense of Thad's life, he might have to worry more about damage to his physical form, but the same cold, calculating mind would remain. Stark would still be a dangerous murderer, now given all the time in the world to do as he pleased.

Stark, unlike Ed Deepneau, is not as incomprehensible in his madness. He has his goals, and he methodically goes about achieving them: eliminating the people who tried to "kill" him and terrorizing Thad into giving him a fuller, more complete life. Stark also knows that, if he does not do these things, he will die anyway. It is unclear what Ed saw as the consequences for *not* attempting to suicide bomb the Civic Center, but whatever Atropos did to him, it convinced him that this was the right way to behave. Stark's motives and actions, compared to Ed's, are coldly logical. With Ed, though, it takes more than a subtraction of empathy to fully understand his aims and his methods.

The same is true with the character who gives his name as "Zak McCool" in *Lisey's Story*. Zak is another of King's "number one fans" whose obsession with an author, combined with mental instability, leads to life-threatening situations. In this case, unlike in *Misery*, it is not the author himself who is in danger. Scott Landon is already dead when the novel begins, and the main character in the position of being threatened is his widow Lisey. Fans and scholars of Scott's work have been impatient with the speed at which she is willing to release her husband's materials, and Zak McCool believes that one of these scholars has given him orders to pressure the widow in more serious, less legal, ways. Despite this interference, Lisey does not "resent or struggle against the fact that her life . . . has remained subordinate to her husband's success and fame,"[10] even when this puts her at risk.

Although Zak McCool is a clear and present threat to Lisey's life, he is almost a background concern for much of the novel. Lisey is more caught up in her memories of Scott and his struggle with either insanity or his strange gift of actually being able to enter a different world, alongside her older sister's current catatonic episode. Since she is being pulled in so many directions emotionally, Zak McCool seems to be more of an annoyance and an interruption than an actual threat that needs to be faced. What Lisey learns from her memories of Scott and her attempt to save her sister helps her to, in the end, eliminate Zak McCool without then having to face legal consequences for it. Lisey, like Rosie in *Rose Madder*, takes advantage of the dangers of another world to lure her prey in and then let someone—or something—else take care of him.

Zak McCool, like Ed Deepneau and George Stark, is fixated on his goal, however strange that goal may seem to the rest of us. He refuses to let anything get in his way or to hear it when the man he thought hired him for this job tries to call it off. Although Zak only threatens one person, it becomes clear throughout the narrative that he will not stop his attempts on her life until she either surrenders her husband's papers—something Lisey, the guardian of Scott's memory and works, does not want to do—or is killed. He cannot be reasoned with, and so he must be stopped.

The same can be seen in *End of Watch*, the final book in the Bill Hodges trilogy. The character of Brady Hartsfield, the multiple murder introduced in *Mr. Mercedes*, has become far more dangerous since this first encounter. Initially a purely normal human being with no superpowers other than his ability to blend in to the background, Brady has since developed a number of abilities that turn him into "a kind of lethally deranged Professor Charles Xavier."[11] No longer confined to his injured, comatose body, Brady discovers that he can jump into other people's heads in order to drive them for his own devices or to convince them to complete suicide. Brady, like Zak McCool and George Stark before him, also fixates on the characters he specifically wishes to destroy: in this case, Detective Bill Hodges and his two companions, who were responsible for stopping Brady's homicidal triumph in the first book.

Here readers are given a longer explanation of why Brady might form this obsession and why his thought processes might not be the ones we would expect of healthy, sane people. Already in the first book, Brady is shown to be a murderer and is given the proper backstory: a dead father, a brother who died at Brady's hands, and a mother who treats her son like a lover. Brady is already a loner, a computer geek who is not respected at his job, and he still lives at home. He is set up to be the perfect sort of mundane serial killer who is merely a face in the crowd and able to continue to murder because of how ordinary he seems.

After being hit in the head at the end of the first book, Brady becomes a very minor character in the second installment of the trilogy, although things are still happening behind the scenes. While Hodges and his two assistants are distracted by a different case, Brady has been given experimental drugs, and these, combined with his injury, help him gain both telepathic and telekinetic powers. Largely stuck inside his own comatose body, Brady has a long time to stew and to meditate on his downfall. All of this helps readers fully understand that, if Brady were allowed to live past the end of the book, he would continue to use his newfound skills in order to induce more suicides and, possibly, to attempt immortality.

Part of the danger of Brady is that he has learned how to take over other people's bodies and so he is no longer confined to a single physical vessel. This puts him more on the level of George Stark than either Ed Deepneau or Zak McCool, who are both still entirely human. When Ed and Zak are, respectively, in a plane crash or eaten by an otherworldly monster, they die along with their bodies. George Stark is carried away by sparrows, not leaving a corpse behind but still moving past the ability to harm any of the others. Brady, weakened during his final confrontation with Hodges and his friends, is unable to leave the badly injured body he is currently occupying and, in the end, chooses suicide rather than waiting for death.

All these characters are set up so that their deaths will in fact be comforting. Readers understand that rehabilitation is not an option. Even when these characters' stories are told from their own point of view, the purpose is not to induce empathy in the reader, but to explain how and why they are monstrous. Readers might consider that his life has not set him up to be a winner, but this does not negate the fact that he has chosen to become a murderer. Any possible empathy is quickly cut off by the cold calculations in Brady's mind, the same way readers are allowed to see into George Stark's thoughts for a personal look at how alien he is.

However, because the genre is horror and even the Bill Hodges trilogy is not made of pure crime novels, death is not always final and the danger is not necessarily contained. Ed Deepneau is dead, yes, but Atropos is still out there and the quest for the Dark Tower goes on. Zak McCool is likewise killed, but the very place Lisey has used to do this becomes a threat of its own, playing not only with her mind but with her physical self. Brady Hartsfield is dead, along with the surgeon who administered the strange drugs that may have played with his damaged brain, but his very existence introduces the idea that the world is not as it seems. George Stark is carried away by the sparrows, but he, like Brady, argues that the supernatural does exist. Readers suspect that Stark is dead but cannot be entirely certain. And, after these strange encounters, the other characters must return to their lives and move on. At least they can do so secure in the knowledge that the dead were in fact evil.

These encounters with madness and characters intent on causing death are not limited to King's novels. Two of his novellas, "Secret Window, Secret Garden," and "Apt Pupil" also deal with central characters whose sanity has broken and who need to be killed in order to be stopped. Mort Rainey, the protagonist of "Secret Window, Secret Garden," imagines a separate personality who hounds him over the plagiarism of one of his short stories, intimidating him by killing his cat and setting his house on fire before moving on to murdering anyone who has become involved. Whether the men were meant to have seen this other person or Mort enlisted them to help him scare the mysterious other man, they end up dead at a surprising rate. At the end of the novella, when Mort and the other personality have fused, he attempts to kill his ex-wife—a task he never could have managed solely as Mort—and ends up being killed himself before he can complete her murder.

Todd Bowden, the title character of "Apt Pupil," likewise slowly unravels throughout his narrative. The warning signs are there for Todd from the beginning since he tracks down a former Nazi officer living in his hometown and blackmails that man into telling him all about the Holocaust. The teenager's obsession builds over the course of years, interfering with his schoolwork and his home life and leading Todd to begin murdering homeless men around town to ease the pressure. In the end he, too, is killed, although unlike Mort, Todd is presumably able to take down victims before his own death, sitting above a highway and shooting at cars below.

Within these shorter pieces, King delves more deeply into the minds of his troubled characters. While George Stark and Brady Hartsfield are both point-of-view characters within their own novels, they are not the protagonists, and they are given only minor segments to narrate. Ed Deepneau and Zak McCool do not command the point of view at all. Mort Rainy, on the other hand, monopolizes his own story until his death. Todd shares narrative duty with the Nazi officer so that, while both voices are protagonists, neither is the clear moral superior.

The benefit of these glimpses into the troubled characters' heads comes in that readers know for certain that these characters are beyond help. They cannot be restored and will continue to be threats to others, so their elimination is necessary. In the case of Mort Rainy, an epilogue with further explanation is also necessary since, from Mort's point of view, the danger is another man and a completely separate character. It is only through others' eyes, especially those of his ex-wife, that Mort's madness is fully revealed. Todd Bowden's obsession with the Holocaust is easily recognizable as problematic, and his actions are clearly attributed to him throughout the book, making his dangerous aspects clearer. Mort and Todd, like the others, must be killed in order to prevent them from killing more innocent people.

PAINFUL AND UNFAIR RESTORATION

Restoration in King does not always come so clear-cut as "the evil is dead and most of the good still live." Although narratives in which the supernatural interferes with "normal" life generally conclude with the elimination of the supernatural, the supernatural itself is not always evil. There are some books in which the deaths, although restorative, make readers uneasy and force them to question more than to relax.

One such instance is in *The Regulators*, where young Seth Garin, an autistic child, becomes the vessel for an otherworldly entity, Tak. The exact interplay between Tak and Seth is never completely revealed. Heidi Strengell argues that the book "introduces the human being as God, stating that a human in the position of God only wreaks havoc,"[12] but it is difficult to parse out which actions are truly from Seth and which are of Tak. By making Seth young, autistic, and nonverbal, King isolates this character from all others and withholds this information from readers. When Tak starts killing Seth's neighbors, only Seth's Aunt Audrey has enough information to even begin to separate Seth from Tak.

The characters have to "keep crucial knowledge hidden away from those who would use such information against those who seek to survive,"[13] which means secret-keeping is a focal part of the story. Tak wishes to keep its presence from the rest of the street, so only Audrey is even slightly prepared for the attacks that come. Seth, on the other hand, wants to keep certain information from Tak, specifically the strange ability he has to send his aunt to a safe place. All the other characters know is that something strange is happening, and that Audrey has finally emerged from her house and somehow puts the blame on her nephew. The others, especially those driven mad by grief from their own recent losses, believe that destroying Seth will be the key to ending the massacre, and both Seth and Audrey are shot and killed before that resolution comes.

Kimberly Beal argues that *The Regulators* "has a positive, uplifting ending"[14] because the book's epilogue reveals that both Seth and Aunt Audrey still somehow exist. Seth had been giving his aunt a safe place to go this entire time, and it seems he has managed to transport both of their spirits there. Without their bodies, but with each other, Seth and Audrey wander the site of one of Audrey's happiest memories, apparently now in the past but otherwise unharmed. Although their physical bodies were killed, Seth has still somehow been able to save the two of them. The other citizens of Poplar Street, however, have no idea that Seth had been helping Audrey in this way, or that the two of them continue to exist somewhere. They only believe that Cammie, driven mad by all the events of that afternoon, wanted to shoot Seth, and that Seth helped her kill Audrey. They also have no idea what truly caused the events of the day, and therefore cannot be reasonably certain that they will never be repeated.

Because the readers have this extra information that has been denied to the other characters, Seth's death, while not necessarily a welcome event, does not need to be a sad one. In this other place, Seth has proven verbal, able to communicate with his aunt the way any child his own age would. And although it seems he cannot bring back any of their dead family members, he can make sure to protect Audrey and keep her in her happy place. It still seems highly unfair that such a young child and his truly caring aunt would have to die, but readers can find an uplifting ending because of this background information.

John Coffey of *The Green Mile* is in a different situation. Coffey "is neither provided with a background, nor does the reader learn about his whereabouts during his adult life,"[15] and so he "embodies the mystery at the center of the novel."[16] All the narrator, Paul Edgecombe, knows is that Coffey has been sentenced to be executed and brought to death row. Coffey himself is not a resource for his past, since, although he is an adult, he is very childlike and seems to find it difficult to piece memories together. His inability to communicate complicated ideas is what led to his conviction in the first place, since he was found holding two dead girls bemoaning the fact that he "tried to take it back, but it was too late."[17] Coffey meant that he was unable to perform a miracle to save the girls, but his words were instead interpreted as a confession to murder.

Despite not being able to see inside his head, readers feel empathy for Coffey because that is what Paul himself comes to feel. As the narrative unfolds and the facets of both his personality and his abilities are revealed, Paul becomes convinced that Coffey would never have murdered anyone. In fact, Paul only sees Coffey use his powers for good: to cure Paul's urinary tract infection, to heal a fellow inmate's beloved pet mouse, to heal the warden's wife, and to dispatch both the most sadistic guard on the Green Mile and the prisoner who was in fact guilty of the girls' murders. Paul and some of his fellow guards come to believe not only in Coffey's innocence, but in his essential goodness.

Coffey is a strange figure in King's lore, since "virtually all of King's characters with inherited supernatural powers turn out to be children."[18] He has managed to grow into adulthood despite his emphasized limited intelligence and the fact that it is so easy for the white majority to believe that such a large Black man would indeed murder children. Physically Coffey is imposing, although he is still very childlike both mentally and emotionally. Killing Coffey is worse than killing Seth Garin, because Coffey has done absolutely nothing wrong and has also been able to fight back against the wrong that was done against him. Killing Coffey is like killing Christ, and the readers, like Paul Edgecombe, would rather speak out against his execution.

However, like Seth, Coffey asks for death. He can examine his own life and search his feelings with enough introspection in order to conclude that he does not want to continue living this way. The world has not been kind to him, and Coffey has been hurt by the ugliness people show to each other. He in fact asks Paul not to speak up in his defense, and to let him die. Even though this is an adult making a decision about his own life, it is a difficult ending because the supernatural that is being eliminated from the world was, for once, on the side of good. However, John Coffey was not the first JC to be executed because of his healing abilities, and his fate as a man with supernatural powers but a lack of cunning or guile was sealed from the start.

Another of King's characters who indeed had the power to "take it back" was forced, in the end, to allow a number of murders to happen. Although *11/22/63* largely centers on the assassination of John F. Kennedy and the main character's attempt to prevent it, JFK's is not the only death that occurs within the novel.

For Jake, JFK was impersonal, unlike the Dunning family of Derry, Maine. Jake was able to stop the family patriarch from attacking his wife and children on Halloween 1958, completely changing the life of the only surviving family member, who was a friend of Jake's. The family massacre is a major emotional linchpin for Jake, since he is shown to cry—something he rarely does—when reading his friend's essay about that night. When Jake is told he has to undo all of his time traveling changes, it is not Kennedy who makes him pause, but Mrs. Dunning and her children. When a stranger arrives and tells Jake he has to once again "reset" the past to what he has always known, he needs time to consider all of the lives that hang in the balance.

Here, Jake's final act is a very clear move toward restoration because the whole purpose is to undo all of his interference. King's Constant Readers once again have the advantage over his characters in that they will likely be aware of the Dark Tower, the Beams, and the idea of the Purpose. The man who orders Jake to reset everything serves the Tower, although he does not explain this to Jake in so many words. Only fans of King's larger body of work, especially those who have read the Dark Tower series, would be inclined to believe this strange man on short notice, because they possess a wealth of background knowledge that Jake does not. The man's hurried explanation, combined with Jake's personal desire to get out of that man's company and to remain as ignorant as possible, means that Jake is not working with all available information. For Jake, it is not a question of the Tower and all levels of existence, but of the lives he has personally seen and therefore influenced.

Readers, then, may be comforted because they know for certain that Jake has made the right decision when he returns the course of history to what it has always been. There is no consolation for the Dunnings, who are consigned to their grisly fates, although Jake does finally give in to his curiosity to learn that his fiancée survived the attack on her own life. He can find her in the present and share one last dance, a scene meant to console both Jake and the readers because the right ending, in this case, was not the fairy-tale version. The cost of restoring order to the world was high.

A CLEAR CUTOFF

At other times the solution to an ongoing threat, real or supernatural, is to kill the living being making the threat. The hope is that death of the living body will lead to death of the threat, although this is not always possible. In the short story "Bad Little Kid," a death-row prisoner explains that he shot and killed a boy because that boy had been haunting him his entire life and was a harbinger—or even simply a bringer—of death. Shortly before his execution, the prisoner told his court-appointed lawyer the whole story. Directly after the execution, the lawyer discovered a note, presumably from that same bad little kid, suggesting first that death did not stop him and second that the curse has now been passed from the prisoner to his lawyer.

"I Am the Doorway," on the other hand, is framed as a written suicide note composed by its main character. There is no lawyer to provide a glimpse into what might happen after the execution. The protagonist here is a former astronaut apparently infested by an alien presence that manifests as gold eyes emerging from his skin. Although he burned his hands years ago to rid himself of the eyes there, he has awakened to find a ring of them on his chest. After he finishes writing his story, he intends to kill himself to stop the infestation from spreading. However, like the death-row prisoner, he has now shared his tale. In this case, it seems to be intended more as a warning for the people who find his body, but in King, sharing the narrative can spread the infection.

Not all of these examples are supernatural. Two of the novellas in *Full Dark, No Stars* deal with realistic serial threats in the form of human beings who can indeed be stopped by death. "Big Driver" tells the story of a rape and attempted homicide victim named Tess who hunts down and executes everyone involved in her experience. She has proof that she was not her attackers' first victim, and that others were indeed murdered. By killing all three family members involved in these attacks, she can prevent any future assaults and murders with relatively low risk.

In "A Good Marriage," a wife discovers that her husband of nearly thirty years is the BTK-inspired serial killer "Beadie." Once again, the female protagonist is in a position of realizing that someone has committed multiple crimes in the past and, if left unconfronted, will continue to do so in the future. While Tess had the advantage in that her attackers thought she was dead, and therefore acted quickly with the element of surprise, Darcy is forced to confront her husband when he realizes she finally knows. The two are then pushed into a stalemate: Bob agrees not to kill any more women, and Darcy realizes she cannot turn her husband in to the police without ruining their children's lives. She has a long, tense period of being forced to pretend that everything is fine before she can kill Bob in a way that looks like an accident. While Tess's future is left to the reader's imagination, Darcy is eventually confronted by a retired detective who had suspected Beadie's real identity. The narrative closes with Darcy and the reader feeling reassured that neither Bob's crimes nor Darcy's own murder of her husband will become public knowledge.

This ending allows the detective to voice what many readers might be thinking: that although Darcy did indeed kill her husband in cold blood, her actions were justified, much in the way that Tess's were. The prisoner in "Bad Little Kid" wants to finally explain his own justification to his lawyer, who passes it off as madness until he receives apparent proof of the bad little kid's existence. Without the backstory, it seems that the prisoner simply shot a child multiple times, an act that can be neither comprehended nor condoned. At least the main character of "I Am the Doorway" ends with violence only against himself.

Both Darcy and the former astronaut tried other tactics before choosing death, Darcy extracting a promise from her husband even though she barely trusted it, and Arthur sacrificing his hands to stop the spread of the alien eyes. Neither reaction proved certain enough, and each was, in her and his own time, pushed to commit murder or complete suicide. The prisoner in "Bad Little Kid" had encountered the strange boy multiple times over the years and eventually concluded that the only way to stop him would indeed be to kill him, if the mysterious eternally young boy could actually be killed. Tess is the one who opted for death in the shortest time span, although regaining consciousness in a culvert next to corpses certainly emphasized how dire her situation was.

Each of these characters recognized a threat not only to themselves, but to other people, and concluded that this threat needed to be eliminated. The world was not safe as long as these beings, be they human, alien, supernatural, or some sort of hybrid, existed. The only way to restore that feeling of safety was to eliminate the threat completely, through murder or suicide, as the protagonists accepted responsibility for acts that other people might never understand nor forgive.

A RETURN TO WHAT ONCE WAS

When confronted with an injustice or an interruption of what the characters consider to be the real world or their normal lives, their reaction is a desire to undo it and make things "right." The evil should be isolated and destroyed, so that it cannot take root again here or elsewhere, and the comfortable, everyday habits and patterns can once again be undertaken. This is not a chance or desire to improve the original state of things, mind, but simply to return to it because it is well-known and understood. Even in the case where a character wishes to improve something, he is foiled by the greater plans of the universe and protectors of the Dark Tower.

The goal is then, largely, for the world to make sense again. Something has interrupted order and expectations and cannot be allowed to stand. It is an affront to reality, not a miracle but an *offense*, as Stan Uris understood the creature It to be,[19] and thus the characters must do whatever necessary to reclaim their original worlds. They are looking for things to once again make sense in the way they apparently always have, and, at times, to prevent themselves from going mad with the memories. If things can be eliminated, then memories can be swept under the rug, and life as we know it does not need to be threatened by drastic change. Once order has been restored, as much as it can be in the wake of deaths and destruction, the characters can breathe once again.

At times the subversion of order is threatening not just to a small town in Maine but to the entire world. Should the Tommyknockers continue to grow and expand their area of influence, or should the vampires in the Lot continue unchecked, or should the True Knot once again grow to its former glory, then it seems as though America, if not the world, would be worse off. Growth of any one of these groups would, it seems, benefit only that group, to the detriment of humanity. Only the Institute offers a too-little, too-late explanation for its own existence that attempts to justify the deaths of children for the good of the world.

King's books are full of characters who "turn out to be monsters beneath their human exterior"[20] and who, because of their monstrosity, need to be stopped. Many of these are people who have succumbed to a form of madness: Ed Deepneau, Zak McCool, Brady Hartsfield, Morton Rainey, and Todd Bowden all begin their narratives as natural human beings and, through the influence of the supernatural or their own brain chemistry, morph into monsters. By the time they reach the end of their murderous paths, it is possible to overlook their humanity in favor of their monstrosity and accept that their deaths are necessary. Characters like George Stark, who are something inexplicably Other than human, are only more difficult because it must first be determined whether they *can* be killed, or how they might be neutralized if death is impossible.

The emotional pain and moral difficulty comes in cases where those who die are seen as innocents or even as forces of good. While Seth Garin provided the vessel for Tak to terrorize a suburban block, he is himself an autistic child and does not seem to deserve death, much less to take his caring aunt with him. John Coffey can perform miracles that draw comparisons to Jesus Christ, and yet he asks for death rather than to continue enduring the evil of the world. Aunt Audrey may not have asked for her fate, but it seems Seth did, for both of them, little comfort though it might be to readers. Only the Dunning family, murdered on Halloween night in 1958, had no say in the restoration of their fate, and readers, like *11/22/63*'s protagonist, struggle with balancing the murder of children against the fate of the Dark Tower. After all, "it is the chance to change Harry Dunning's life—rather than the more than utopian idea of saving JFK—that motivates Jake to travel back in time"[21] in the first place. Everything that happens only had the chance to occur because Jake wanted to save the Dunnings.

It makes more logical and emotional sense to readers when a death can be seen as the sole means of halting a series of wrongdoings. In many of these examples, "confusion and guilt translate into bravery"[22] as characters confront not just the serial evil, but their role in allowing it to continue. The death-row prisoner had to shoot the bad little kid to keep the kid from harming his loved ones; Arthur had to kill himself to prevent the alien eyes from overtaking his body and continuing to commit murder; Tess must rise up after her rape and attempted murder to stop the three responsible from killing any more women; and Darcy Anderson takes steps to prevent serial killer "Beadie" from committing further murders and taunting the police. Each of these involves a struggle not only with personal responsibility for what has already happened, but with what likely *will* happen if they do nothing. Once they have accepted the inevitability of the future, they can act in order to return the world to its previous level of safety.

It is generally comforting to both characters and readers when this restoration occurs. Although something strange and mysterious has indeed threatened reality, it can be destroyed, and the world can still keep spinning. People are hardier than the threat was strong, and the old, comforting ways can still endure despite these interferences. There may be wonders out there that have yet to be described, but, even if they were to be, that knowledge would quickly be hidden so we could continue on with our lives and our sanity intact.

There are only a very few instances in which King's characters have the knowledge of his readers: that, although it might be defeated for now, the evil can return. Sharon Russell points out that, in *The Dark Half*, King relies less on mystery or crime fiction generic expectations and instead reaches for supernatural conventions[23] when he has his own characters wonder if, perhaps, this could happen again. The resolution expected in other genres, including horror, is not a necessary part of the supernatural. Although King frequently concludes his books with the idea that, even if the horror is not entirely over, it is at least over for now, in this place, he is willing to end some of his narratives with the idea that even this might not be true.

But the vast extent of King's books follows these generic expectations, giving readers at least one surviving protagonist and the suggestion of a way to defeat the horror and therefore a return to normal life. The escape itself is horrific, considering the deaths and sacrifices necessary to enact it, but it can also be completed. Even if the horror does crop up again in the future, readers are aware that it can in fact be defeated. Restoration, however, does not come without a price. Even the King narratives with relatively happy endings include deaths as the protagonists confront the interloper, and not all of those occur on the side of evil. No matter what the threat or the main characters' response to it, readers can be sure that the level of danger will include loss of life.

NOTES

1. Newhouse, "A Blind Date with Disaster," 274.
2. Russell, *Revisiting Stephen King*, 66.
3. Mary Findley "The World at Large, America in Particular: Cultural Fears and Societal Mayhem in King's Fiction since 1995," *Stephen King's Modern Macabre: Essays on the Later Works* (Jefferson, NC: McFarland & Company, Inc., 2014), 51.
4. Magistrale, *Stephen King: The Second Decade*, 83.
5. Strengell, *Dissecting Stephen King*, 184.
6. Magistrale, *Stephen King: America's Storyteller*, 69.
7. Stephen King, *The Tommyknockers* (New York: Signet, 1987), 642.
8. McAleer, "Untangling the True Knot," 232.
9. Davis, *Stephen King's America*, 41.
10. Magistrale, *Stephen King: America's Storyteller*, 89.
11. Simpson, "From Meat World to Cyberspace," 121.
12. Strengell *Dissecting Stephen King*, 234.
13. McAleer, "The Fallen King(dom)," 179.
14. Kimberly Beal, "Bachman's 'Found' Novels: *The Regulators*, *Blaze*, and Author Identity," *Stephen King's Contemporary Classics: Reflections on the Modern Master of Horror* (Lanham, MD: Rowman & Littlefield, 2015), 166.
15. Strengell, *Dissecting Stephen King*, 213.
16. Russell, *Revisiting Stephen King: A Critical Companion*, 68.
17. Stephen King, *The Green Mile* (New York: Pocket Books, 1996), 20.
18. Strengell, *Dissecting Stephen King*, 208.
19. King, *It*, 412.
20. Strengell, *Dissecting Stephen King*, 210.
21. Stefan L. Brandt, "Time *Ravel*: History, Metafiction, and Immersion in Stephen King's *11/22/63*," *The Modern Stephen King Canon: Beyond Horror* (Lanham, MD: Lexington Books, 2019), 189.
22. Magistrale, "The Rehabilitation of Stephen King," 14.
23. Russell, *Stephen King: A Critical Companion*, 95–96.

Conclusion

"It Seemed to Mean Something"
Confronting Death and Multifaceted Horror

Death is a constant in King's works, but as a subject, it is a complicated one. There is no one single function of death within his narratives, although deaths occur frequently. Readers can expect and anticipate death simply because they are consuming a work by King, although their expectations are not always fulfilled. The good can die along with the bad, the young along with the old, and the intelligent alongside the stubborn. In real life, "[t]hat instant of death is the only true universal rite of passage,"[1] and in fiction King engages with this universal horror by approaching it from multiple angles and examining it with, as he has argued, the curiosity of a child instead of the disgust that has grown up with the societal taboo surrounding death.

Americans have a complicated relationship with death and with questions of what, if anything, comes after. In King's works, death is still largely the end, with few instances of characters being told that something, anything, awaits them afterward. *Duma Key*'s ship of the dead and *Revival*'s Mother are two examples of characters who have peered into life after death, and neither is entirely encouraging. As bad is this life may be, something worse awaits them, death is still horrific, and "[k]nowing the truth, it turns out, is . . . much worse than not knowing."[2]

In King's novels, like in real life, death can occur at any time and affect anyone. There is no guarantee of safety, and the characters who act selfishly to attempt to protect their own lives above the lives of others will likely die themselves before the book is through. Readers can at least be comforted by the fact that they are engaging with a novel instead of experiencing the deaths in real life, and that the format of the narrative can allow for meaning and sense to be made of the deaths. Although not all unnatural death within the narrative has a specific purpose, many of them do in King's books, providing an explanation for why a character must die and possible comfort surrounding the horror.

In books, unlike in real life, the narrative intention can be made clear and closure explicitly possible, although readers still must slog through pages and pages of death in order to reach it. And, of course, part of the horror is that closure might not in fact be possible, after all.

THE LABEL OF HORROR

Readers who flock to King because he is a known name, or who pick up his books because they are categorized within the genre of horror, come with their own expectations. We categorize narratives based on their function. Is it a story meant to make us laugh, cry, or feel love or fear? Do we expect the book we pick up to leave us dangling with narrative threads unresolved or to feel some sort of catharsis in a conclusion that returns the world to normal? Do we expect to be able to put down and pick up the book at our leisure, or to be forced to turn the pages as fast as we can, breathlessly awaiting the narrative outcome?

As a horror writer, King finds himself working within, and sometimes against, horror expectations. Especially since King has become a household name, and since his name has been written in bigger type than the book's title, Constant Readers have been able to narrow their expectations not just based on the genre, but on the author himself. There are certain elements that make a Stephen King book a Stephen King book, and although the author continues to play with those aspects, including self-reference and even self-insertion, the basic expectations still hold. While a Stephen King book might be an easy read, with no necessary deeper philosophical meanings or convoluted vocabulary, it will also likely be an intense read. Even when mocking the trope, such as in *The Colorado Kid*, when no satisfying concluding explanation is possible, King plays fully with the idea of keeping his readers on tenterhooks.

Death and Suspense

There are three main points within King's plots where deaths occur: the introduction of conflict, during the rising action, and during the climax. Rarely do deaths occur during the exposition and resolution, the two points in the plot in which "normal" life can be observed. Generally, the protagonists like that normal life, and the main characters spend their narratives attempting to restore it. The deaths that occur on this journey can themselves be important plot points, giving readers, if not characters, clues to guess at what might happen next.

Deaths that occur earlier in the plot, perhaps even before the narrative begins, are frequently revealed to the readers before the characters pick up on their importance. When readers have knowledge that characters do not, including the suspicion that some small throwaway comments will be important later, this sets up the necessary conditions for suspense. Readers have more knowledge than the main characters and can worry that the characters will not come to the right conclusions in time to save their own lives.

These early or pre-narrative deaths set up readers' expectations for further deaths within the novel. Depending on the situation surrounding these early deaths, readers might anticipate more of the same sorts of deaths to occur throughout the plot, as in the threat of a serial killer, or the deaths might help establish the power of the book's antagonist. The knowledge that a death is a part of a series or that the threat still exists heightens the suspense, especially when readers are able to witness some of these gruesome acts in ways that the main characters cannot. The narrative allows readers to follow, for example, Pennywise, Christine, or Cujo in their confrontations with other characters. Even though Cujo is a dog, King allows us to "read his thoughts"[3] and gain a dog's perspective on events. The dead characters are unable to warn anyone else of the threat, and the living characters do not have all the tools provided to readers.

Even within these series of deaths, frequently one of them stands out enough to mark the beginning of the narrative, even if the narrative does not in fact begin with the very first death. Serial-murdering characters such as It, the True Knot, the Outsider, and human figures like Frank Dodd and Bob Anderson are not followed from their very first murder. The story is picked up in the middle, with the death that means the most to the central characters in the book. Even in these cases of serial murder, not every death is discussed or covered. King picks and chooses to carefully control the release of information to the reader, while at the same time differentiating the information available to the main characters. Especially in his texts that more closely follow the police procedural, a death is necessary early on to establish both the genre and the stakes.

It would be an oversimplification to say that the impending death of any character is enough to create this tension and suspense. Readers do not always fear the deaths of King's characters. When they are antagonists, readers find themselves cheering for those characters' deaths, and hoping that they come quickly and with minimal consequences. When secondary characters die, especially if those characters have not been painted as "good" people, the impact of their deaths is not as strong. Gary Pervier and Joe Camber fall victim to Cujo early on, and although their own deaths are perhaps no great loss, the bloody scenes establish the tension around the fate of young, and clearly innocent, Tad Trenton. Similarly, Christine's first victims are largely those who have bullied her new owner Arnie or who have trashed her for no apparent reason. Even the bullies themselves understand why they are being pursued and therefore the reason for their deaths. When Arnie's best friend and girlfriend also find themselves the target of her wrath, however, readers no longer wish to see how Christine outwits her prey, but how Dennis and Leigh might triumph.

These deaths of secondary or "bad" characters work to heighten the tension because they narrow the focus of the antagonist toward the protagonist group. Having dispatched the secondary characters with less emotional impact, the antagonist, now proven to indeed be a deadly threat, can turn toward the protagonist. Readers who have witnessed these murders in action can more clearly imagine what might happen to their own favorites, should the protagonist underestimate the enemy. Readers have been privy to the protagonist's private conversations and explanations for the supernatural or human evil they are about to face, and readers can therefore also measure the gap between the protagonist's expectations and the antagonist's reality.

As well as narrowing the focus by eliminating other characters as possible victims, these secondary characters' deaths can also then heighten the tension by imposing a more immediate time line. The death of trooper Duane Kushner in *Misery* alerts both Paul and his captor Annie that their time together is now short. Although Paul had previously been aware that Annie was capable of murder, as well as "suck[ing] out Paul's inspiration and creativity in order to fashion a self-enclosed world,"[4] the quick and brutal death of the young officer in front of Paul's eyes, and then blamed on Paul himself, brings her ruthlessness fully onstage. Annie's other murders were only uncovered through a scrapbook, clearly in the past and having occurred to characters who were dead before the narrative began, but this is the first time that readers and Paul have witnessed her actively murder someone. Although Annie can work quickly to cover up the murder as well as she can, Kushner's absence will be noticed and investigated, and the outside world will intrude. If the resulting search is thorough, Paul himself will be discovered and the narrative brought to a premature end by his own murder.

King also carefully controls the knowledge of past deaths through instances such as Paul's discovery of the scrapbook or the way in which he intercuts scenes in *Dreamcatcher* between the past and the present to stop his characters from revealing crucial details just yet. Savvy Constant Readers can pick up on the fact that information is being withheld for plot purposes and can speculate on what that information might be. The assumption is that, if King prevents one of his characters from saying something, it must be important and have a bearing on the climax of the novel. This is information that the characters themselves might not possess, because, even though their trains of thought are interrupted, they are not aware that this interruption is part of a narrative structure.

Further, King's use of revealing and concealing information can allow the same death to occur at multiple points within a narrative. In *Bag of Bones*, Sara Tidwell is known to be dead before the narrative begins simply because the time period in which she lived was long enough in the past that she would have died of old age by now if nothing else had happened. Although main character Mike Noonan owns a summer place named after Sara, and although the history of Dark Score Lake includes the presence of Sara and her bandmates, her actual existence did not factor into his life until her spirit presented itself in a more direct form of "the past shaping the present."[5] In visions and dreams, Mike is able to interact with Sara as though she were still alive, and to witness the murder of her and her son. Sara's death, a simple foregone conclusion at the start of the novel, turns into multiple murder and the demand for revenge.

This is similar to the way King presents Luke Ellis's kidnapping in *The Institute*. Readers watch it through the eyes of the kidnappers themselves and are therefore fully aware that Luke's parents are murdered that night. Luke does not witness it, and he is in fact later told that his parents are still alive and waiting for his return. A child genius, Luke even realizes that he is putting off the revelation of this knowledge when he refuses to search for the news of his parents, even when he finds a way to access the internet. Luke knows that reading it will make it real for him, even though he said he suspects that it is indeed the truth, and he puts off the discovery of this knowledge as long as he can. The suspense here comes in wondering how the twelve-year-old will react emotionally to this confirmation. His IQ might be immeasurable, but Luke is still only a child, and an imprisoned child at that.

All these different ways of revealing, concealing, and repeating deaths are used to create and heighten suspense within King's works. This is most easily achieved when readers have information that the protagonists do not, and that the protagonists may not be able to uncover. The narrative structure allows readers to witness things that could not be seen in real life, or that the main characters themselves have no way of knowing. By providing readers with more information about the antagonist, proving their identities and level of danger, King works to ensnare the attention of his readers from page one and pull them along to the end of the book.

Death and the Genre

King is, first and foremost, a horror writer. He has written frequently of his first agent's concern that he would be pegged as this and solely this, bound to a single genre to his detriment, although his body of work has shown that this original fear was misplaced. As the master of horror, King finds it difficult to write anything that steps out of those bounds. Even *Mr. Mercedes*, the first book in the Bill Hodges trilogy, may have been written solely as a realistic police procedural that explores the danger hiding behind Brady Hartsfield's "bland anonymity and computer skills,"[6] but it set up the circumstances necessary for the second and especially the third book to embrace supernatural horror once again.

Even then, King does not always confine himself to generic expectations. He likes to subvert them, and then later subvert his own subversions. While Constant Readers might have a better chance at predicting how characters will act or how a narrative might unfold, prior knowledge of King's plots and narrative devices does not always lead to accurate predictions. While deaths can be expected, they do not always occur in the same manner, in the same part of the narrative, or to the expected characters. Sudden, senseless death can occur at any time, felling reader favorites alongside the antagonist.

King plays with the conventions of the horror genre, at times keeping his supernatural monsters in the dark for both the readers and the main characters, and at other times allowing the readers a peek into the mind of the monster. While many horror narratives attempt to make an argument in favor of the antagonist in some way, King at times uses these glimpses to reassure readers that there is nothing salvageable in the antagonist. And while King can make use of the false ending in which the antagonist is shown to still be alive and capable of rising again, at other times it seems as though his protagonists have indeed conquered and triumphed.

These generic subversions are seen even in his human characters, especially the serial killer. Frank Dodd, the monster of Castle Rock, is frequently mentioned in his books that take place in the city. Dodd casts a long shadow and has developed his own mythology within the Rock, looming large over generations that follow his death. However, Dodd is not the central character of his own story. He exists as a minor character in the tale of Johnny Smith, given a few meager lines to speak before bowing out of the story forever via suicide, and "Smith, like the narrative, does not dwell on the hows and whys of Dodd's crime spree, but quickly moves on."[7] Dodd's psychopathy is examined only enough for readers to conclude that this serial killer is a human monster who will not stop until he is caught, and whose strange ideas of women and sex were implanted by his overbearing mother. Dodd is shown sufficiently for readers to be sure that he fits usual expectations for a serial killer before Dodd confirms his identity for the other characters by killing himself.

The same approach is seen in the novella "A Good Marriage" in which the point-of-view character, Darcy, realizes that her husband is in fact a local serial killer. Through Darcy's eyes, Bob Anderson is seen as very much human, and perhaps even boring, an accountant who collects coins in his spare time. Their life together is unremarkable until her discovery, and the crisis comes when Darcy must decide what to do about it. Bob is given more of a chance than Frank Dodd to explain his actions, but the explanation, like the scenes in which Dodd is seen mulling over his mother's treatment of him, is almost unnecessary. Fans of serial killer stories have heard it all before. It can be largely dismissed to focus on what King finds more interesting: the reaction of a wife to realizing that she barely knows her husband of twenty-seven years at all.

Although there are some elements that can be seen to commonly hold across all of King's works—it is, for example, bad luck to be a dog in any of his stories, while pregnant women rarely need to fear for their lives—very few of them apply to every single narrative. A senseless and sudden death can pop up quite suddenly, even when characters and readers believe they are in the midst of safety. A character's hard work, commitment to the greater community, and purity of heart are not enough to ensure that he will still be alive on the final page of the book. While the antagonist and his top supporters are usually vanquished during the climax, he might rise again in the epilogue or in a later narrative. Other antagonists can therefore only be said to have been killed or conquered merely for now. In the best horror tradition, the monster can always rise again, should King think of a narrative it would benefit.

HUMANITY, COMMUNITY, AND EMPATHY

Alongside the usual generic expectations that occur within a Stephen King novel, some common themes within King's works involve a sense of community. King is very interested in dealing with large casts of characters, dividing them into groups or perhaps solitary figures and then considering the motivations and morals of those factions. It is not enough for characters to work for the good of their own small group if this means going against the best interests of humanity in general. A small, isolated group could be just as bad as a single isolated individual.

Characters' choices of allegiance are just as important as the motivation for those choices. Frequently King offers glimpses inside his characters' heads, both protagonists and antagonists, so that readers can have a more complex understanding of why those characters make the choices they do. Even then, understanding is not always meant to lead to empathy or agreement. It is possible to comprehend the reasoning behind characters' poor choices without condoning the actions that follow.

The characters who see themselves belonging to a group rather than standing outside of it are more likely to cling to each other for survival rather than striking out on their own. It is possible for characters to choose to ally themselves with the "wrong" side, turning their back on their own humanity, as well as acting for their own individual interests. In King's books, other people, and especially family members, are often the key to survival. If characters choose the proper group, whether blood relatives or found families, and put the survival of the group above their own, they might still die, but they will be more likely to die well. Their choices and alliances are what help make their deaths meaningful and their sacrifices noble.

Complicated Motives for Death

Not all of King's evil characters are inhuman, and not all of them are inexplicable. For a number of his characters, the discovery of the antagonist's motivation is part of the protagonist's path to first identify and then defeat them. If they can understand why the antagonist is killing, they can hopefully then both predict the identity of the next victim and stop the monster from killing again.

The completely human murderers are perhaps the most explicable. They are not killing to feed themselves and prolong a near-immortal life, but rather for reasons that we, as fellow human beings, are meant to at least nearly understand. If a human killer has a longer and more detailed backstory, then readers and other characters, are more likely to feel empathy toward that character.

Carrie is a prime example. When first encountered, she is a teenage girl suffering from both her classmates' bullying and her mother's lack of explanation about the transition from girlhood to womanhood. She is singled out for ridicule and has been all her life, the object of "communal finger-pointing"[8] both before and after her death. The more readers learn about Carrie, the more they hear about her social and emotional isolation, as well as her telekinetic powers. When Carrie goes on a spree killing throughout her town on prom night, readers have enough information to see that the so-called prank with the pigs' blood was only one in a long string of offenses against her.

At least one survivor of prom night, Sue Snell, also seeks to hold Carrie and her memory as human and not as monstrous Other. Some of those who were present in the town of Chamberlain, as well as those who make up the White Commission, want to frame Carrie as inhuman and assign blame solely to her telekinetic powers and not to social interactions. Because those who bullied Carrie, and especially those who dumped the buckets of pigs' blood on her, died on prom night, considering their roles in the event might feel too much like blaming the victim. It is easier for them to place all the blame on the social outcast who had no friends in life and who has very few people able to defend her after her death.

On the opposite end of the scale are characters like Brady Hartsfield and Bob Anderson. Within the first book of the Bill Hodges trilogy, Brady is still "merely" Mr. Mercedes, a fully human serial killer without any superhuman powers. Readers are allowed glimpses into the lives and minds of both Brady and Bob, more intimately seeing Brady as the point of view goes into his own mind and seeing Bob through the lens of his wife of more than a quarter-century. Readers learn the hardships and difficult childhoods that the characters had to endure through both Brady's thoughts and Bob's story told to Darcy. They each try to explain to the reader why someone in their position would have committed these crimes.

These justifications, though, are not meant to make readers feel a deep empathy. Readers are not meant to relate to either Brady or Bob, but to be repelled by the cold, calculating thought processes revealed. Each of these men has his own term for his victims, showing how he dehumanizes them in his mind, and clearly separates himself from the others. While Carrie wanted to fit in with her classmates and struggled because of the upbringing forced upon her by her mother, Brady and Bob leaned into their difference and killed other people as a means of asserting their dominance and superiority. Carrie's reaction was personal. Bob's, and Brady's initial murders before he focuses on Detective Bill Hodges, were highly impersonal.

In this way, Bob Anderson is the most like King's other fully human serial killer, Frank Dodd. Although Dodd gets transformed into a mythical monster after his suicide, and although he exists in a story that includes the supernatural, Dodd himself has no such abilities. He is eventually caught by psychic Johnny Smith, but Dodd was merely human. Readers are allowed glimpses inside Dodd's head the way they are inside Brady Hartsfield's, showing more intimately the way his mind works and his thought process during the actual events of murder. Dodd, like Brady, is suffering from an overbearing mother who forces an intimate sexual relationship on her son. However, this explanation is provided as background and again, not to allow readers to feel empathy toward Dodd. Readers want the killer to be caught, no matter how much of him they see and are allowed to understand. Even when he is human, he has broken the expectation of community when he chooses to murder others.

The inhuman, monstrous Other can also be accompanied by an explanation of motive. Fully supernatural creatures such as It or the Outsider kill children for their food. They need to eat, and although most of their sustenance seems to come from the child's fear or other emotions rather than death and consummation of flesh, death is still a necessity for these creatures' own continued existence. However, "taste is actually immaterial when it comes to mere survival,"[9] and these supernatural beings engage in torture purely for flavor's sake. The Outsider is not given much of a backstory, but It is shown to be completely alien: not human, and not of this Earth. They cannot be expected to look upon humans as equals, the way many humans make distinctions between themselves and the animals they choose to consume.

Other supernatural killers such as vampires or the True Knot are not human any longer, but once were. Vampires need to drink human blood to survive, condemning their victims to a similar existence and killing those who begin to suspect what is happening. The True, on the other hand, can only feed on very specific people: children who produce steam, otherwise known as children who shine. Like It and the Outsider, the True Knot torture their chosen meals to purify the steam and make it taste better.

Vampires and the true are thus selecting victims that, at one time, they should have recognized as being like themselves, showing how "one group *chooses* to position itself over another."[10] However, from the one demonstration of the True "turning" a human being into a new member, it seems that all of them possessed their own unique abilities prior to their transformation. Snakebite Andi is given a backstory of sexual abuse, like Brady Hartsfield and Frank Dodd, as well as her own supernatural ability to make others fall asleep, already separating her from other people before she was physically transformed into something other by taking steam. Vampires, like Snakebite Andi, are no longer human and therefore view people as possible sustenance.

Many of those who are turned vampire in 'salem's Lot are also shown to be less then fully contributing members of the community prior to their transformation. They are not "good" people who are haphazardly felled by the bite of the vampire, the way Cujo was a good dog until he encountered the rabid bat. Kurt Barlow, like the Tommyknocker ship, descended on a town that was already fractured and petty, with members working to undermine or cheat each other. The success of the supernatural in these towns was due largely to this lack of community and the stark divisions already present.

It is this fracturing that allows monsters to rise. Just as King strongly believes in a group banding together to defeat the monster, forming a ka-tet to merge their strengths and compensate for each other's weaknesses, he presents this fracturing or lack of community as being a central point of failure. If even one member of the community strives for independence or otherwise breaks their bonds, the entire community suffers, and success is in doubt. Therefore, King's human characters, or his characters who were once human, that prey on human beings are a recurring threat.

Even when the antagonist is a supernatural, inhuman creature, it makes use of this lack of community to find its victims and also to secure an assistant. King's Renfields are outsiders before they throw their lot in with the supernatural creature, like the Outsider. They already do not feel as though they belong to the community and hold grudges against those who fit in so neatly. Rather than attempting to find their own place within it, these characters strive for independence and greatness by allying themselves with the Other in an attempt to raise the self above other members of the community.

These Renfields have bought into the belief that the individual human life is not worth preserving if it can be sacrificed for something greater. They simply believe that their own lives are not ones that should be sacrificed, and that by deserting their fellow humans and aligning themselves with the monster, they will be able to make themselves better in the monster's eyes. Although this is frequently framed as a decision made for personal survival, it is also one that comes at the cost of other human lives. While a Renfield believes that he is saving himself and setting himself up for a good position in the New World once the revolution is complete, he has betrayed his fellow man and cannot be allowed to live. Even the monster he has chosen will not work to save a Renfield's life because the monster is always more concerned with itself.

At times the monster is not as explicable as a vampire, which has its own mythology preceding King, or the other various antagonists who are given backstories within the work. Sometimes the evil is not fully understood by either the characters or the reader. For example, there is no easy or full explanation for why the Overlook Hotel seeks people with the shining, or what, exactly, Perse wants and searches for in the artists who live on Duma Key. Readers and characters alike are aware that the Overlook somehow feeds on the shining and wants to kill Danny, and that Perse is not above committing murder to force Edgar to do what she wishes, but the overall background is still fragmented. Jack Torrance uncovers a salacious history of the Overlook, and Edgar and his friends learn more about the artist Perse controlled previously, but the full motive of the antagonist is not completely understood. They know what the antagonist wants, but not the comprehensive story of why.

Whether or not the murdering antagonist is given an explicable backstory that allows readers or the characters to empathize, it is important to note another area in which King subverts the genre. In a battle between the supernatural and the human, the supernatural is not always evil and the human is not always good. Possessing supernatural powers within a King novel is not an immediate marker of where the character falls morally. As always, things are more complicated than an initial glance might indicate.

Dan Torrance, as a young boy in *The Shining* and as an adult and *Doctor Sleep*, is one example. He is the proposed victim in his first story, the focus of the Overlook and the entire reason the Overlook has been catering to Jack. Since he is just a child, Danny uses his gift to call for help during the climax of the book. For King, "children basically possess the true weapons for survival—a productive imagination, a love for simple things, a gentle nature,"[11] and yet children rarely triumph on their own. In *Doctor Sleep*, he has become that adult when a child with the shining also needs help. In both cases, Danny uses his supernatural gift for the side of good to fight off other supernatural forces, be it whatever haunts the Overlook Hotel or the murderous attention of the True Knot.

A more recent book, *The Institute*, places children with telepathic and telekinetic abilities in direct confrontation with purely human adults. Although the children do manage to get other adults on their side, the human faces of the Institute are presented as the real antagonists who must be destroyed. Following in the footsteps of Charlie McGee from *Firestarter*, the children use their powers to take down not just individuals but an entire institution that would have used them up and kill them if it had its way. However, as adult Dan Torrance demonstrates, the division between good and evil cannot also be drawn between children with powers and adults with the same. It is a more individual choice of the author and the narrative so that the age of the character and the character's relationship to the supernatural cannot be used to make snap judgments about the moral alignment of that character.

Likewise, the consequences for a character betraying his fellow man are complex. Disloyalty does not always lead to immediate death, and although safety is found in community, it must be the *right* community. Choosing the wrong partnership can be just as dangerous as attempting to proceed alone.

Alliance, Betrayal, Community, and Isolation

Again and again, the monstrous outsider is able to find human allies and strengthen itself through their alliance. These human characters, however, are not meant to be sympathetic prior to their seduction. It is not, in fact, a loss for the human race when these characters choose to defect, even though this choice will ultimately end in their deaths. In King's works, it seems impossible for the inhuman antagonist to seduce a "good" human character. Morality is already set before the time for decision appears.

The ways of betraying fellow men are many. Jack Torrance, for example, finds himself isolated in the Overlook Hotel with the only people in the world who still might believe in him due to his alcoholism and anger issues. He is desperate to function as the proper head of a household, the breadwinner for his wife and son, and to follow his dream of becoming a great American author. The only path left open to him after he is fired from teaching at a private school is this caretaker's job, and he needs help to be offered even that. Jack is resentful that the world, his wife and child included, does not recognize his brilliance or praise him as he believes he deserves to be praised. Jack has already isolated himself and withdrawn in his heart before his small family is left alone in the hotel for the winter.

Similarly, other individual characters are shown to give in to the offers and temptations displayed by the supernatural. Jack thought that whatever inhabited the Overlook would help him achieve his goals of obtaining immortality through his amazing writing. Jud Crandall, who knew the secret of the pet sematary, was seduced by the knowledge of its power and therefore attempted to pass it on to his new neighbor, Louis Creed. Where Jack believes that the Overlook holds the power to help him write a bestseller, Jud knows that the burying grounds past the pet sematary also hold power over death, and "it is always white males who seek to impose their will without respect"[12] for the tradition in which supernatural powers began. Each man is weak in the face of this temptation, and although Jack manages to take control long enough to save Danny's life and Jud does his best to help the Creed family, each man's fate is death.

In contrast to Jud, who honestly seems to think that he is acting out of the goodness of his heart and for everyone's best interest when he tells Louis about the burying grounds, most characters seduced by evil are not looking out for anyone but themselves. This can be on an individual basis or can also affect an entire town. 'Salem's Lot can be overrun by vampires and Haven by Tommyknockers through a number of smaller decisions that lead to mass capitulation and the "reluctance to shoulder responsibility."[13] Those who attempt to take a stand against either the vampires or the aliens must be killed or run out of town, where they will be prevented from telling anyone else what is happening because of how unbelievable their stories sound. Those who are seduced by the stories and promises are the ones who stay.

The town of Castle Rock, very nearly destroyed at the end of *Needful Things*, is another example. When an outsider, this time a not-entirely-defined shopkeeper named Leland Gaunt who happens to be "a character who represents absolute evil,"[14] arrives, he can masterfully manipulate the already existing grudges and divisions he finds there for his own devices. Gaunt, like many of these other antagonists, seeks to play with people's emotions in the hopes that they will not stop to think logically about their actions and will therefore be prompted to violence instead of reason. He even manages to do this without transforming the town into vampires or aliens but keeping them fully human and turning them on each other all the same.

Needful Things is another example of the basic unfairness of what happens when evil overtakes a town instead of an individual. 'Salem's Lot is now a ghost town where all citizens are either vampires or run out, and Haven no longer exists because those who resisted the Becoming were killed before the ship flew and all of the remaining members died after. In Castle Rock, however, many of the people who die had themselves entered personally into one of Gaunt's bargains. They purchased something they desperately wanted at his shop for a small monetary price and the promise of a prank, since "Gaunt possesses the essential understanding that Americans have a need for things, and that they must work and compromise themselves to have their things."[15]

Willing to play evil tricks on others, they then found themselves at the mercy of other such pranks. Their consequences were literally bought and paid for.

During the final cataclysmic night in which many of these grudges turn deadly, readers are told of Antonia Bissette, "who had not bought a single thing from Mr. Gaunt or participated in any of his little games."[16] Unlike some of the others, suffering slow deaths from poisoning, this woman died quickly of a broken neck. However, because she had nothing to do with Gaunt and his store, her death seems the most senseless. She is caught up in the wrath of the town, and indeed was attending a meeting for one of the feuding churches, but she had done nothing to harm another person. She, like Ruth McCausland in Haven, became collateral damage in spite—or perhaps because—of the fact that she clung to her own basic humanity.

Characters like Ruth and Antonia are, however, in the minority. The towns antagonists like Gaunt choose to haunt are made up of morally gray people. Even the "good" ones like Sheriff Alan Pangborn can have their morals overcome by strong emotions and face moments of doubt. But the characters who more or less willingly help the antagonist, especially those who enter into bargains knowing for certain that they will harm other people, are not those of the Alan Pangborn type.

While anyone, including children, can be tricked into helping the antagonist, those who commit themselves to the antagonist for personal gain are never framed as good or innocent people. These are characters who have already been shown to be violent, or to harbor hatred against the book's protagonists, and who could be expected to hurt the protagonists without any outside interference. The appearance of the antagonist, however, introduces new ways to harm and new levels of weaponry. Characters like Ace Merrill or Jack Hoskins throw their alliance in with the antagonist because it gives them support and yet another reason to harm the characters they already disliked.

These characters have betrayed their community before readers first encounter them, and the readers are not set up to cheer for them and their personal success. Because they are only looking out for themselves, it is unsurprising when they decide to become the antagonist's Renfield. For them, betraying humankind is a mere step on the way to achieving personal success. For King, their desertion is a sin.

While King's protagonists frequently form small groups to achieve their goals, his antagonists are usually lone characters who accept an assistant not as an equal, but as a subordinate. Community is sacred, and largely reserved for the side of good. When King's antagonists form a community and "choose to live in a particular manner at the cost of another's life,"[17] such as the True Knot in *Doctor Sleep*, it becomes a mockery of all that is good. The True have united to commit torture and child murder. While this could indeed be seen as the usual goal of a community—to protect itself and its continued existence—the True have all made the choice to become inhuman and have therefore turned their backs on the form of community that truly matters. Found families are good, and dedication to the group over the self is prized, but not when any of these things come at the expense of humanity. Each member of the True only stays because they need the group to personally survive, and so their decision is, at its base, still selfish.

Once a character has shown an allegiance to the supernatural or inhuman, he can no longer be trusted or allowed to survive. Someone who has already abandoned the community cannot then be a trusted member of that same community afterward, since he has clearly shown himself to be easily swayed to betray his fellow man. Unfortunately for such characters, the antagonist has no interest in forming a true community or watching out for those around it. The antagonist, like the Renfield, is only interested in his own goals.

All the same, one human character's allegiance to another does not always mean salvation. Jim Gardner and Jack Torrance each found themselves isolated with perhaps the only other human being who still believed in them. Gard had Bobbi Anderson, the last of his friends whom he had not alienated, and Jack had his abused wife and child, who supported him in his sobriety and understood that a winter in the Overlook was his last chance at proving himself to himself. In each case, the loyalty went awry. Bobbi Anderson, after encountering an alien spaceship, began to turn alien herself, and Jack Torrance was corrupted by the spirits that inhabited the Overlook. Gard gave his life to save the world, the same way Jack gave his to allow his son the chance to escape. While Danny and his mother Wendy did make it out of *The Shining* alive, neither was unscathed. Wendy suffered immense physical harm, and both she and Danny were haunted by the Overlook in different ways.

Noble Sacrifice

As characters like Wendy Torrance and Jim Gardner learn, their choices of alliance and commitment do not come without a cost. Wendy's sacrifice at first blush appears to be lesser, since she lives and many other of King's heroes die, but it is a sacrifice all the same. Perhaps Wendy, more than others, can be blamed for getting herself into a situation and for waiting almost too long before acting as a hero, but she still finds herself in the same sort of life-or-death situation as others of King's heroes. The reason she waits so long to act is echoed across so many other narratives: the risk is great, and while heroic action might preserve something important, there is also much that can be lost.

Many of King's heroes struggle with the idea of risk, especially when it seems clear that they are going to their own deaths. It is easiest in a moment of active threat, when the character or their loved one is clearly in a life-or-death situation. This is the time when a character can no longer argue to themselves that things will turn out all right, that another character will get himself under control, or that the cavalry is coming to save them. Even the bravest characters must steel themselves for final confrontations when the outcome is likely their own death.

Characters who have more time to think about their actions, especially characters who must travel in order to meet their fates, also have more time to reconsider. When Glen, Ralph, Larry, and Stu leave Boulder for Vegas in *The Stand*, they are told to go on foot, prolonging the journey. Part of this seems to be a test: will any of them falter along the way and decide not to continue, because they know they are being sent to be sacrificed? Part of it, as Glen muses, is an emptying out and recharging, as though they are batteries. Although Glen is the group's most scientific and logical mind, he has agreed to go on this religious quest at the behest of Mother Abigail's God and to perhaps rationalize it to himself along the way.

The four men have more tests than simply the thoughts inside their heads. When Stu, the initial leader of the group, breaks his leg and must be left behind, second-in-command Larry encounters a crisis of conscience—after all, "[i]n King a minor catastrophe seldom makes a difference,"[18] and Larry needs sterner tests of his character in order to prove his mettle. While the long-term goal seems to be to obey Mother Abigail and, in their deaths, save the Boulder Free Zone, a more immediate life-or-death struggle is staring Larry directly in the face. Stu, Glen, and Ralph all agree on what must be done, and that the original plan should still hold, but it is a crucial moment during which the entire balance of the world seems to hang at stake because of a single man's life. The other three must leave Stu, thinking they sacrificed him in a way that will make his death somehow less meaningful, even though Stu's own willingness to be sacrificed means that he is the only one of the four to ultimately survive.

This journey is paralleled in *Dreamcatcher* when the characters of Owen Underhill, Henry Devlin, and Duddits Clavell find themselves in a race against the clock to save the world from an alien invasion. Their journey is much faster, and accomplished in a car instead of on foot, but it still lasts long enough for Owen especially to have his doubts. While Henry and Duddits both have the knowledge of Duddits's abilities and the comfort from Duddits's certainty, Owen is the outsider who has been roped into this mission not because of any personal feelings for the man they are pursuing and his safety, but because Henry was able to tap into guilt from Owen's childhood. Unlike the four who travel from Boulder toward Vegas on foot, Owen does not undertake his mission with any divine assurance that he will be successful, or that the world will be saved. He must trust in his fellow man and in his own gut feeling that what he is doing is necessary and right, and in the end "Owen dies happy in the knowledge that he has become the hero he always wanted to be."[19]

The concept of guilt leading toward heroism is a repeated one. Numerous deaths within King's novels occur to spur the main character on to action when he or she was otherwise frozen and unsure of what to do. In the face of such a large threat, against the self, the community, or the world, characters often find themselves uncertain. They tend to enter a period of stagnation during which they can only hope not to make anything worse, while fearing that any action they do undertake might only be fuel for the fire. These characters, like Wendy Torrance, find themselves unable to fully grasp the enormity and possible repercussions of their current situation until it is so dire that they are forced to react to something instead of choosing to go on the offense.

At times the deaths that spur the characters onto action are caused purposely by the antagonist, although the antagonist usually hopes that these murders will convince the protagonist to slink away instead of to gear up for confrontation. George Stark of *The Dark Half* is one such example because he commits murders and threatens more in an attempt to convince Thad to bend to his wishes. Thad, however, decides that he will not be bullied and instead screws up his courage to save his wife and children as well as himself.

Deaths that are caused by characters other than the antagonist are more likely to result in the action those characters desired. Ray Huizenga of *Cell*, for example, completed suicide as part of an overall plan to save the small group he was traveling with. He could only hope that the others, the current survivors, would be able to puzzle out why he did it and then to act in time to save themselves. Ray's death, unlike the ones caused by George Stark, was selfless and geared toward saving the community over an individual. Therefore, his suicide was allowed to have meaning and to spur the others onto action in a positive light.

For these deaths to be centered in the plot as heroic, the character involved frequently needs to struggle with the idea. The resistance to action considering their possible death and the resulting hesitation are not markers of a lack of courage, but of relatable humanity. No one wants to die a meaningless death, especially when their loved ones are still in a situation that threatens their lives. They want to look for other ways to help the community that involve still being there to watch as the community thrives. The decision to finally approach their own death, especially in cases such as Larry Underwood or Owen Underhill, is one of major character development where they widen their focus from the personal to the entire world. These men die as heroes because readers and other characters have seen that, in their initial encounter, these men never would have chosen such an action. Larry Underwood, after all, was "no nice guy," and Owen Underhill served under the vicious and murderous Abraham Kurtz for years.

Some such sacrifices are highlighted while other heroic deaths might be overlooked. Ralph Brentner, who died side by side with Larry Underwood in Vegas for the good of the people of Boulder, is not given nearly the same attention as Larry. Although Ralph becomes one of the leaders of Boulder in its early stages, and although he is part of the first group that meets Mother Abigail, Ralph's backstory is not told to the same extent as Larry's. Ralph is, in fact, a secondary character picked up in Nick Andros's story. Although he is both a rock during the initial weeks of the Free Zone's formation, and one of the four sent to Vegas by Mother Abigail and her God, he is not even the point-of-view character at the time of his death. Larry Underwood is the one who allows readers to witness that final confrontation.

Ralph, it seems, was always a good guy. He threw his allegiance in with Mother Abigail early on and did everything he could to help the community. Unlike Larry, he didn't have to undergo great personal change to be that sort of person. From the time readers first encounter him driving down the road and stopping to pick up Nick and Tom, Ralph is an affable hard worker who will do what Mother Abigail and the community need him to do with good cheer and without complaint. Although he does not make himself a martyr until the very end, it is not surprising that Ralph would agree to the journey and his likely death in service to the Free Zone.

CATEGORIZATION AND CHARACTERIZATION

The ability to label a character's death as noble or meaningful is largely tied to contrasting ideas of value and usefulness. It is indeed possible for a character to personally believe that his death is a noble sacrifice without the reader agreeing. This is shown in the many examples of King's Renfield. For the reader to agree with the character's assessment and to view that death as having a larger narrative meaning, the reader needs to see how it fits within the story's larger framework.

In some of his books, especially those tied to the Dark Tower, King clearly introduces the ideas of the Purpose and the Random. The structure of the world in relation to the Tower already labels each individual life as one or the other. There is, then, a wider purpose to not only our world but all worlds, and one life can be so important that all worlds pause and wait to see the outcome if that life is threatened. Readers—and indeed characters—need not come up with their own explanations for why and how a character's life or death is necessary or impactful, because it is bluntly stated within the story. "Our world moves along without real endings,"[20] but those who live within the shadow of the Tower can mark both endings and their Purpose because of their connection to it.

In other cases, meaning and a sense of purpose are imbued through a character's choices, motivations, and the consequences of those choices. The character him- or herself might not be alive to find meaning in those consequences, but readers, through the more omniscient narration, can draw these conclusions themselves through the aftermath and the epilogue.

Just as the protagonist can be sorted into categories such as the Purpose and the Random, so the antagonists can be categorized based on whether they can be described as still reasonable or if they have given into madness, or if their continued relationship with humans is parasitic or symbiotic. Both of these carry meaning and expectation when it comes to deaths, those of the human protagonist and that of the inhuman antagonist. These characterizations provide readers with the scaffold on which to base their expectations of how the book will unfold and how and when the deaths will occur. Although no one is ever entirely safe, some characters, given their choices and alignments, may be safer than others.

The Purpose and the Random

The vast majority of King's plot arcs follow the genre of horror in that the narrative opens with a seemingly "normal" day that is quickly interrupted by the arrival of the supernatural. The ultimate goal the characters face throughout the plot, then, is restoring what once was and returning to their normal. The main characters, positioned on the side of good, thus steel themselves to define and confront the threats, frequently deciding that restoration is worth the possible cost of their own lives.

These characters regularly desire to take control of the situation and therefore actively pursue restoration rather than sitting back and letting things happen around them. Generally, the intrusion of the antagonist involves death, so characters can be forgiven for hesitating to confront the situation at risk to their own lives. Frequently, King's main characters encounter meeker others along their way, and are told that they are being stupid or reckless for choosing to act. In *Cell*, for example, when the main group is shunned for destroying a flock of Phoners, teenager Alice Maxwell responds to a dismissive passing band of strangers by asking, "What did *you* do?"[21] Although Alice and her friends have been marked untouchable and slated for public execution, they still take some comfort in having acted instead of passively submitted to what is happening.

The unfortunate thing is that being a "good" person does not always save King's characters from death. Alice herself dies shortly after this confrontation, not at the hands of the Phoners but through random violence. Even as she lays dying slowly from a mortal head injury—"King doesn't afford either the reader or Alice the dignity of a quick death"[22]—other passing groups of

Normals refuse to help because she has been marked. She, like Jimmy Cody of *'Salem's Lot*, dies what seems to be a senseless death before the final confrontation. While Jimmy's friends then go on to confront the vampire Kurt Barlow in part as revenge for Jimmy's death, Alice is largely forgotten during the climax of *Cell* in favor of Ray, whose suicide delivered the others a means of survival, and the Head, whose death provided young Jordan with the resolve to make the final confrontation more deadly. Jimmy's death was directly caused by the Lot's vampires, while Alice's seems to be all the more meaningless because it came at the hands of two other human beings: men who, at the time of the book's climax, had already themselves been murdered in retaliation for their actions.

It is far less comforting to read of the deaths of such innocents or people on the side of the protagonist than it is to read about deaths that have, in their own way, been earned within the narrative. In *Christine*, the possessed car methodically goes about killing the people who have harmed her or her new owner. The high school bullies are first on her hit list. Readers have already seen how the bullies attacked Arnie Cunningham and his new car, and even the lead bully himself realizes why his death is quickly approaching when he recognizes Christine. Christine specifically hunts down those against whom she has a personal grudge, making her actions more understandable. These characters, like the Renfields, have already shown that they do not desire to be part of the community with the protagonists and have therefore set themselves apart in a negative fashion.

Even in *Christine*, however, the lines blur. When she pursues lead bully Buddy Repperton on a slick winter night, he has other people in his car, and one of them was not involved in the attack on Christine at all. This younger boy just happens to be in the wrong place at the wrong time and to die along with the others even though he, like Antonia Bissonnette from *Needful Things*, had nothing to do with the supernatural antagonist. Choosing to hang around with Buddy Repperton's gang is hardly enough to merit a death warrant.

For Christine to be seen as evil, she must threaten the good along with the bad. If she only sought revenge against those who have already proven themselves to be bad, and readers agreed with her assessment of each individual's character, then she would not need to be stopped. Instead of the villain, she would turn into an avenger, protecting her outcast owner against the evils of high school. Instead, she also focuses on innocent victims, from the younger boy in Buddy Repperton's car to main characters Dennis and Leigh. Unlike the younger kid, Dennis and Leigh are fully aware of what Christine is, and therefore they decide to attempt to stop her.

Characters who recognize the evil within their own narrative, decide to believe in it despite its supernatural explanation, and then move to confront it realize they are risking their own deaths. They can only hope that their sacrifice will be for the greater good and make some sort of mark on the world that their own lives could not. At times, characters are helped along by the supernatural elements of the story. In *The Stand*, the four men who are sent to their deaths in Las Vegas understand that they are going because of the will of God. They do not have to wonder if a higher power is out there, ensuring that their sacrifice will be worthwhile. They have Mother Abigail to tell them exactly what they must do, even if she cannot then also explain how their deaths will benefit the community. They still have the comfort and benefit of following someone else's plan instead of having to come up with one of their own.

Ralph Roberts, of *Insomnia*, has also had dealings with a higher power throughout his narrative. He has been shown an image of the future in which a girl he dearly loves is killed in an accident, but he has also been offered the chance to prevent this from happening. He knows for a fact that he will have to die to save her, but he has also been promised that her life will indeed be saved. He does not have to worry about running into the street and getting both of them killed, because he has managed to strike a deal. Ralph has clearly chosen his own death in exchange for Natalie's life, and his biggest concern is that his wife will do her best to prevent him from being able to keep up his end of the bargain. But Ralph, however, exists in a book that is connected to the Dark Tower and in which clear discussions of the Random and the Purpose take place.

However, outside of the Dark Tower books, the vast majority of King's characters, like those of us going about our own daily lives, do not realize that they are living with in a narrative. They are not allowed the same knowledge as readers, including the different points of view frequently presented to put events such as death within a broader context. Many of the characters going to face their deaths do so without knowing of these wider structures and therefore the greater implications of their actions or inaction.

Readers' knowledge of the narrative can help them put otherwise senseless deaths into context. The suicide of twelve-year-old Brian Rusk in *Needful Things*, occurring in front of his younger brother, seems both horrific and senseless to the characters who are still in their own right minds when it occurs. Following Brian's suicide, Sheriff Alan Pangborn and Brian's little brother, Sean, meet for the first time. Neither of these characters has encountered Leland Gaunt, by now making them the minority in Castle Rock, and the conversation the two of them have opens Alan's eyes to the situation. While it can be little comfort to Brian's remaining family members, his suicide was the push that Alan needed to finally confront his town's newest store owner, and to triumph against him.

Even though their situations are similar, Brian Rusk's suicide is worse than that of Ruth McCausland in *The Tommyknockers*. Ruth is given her own backstory, including the double sorrow of infertility and widowhood, but she is also depicted as a rather stubborn woman who knows her own mind and is willing to endure physical and emotional pain to get what she wants, even if this means fighting against the Tommyknockers' "need for ultimate control over people and situations."[23] Further, Ruth is no longer twelve years old. She is a grown woman, much more capable of making up her mind and acting in defense of her town. Even though Ruth understood that her plan would threaten her life, she chose to do her best to alert the outside world, anyway. Ruth was a woman on a mission; Brian was a lost little boy. Each was isolated in a town that had, up until then, been generally welcoming, but Ruth was able to make the decision to risk death during a cry for help that would serve others. Brian completed suicide because he was overwhelmed with guilt and felt helpless.

Because of the amount of information withheld or revealed within the narrative, both before and after these sorts of deaths, readers can assign meaning to them in a way that the characters cannot. They can see into more minds and witness more situations than any single character in the story, and they are able to see the repercussions that follow these deaths. While still tragic, Brian's suicide finds meaning in the way it spurs Alan Pangborn onto action. Rather than being solely the end of a life, it also becomes an instigating event in a battle for the town's souls.

Adding to the tragedy of a character's death is the amount of time a reader has to get to know them prior to it. Brian appeared on the first page of chapter 1 as the first citizen of Castle Rock to meet its newest shopkeeper. Ruth McCausland, on the other hand, appears much later in *The Tommyknockers* and her backstory is only given after readers already know she is dead. King chooses when to reveal a character's fate in a way that impacts the way readers will then encounter that character. If readers already know that a character is dead, or if they know that he will soon be, as is the case for Bradley Trevor in *Doctor Sleep*, then readers approach the unfolding action already aware of the outcome. It is not a question of if someone will survive, but how much they might accomplish before their death.

King creates suspense in situations where readers have no foreknowledge of which character will die next, but where the threat is so great that a death is clearly anticipated. By allowing readers to get to know and to like his main characters, following them around throughout the course of the book rather than introducing them only to kill them off, he allows space for the deaths to become more emotionally resonating. Although he makes the point that Ruth McCausland's death robs Haven of such great good and potential, readers may not have had the time to connect to her emotionally on a level that would clearly let them feel how much has been lost. The death of a child already invokes more pathos than the death of an adult, but knowing a child's hopes and dreams and fears, the way readers can see into Tad Trenton's head in *Cujo*, allows them to feel that a more complete human has been senselessly killed and that wide swaths of opportunity have been lost.

The same goes for characters like Alice Maxwell in *Cell*, who was one of the first normal people encountered by the protagonist and is therefore present for much of the book prior to her death, or the boys who most closely befriend Raymond Garraty in *The Long Walk*. Characters and readers can get to know them in more complex ways prior to their deaths. While it can be incredibly sad that a child must die, other instances in which the child character is introduced with a rushed backstory prior to his death so that he does not have the chance to interact with the main characters, like Bradley Trevor in *Doctor Sleep*, do not have the same emotional impact. Children's deaths are still meaningful and terrible, but in this case, it is simply because a child has died, and not a specific human being.

Bradley Trevor is not, however, one of the most senseless deaths within King's works. Although he becomes a victim of the True, his murder allows central character Abra to identify the True Knot as a threat, to connect more deeply with Dan Torrance, and to strengthen their resolve when it comes to defeating the True. Further, because he was not vaccinated, Bradley was able to infect the True Knot with measles, which also led to their downfall. Although it is absolutely no comfort to the character himself or to his grieving family members, readers can see how Bradley Trevor's death ended up leading toward the triumph of the good characters against the inhuman True Knot. Brad's death is therefore still terrible but can be given meaning within the wider narrative arc.

In contrast are the deaths that seem senseless even given the broader understanding that comes with being a reader. At times King mitigates these deaths by allowing them to occur to characters that readers and main characters barely know. For example, in *The Dark Half*, newly risen inhuman George Stark murders a series of people whom Thaddeus and Liz Beaumont have met only briefly. Stark's first New York City murder involves a "Creepazoid" who had attempted to blackmail Thad, and whom the Beaumonts did not wish well in the first place. When Stark kills the author and photographer of the article in which he was revealed to be a pseudonym, the Beaumonts are horrified, but not as much as when the deaths occur to people they have known and cared about for years. As he gradually works his way along the list of people he sees as being complicit in his own demise, Stark also works closer and closer to characters we have met and who matter in a deeply personal way to Thad himself.

While the blackmailer and photographer are especially portrayed to be people whose morals are perhaps not entirely intact, Stark's very first murder, immediately after he rises from his grave, is of a completely innocent man the

Beaumonts knew because he was the caretaker of their summer place. Homer Gamache's death is more ruthless and senseless than the others because Homer himself had no connection to the creation or destruction of Thad's pseudonym. Further, Homer was beaten to death with his own prosthetic arm when Stark could have just thrown him out of his truck and stolen the vehicle. Homer did not have to die, and the fact that he was beaten and then abandoned works to cement Stark's ruthlessness and lack of morality from the very beginning. While the others are murdered purely to drive Thad to agree to Stark's proposal, Stark killed Homer simply because he is the sort of person who enjoys killing. Any death at the hands of a person like that feels incredibly senseless.

The rest of Stark's murders set up an example of what can help make a character's death meaningful: if they can be fit into an established series, that series can be used to define the intention of an antagonist. It may not be a comfort to know that children are being killed to sustain supernatural monsters, or that a completely human serial killer was the cause of their death, but it is more of an explanation than solitary deaths are usually given. It is no more comforting to Charlie McGee that her mother was murdered because an organization called The Shop had their own plans and expectations, but this backstory can help readers make sense of Vicky's death in a way that the seven-or eight-year-old cannot. Vicky's own apparent innocence in the situation—she was not made fully aware of the experiment performed on her and Andy when they were in college, and no one anticipated that their child would have such incredible pyrokinetic powers—combined with the Shop's ineptitude in keeping track of young Charlie, makes her death senseless and unnecessary. Readers who can grasp the situation much better than a child therefore anticipate that, one day, Charlie must use her powers to revolt against the institution, and that anyone who works for the Shop has it coming.

Vicky's innocence mirrors those of the victims Norman Daniels kills throughout *Rose Madder*. From his wife Rosie's unborn child, to a case of mistaken identity during a drug bust, to the string of people who helped Rosie begin her new life in a new city, "[e]very time we counter Norman he commits another violent act."[24] His method of murder, involving biting, is likewise horrific as it prolongs the death agony of his chosen victims. This series of murders is meant to put Rosie in a difficult situation, as she resists going to the police since Norman is himself a cop, and the others in her life, men and women alike, dismiss the threats. At least one of those, the woman who heads the safe house Rosie lives in when she first moves, becomes one of Norman's victims herself. Readers are the only ones apart from Rosie fully aware of the danger that Norman Daniels presents, and how he will use all the cunning in his power to track down his wayward wife and punish her along with anyone who helped her.

Because Norman is lured through Rosie's mysterious painting into another world and killed by a goddess who lives there, he is no longer around to face the consequences of his actions. Although Norman's murders, like those of George Stark, took place in the real world and would have plenty of forensic evidence to identify him as the murderer, Norman, again like Stark, will not face any real-world legal consequences. The difficulty of explaining what, exactly, happens to either Norman or Stark is glossed over as the main bulk of the narrative ends. Rosie's new life is told in snapshots over the next few years, as she comes to terms with her own anger in the wake of Norman's death, while the fate of Thaddeus Beaumont is only revealed in a later Castle Rock book. The closure for readers and characters alike comes in the supernatural way the killer is destroyed and therefore rendered inert, even if the real-world policemen are not allowed to have that same satisfactory ending.

King's first novel, *Carrie*, deals most directly with this unfairness of death taking a murderer out of our reach. Interspersed with the story of that final high school semester and the now-infamous prom night are various interviews, newspaper articles, and testimony coming from after the event. Carrie, much like Charlie McGee, has finally reached her limit and used her powers to defend herself against those who have been bullying her for her entire life. Carrie starts at the gym where prom is being held and walks her way through town, causing all kinds of death and destruction in her wake. She tries going to the church for solace and to her mother for acceptance but finds neither. The only person to directly confront Carrie White and be allowed to live is Sue Snell, whom Carrie concludes is innocent of any evil intent. Unfortunately for Sue, her life sentence means that others can turn on her in the wake of that disastrous night, because they need someone on whom to vent their anger and Carrie herself is dead.

It is rare for King's books to deal so much with the aftermath of the climactic event, especially when it involves a supernatural power. More frequently, readers see that good has triumphed over evil, and, if there is any information provided after the fact, it comes through an epilogue months later. The initial confrontation between the triumphant humans and the outside world is glossed over so that readers might find out what a group such as the White Commission has decided, without the more meticulous ins and outs of interviews, testimony, and the laying of blame. From the beginning of her story, Carrie is presumed to already be dead, unable to answer any questions or attempt to defend herself. The supernatural threat has therefore been defeated, and the question of *Carrie* is not so much "Will they be able to stop her?"— they will not; Carrie will run herself down and collapse—but "How much can go wrong in trying to move past her?" The White Commission wants to assign blame and enact justice of their own making so that the story can be buried, and they can move on. It is an attempt to make Carrie's death, and her life, meaningless so that larger questions of supernatural abilities do not need to be confronted.

Where Carrie White dies, Charlie McGee lives, although she is not given as much of an epilogue to explore her choices following her own cataclysmic events. While Carrie has clearly already been written up in multiple venues, Charlie is last seen approaching *Rolling Stone*, wanting to tell her story and make it public. The reception of anything printed about Charlie McGee and the Shop is left to the reader's imagination, since we are not provided with text from the publication or mentions of public reaction following the reveal. At the end of their stories, Carrie and Charlie are both orphans who have witnessed the death of their remaining single parent. A wounded Carrie gives in to her own death, unable to control her powers enough to keep them from destroying her, while Charlie attempts to honor her father's memory not only by using her abilities for good, but by telling the world about them. Alive, Charlie at least has the chance to be in control of her own narrative and to show how "[h]er essential strength . . . lies in her ability to recover,"[25] while Carrie's narrative ends up resting largely on Sue Snell.

This sense of characters controlling their own narrative, which can include making choices to either cause or prevent their own deaths, is frequent within King's works. Even sudden deaths that seem senseless because the character has not done something wrong enough to "earn" it can function to spur other characters onto action that will save many people. Rarely does a character in King die solely because he or she has worn out his or her usefulness, although the one instance in which King has confessed to killing characters purely to rid himself of writer's block may come as a shock. In *The Stand*, Nick Andros's death via a bomb feels almost desperately unfair, especially since divine inspiration came only slightly too late for him to disarm it in the first place.

The further unfairness that unfolds months after Nick's death comes in how the initial leadership of the Boulder Free Zone is ultimately reduced to two surviving characters who, in the face of changing politics, decide to depart for Maine instead of sticking around. Although Nick's death apparently allowed him to appear in visions, meaning that Stu Redman's life could later be saved, a bomb still feels like a senseless way for one of the characters King has been following since the beginning of his narrative to be written out of it. This unfairness is amplified when Harold Lauder, who set the bomb, is unable to follow through and reap the rewards he had anticipated for setting it off. Harold Lauder's life is wasted, just as he—or King—wasted Nick Andros's.

Reason and Madness

Harold Lauder is also an example of King's characters who struggle between sanity and insanity. For a world to progress and flourish, its leaders and the vast majority of its population must adhere to a common definition of sanity. They must accept that the world works in a certain way, as explained by the wider community, and therefore not undermine the expectations or well-being of the group. Tempted by the Dark Man, Harold fights for a while to wear a mask of sanity and cooperation before planting the bomb and abandoning Mother Abigail's people in search of glory in the West.

While Harold would argue that he is in fact the most reasonable of anyone in Boulder, his final moments and written confession reveal that he understands the fine line he has been walking. Abandoned and left to die by both the Dark Man and his up-until-then accomplice, Harold writes that he chooses to die in his right mind.[26] Rather than wait around for the impending death caused by his broken leg and resulting infection, Harold chooses to embrace the idea of the man he could have been in Boulder and to complete suicide of his own free will.

In this way, Harold differs from other antagonists who neither benefit nor suffer from last-minute clarity. Characters such as *Insomnia*'s Ed Deepneau and *The Dark Half*'s George Stark cannot be swayed by reason. Stark is willing to continue to commit serial murder, even that of his twin/creator Thad Beaumont, to secure his own existence. Deepneau, fueled by his own wild beliefs about abortion as well as influenced by a being from another level of existence, intends to commit mass murder in a kamikaze run while gazing upon a photograph of the wife he has frequently abused and their young daughter. From their first introduction, each of these characters is shown to be operating in a different sort of reality than the fully human, apparently sane, protagonists.

Unlike Harold Lauder, who causes damage but eventually awakens to the reality of his thoughts and actions, Stark and Deepneau will not stop on their own. There is no hope that either will regain a sense of sanity or clarity, or that a reasonable discussion would prevent them from continuing their courses. The only way to stop characters who cannot see reason is through their deaths.

And they must be killed for the world as established at the beginning of the novel to return. Madness and murder are intrusions into the expected way of things and must be eradicated for restoration to occur. Stark needs to be killed so that Thad will no longer worry that his wife and children, as well as any other associate, might be murdered, and Deepneau likewise must die so that he does not fly his plane into the Derry Civic Center. In this case, it is a single life that must be saved—one of great importance to the Dark Tower—but, when Deepneau is thrown off course and crashes in the parking lot instead, it greatly decreases the possible loss of life that night.

Each of these characters has fixated on a goal and refuses to be swayed. Because Harold's death is much longer and drawn out, he has time to contemplate his decisions and his actions and to conclude that he was in the wrong. Stark and Deepneau must be dispatched much more quickly, because they are in immediate danger of murdering more people. If Harold had lived, he may have been able to turn his life around and become an asset to the community, but he is not given that choice. Madness must be stopped and stopped as permanently as the protagonists can manage. In these cases, disposing of the immediate threat is also cause to breathe a sigh of relief because it is a single occurrence of spree or mass murder, rather than being a threat of serial murder.

Symbiote or Parasite

While the understanding of a death as part of a cycle can help characters in readers make sense of the deaths in a different light, it also adds another layer of threat. If the antagonist continues to exist, so will the horror. Creatures such as It and the Outsider are clear, continual threats to children. While it might be possible to get out of their hunting grounds, either by leaving Derry or by waiting for the Outsider to move on, there is little bravery in either. Protecting only the people closest to oneself, or perhaps even simply oneself, is selfish and frequently punished within King's works. Once the supernatural threat has been acknowledged and identified, something must be done to stop it before it kills again.

The difficulty is increased when the threat is like It and a symbiote instead of a parasite. In return for a slew of child murders every twenty-seven years or so—"there is no single group more oppressed or expendable than Derry's children"[27]—It blesses Derry and helps the town to prosper. Although violent acts and anger are far more common in Derry than other similar cities, Derry has been able to thrive out of proportion, as well. Between 1958 and 1985 when the main characters first grow up in, and then return to, Derry, they are amazed at how much the city has grown. Pennywise not only lives underneath the city, emerging to commit murder, but more or less farms Derry's citizens in order to guarantee Itself continued meals. In turn, the people of Derry willingly ignore or participate in acts of violence that fuel and feed It.

The same relationship is seen in both *The Long Walk* and *The Institute*, albeit in relation to an institution instead of a creature. Boys in the world of *The Long Walk* apply for the chance to participate, undergoing various tests of their own free will. The Walk is supported by the media, who eventually cover it constantly; by the army and the police, who keep the roads clear and follow the rules for "ticketing" Walkers; and by the American population in general, who travel for a spot to view the Walkers in person and who place bets on their favorites. The Walk itself is an annual event and no secret. In fact, speaking out against it is a good way for characters to make themselves disappear.

The Institute of the book with the same title operates on a smaller scale and draws comparisons to Holocaust death camps rather than game shows. Instead of being broadcast with the children filmed for nationwide coverage, the Institute is hidden deep within the Maine woods. The nearby town, supported by those who work at the Institute, finds itself in very much the same position as Derry: they are willing to turn a blind eye to what is happening so that they can continue their own lives as planned.

The main symbiosis enacted within the Institute is seen between the organization and its staff members. Doctors can operate without the oversight of any outside governing body, and aides can indulge in their desires to mentally, emotionally, and physically abuse children. They have all bought into the same sort of patriotism that supports the Long Walk and believe that what they are doing is for the good of the country. The Institute even promises to help workers with incredible personal debt and otherwise finds ways to both support its workers and tie them to the Institute for the rest of their lives. It seems almost impossible to stop working there once employment has begun, short of suicide, and readers are allowed to see into the mind of the woman at the top. Mrs. Sigsby, the director, passionately believes that she is doing the right thing, although she refuses to provide either the children or the readers with the full explanation for her belief.

While Ray Garraty is far too caught up in the Long Walk to get himself or others out of their predicament, Luke Ellis is the first child to ever escape the Institute, and he does not let his story and there. Luke, like the Losers in Derry, puts his own life at risk to save his friends. Those who were meant to be sacrificed to the ever-hungry entity fight back, not just for themselves but for others like them, known and unknown. The children are willing to stand up and say that, whatever benefits that entity might provide, it is not worth their lives.

These characters are all able to recognize that their own survival does not necessarily mean success. Although the Losers initially seem to triumph over It in 1958, and although Luke Ellis manages to escape the compound, the seven Losers all promised to return to Derry if It did, and Luke did not leave with the intention of forgetting that this ever happened to him. These children summoned up the courage to confront a danger facing all children like them, and to fight it, even when the adults around them would have argued that this was a bad idea.

The same cannot necessarily be said for the adults within King's novels. Although Ben Mears returns to 'salem's Lot with young Mark Petrie in tow, and sets a fire meant to burn most of the town flat and therefore give the vampires inhabiting it fewer hiding places, the pair does not manage to eradicate the vampires completely. Later short stories and references reveal that the Lot is still home to vampires, and those living in the small towns around it are fully aware of the threat, even if they do not name it directly. Alan Pangborn, who was there to witness the demise of George Stark and was later able to run Leland Gaunt out of Castle Rock, seems not to consider the fact that Gaunt is an itinerant salesperson. Robbed of the souls he had collected during his time in the Rock, Gaunt presumably opens the new shop referenced in the book's epilogue, allowing the novel's disastrous occurrences to start all over again. Alan and his friends are not shown to attempt to warn anyone else of the danger, or to track Gaunt down to his new city and his new name. Once he has been driven out of their hometown, they are satisfied with the outcome.

Unlike the vampires, who seem to remain bound in one place, Gaunt's methods mimic those of the Outsider: a creature who travels from town to town, hiding its true identity in order to wreak havoc before moving on. Although Gaunt appears to offer people the things they dearly want or perhaps need, neither he nor the Outsider qualify as symbiotes. They are instead parasites that suck their victims dry and must continually be on the move and on the lookout for new fuel. In their choice of victims, they may or may not be as selective as the True Knot, but their defenses are remarkably similar. Rather than drawing upon the supports of a community, they sneak in, take what they want, and then leave before they can be caught or blamed for the chaos left behind. Although they are still alive, unlike Carrie, they are also not brought to justice for their actions through courts and the American legal system. While both the True Knot and the Outsider are killed or destroyed, Leland Gaunt is merely run out of town. He may or may not even be truly weakened and might merely be mad and hungry, making him all the more dangerous for the next town on his list.

Some parasites within King's works are doomed from the start, such as the byrum which appear in *Dreamcatcher*. Although apparently meant to live in the host's intestines and offer up telepathy in exchange for life, the ones seen in this novel are far too hungry. They outgrow their hosts and kill them by eating them from the inside out. Even though they seem to be an incredible threat to humanity, these byrum and the strange fungus that accompanies them cannot be fully supported on humans and the environment of planet Earth. Because these parasites malfunction, the danger comes in the one person who can indeed support this alien lifeform. Without the man dubbed "Typhoid Jonsey," some lives would be lost, yes, but the threat itself would burn out quickly. The byrum cannot even survive as well as the vampires in the abandoned 'salem's Lot.

What protects the Outsider, Gaunt, and the True Knot, as well as making them more threatening, is their ability to blend in and pass for human. Instead of being horrific monsters like the alien byrum, incubating deep within human bodies, they look relatively normal and make full use of their appearance in their search for their next victims. This is more in line with Its disguise of Pennywise the Clown rather than Its other, more horrific faces, since even Pennywise is largely overlooked by the adults of Derry. Readers are aware of the threat posed by these supernatural beings with apparently human features long before the main characters come to the same realization, and thus readers fear that the main characters' lack of recognition will lead to their deaths.

MENTAL AND EMOTIONAL TOOLS OF SURVIVAL

King frequently plays with contrasting themes and ideas that heavily influence the fates of his main characters. At times, these concepts also factor heavily into the way the narrative is revealed to the reader, such as the concealment or revealing of crucial pieces of information. While characters keep secrets from each other, the narrative can also structure itself to keep readers guessing, too. This information can be a confidence shared among some of the characters but concealed from the reader, or a crucial piece of the puzzle that no one has yet figured out.

While readers themselves are not threatened beyond the possibility of a few sleepless nights, the protagonists are in a struggle of life and death. The outcome of this battle is not merely dependent upon the physical prowess of the character—and indeed possibly does not rely on physical strength or capabilities at all—but does often center on a character's intelligence and ability to adapt to new information. Refusing to believe in a monster simply because it does not follow the scientific rules and expectations does not save a character from being killed by the monster, and in fact decreases the chances of survival.

Finally, the emotional toll that accompanies these situations and the deaths that occur is frequently ignored. Characters are not given a chance to mourn in the middle of their own life-or-death battles, and the immediate fallout after the climax is skipped over in favor of an epilogue occurring weeks or months later, after the situation has once again settled down. It serves King's characters best to be able to withstand the emotional assault alongside the mental and physical, pushing themselves to complete their tasks before allowing themselves to collapse and, perhaps, recover.

Revelations and Secrets

The way King controls the release of information in his narratives sets up both reader and character expectation for how the plot will unfold and how dangerous it might be. While the protagonists might not see it this way, readers will encounter a death early in the plot and consider it an indication that further such deaths will either occur or be uncovered. While characters might not wish to look for serial killers at every turn, a Constant Reader is more likely to wait with bated breath to see what further deaths an initial death will uncover. Between King's human and nonhuman serial-killing characters, he has created the expectation that an early death will not come alone.

Character deaths can uncover secrets in more than just the autopsy room. Conversations with those who have witnessed a suicide or even with oneself can point characters in the right direction. Sheriff Alan Pangborn finds himself all but paralyzed by recent occurrences within Castle Rock until his hospital-room conversation with Sean Rusk, younger brother of the recently deceased Brian Rusk, clearly puts new shopkeeper Leland Gaunt at the center of everything. Jim Gardner in *The Tommyknockers* and Clay Riddell in *Cell* each have their own suicide to ponder and their next actions to plan if they have any hope of saving the remaining humans in a world gone either alien or Phoner. Each of these deaths allows the protagonist to finally admit to himself the depth of the problem at hand, and to spur him on to action where previously he felt paralyzed.

Complicating the suicide of Ray Huizenga in *Cell* is the other way in which deaths in King can work to reveal or conceal. Ray completed suicide to prevent the telepathic Phoners from learning that he had concealed a bomb in the group's bus and that he wanted them to use it to blow up the Phoner flock. This suppression was the entire purpose behind the character's decision to kill himself. He made the sacrifice so that the others might be able to survive, if they figure out his secret in time. Because readers can only see inside Clay's head and glimpse Clay's thoughts, they are just as much in the dark about Ray's motivations as Clay and the other protagonists. It is a secret that must be uncovered, and quickly, before the other characters are led to their deaths.

The death of Elizabeth Eastlake in *Duma Key*, while not a suicide, was caused by the antagonist to keep Elizabeth from warning or better preparing the three protagonists who will go to fight Perse. Throughout the book, Elizabeth's Alzheimer's and the men's lack of understanding about the situation prevented these conversations from taking place. Once Elizabeth realizes how much power Perse has amassed and is clearheaded enough to start telling Edgar and the others about her concerns, Perse afflicts her with a seizure and a mortal stroke. The entire time Edgar has been on Duma Key, Perse has been working to both strengthen his power and keep him in the dark about everything she is doing and everything she has done before. Edgar and his friends must therefore find another way to access Elizabeth's memories, a goal that is indeed possible thanks to the powers they have been gifted by either Perse or the island itself. The main theme of the book is one of memory, especially memories lost, but in this case, Elizabeth's persist even after her death despite Perse's desires.

The memory of a death can itself be kept secret as seen in *Bag of Bones*. Sara Tidwell, who cannot be traced in the history books after the early twentieth century, is a strange example of a known local historical figure but also a forgotten person. Those who live around Dark Score Lake remember Sara and the Redtops, both as a band and as a group of people who once lived on its shores, but any explanation for why they would have left the area is largely unspoken. Mike Noonan discovers that Sara Tidwell is just one of the many subjects he should not pursue with any of the locals. Sara, like Perse, operates best in secrecy.

Also like Perse, Sara is a serial killer. She is not content with a single instance of mass murder, the secret concealed by Ray Huizinga's death, or even murder confined to a single generation. While Perse has been sleeping and inactive for decades by the time she arises again in *Duma Key*, Sara's spirit—or the "outsider" that Sara's spirit has become—has been taking victims from multiple generations ever since her death. Since several young men raped her and then killed both her and her son, the situation "blur[s] the concept of evil in an intriguing way."[28] Sara has induced members of those men's families to kill their own children, all the way up until the present day, but she was the one who was first wronged. When Mike's wife came close to uncovering her secrets, it seems that Sara was the one who caused her fatal aneurysm.

These deaths, purposely caused by antagonists to keep information from the reader and protagonist both, clearly have meaning in each of the narratives. Although it seems highly unfair that the gathering or transmission of knowledge should turn out to be a death warrant, these deaths are at least connectable and explicable once the antagonist's motive is uncovered. When the protagonists and the readers realize that these deaths have meaning, they are able to use them to help with planning how to defeat the antagonist. These deaths also largely serve the function of strengthening the remaining protagonists' resolve and therefore setting them up as more than equal to the task of facing down the antagonist.

Belief, Imagination, and Death

Just as knowledge can provide a death sentence even for a "good" protagonist, so can unbelief. In fact, unbelief and intelligence frequently go together.

In King, unbelief is often a tool of the supernatural, since it relies upon the age of reason and science in order to continue stalking its victims.

Protagonists who find themselves threatened by the supernatural antagonist can often be slow to conclude this or convinced to pursue wrong action because the interplay between knowledge and belief is imbalanced. Here, King's author characters more often find themselves at a loss. Although they can spend their days making up stories for other people to read, they have a hard time believing when it seems that one of their beloved horror stories has come to life. This lack of belief, as seen in so many of King's stories, does not render the supernatural nonthreatening. As Eddie Corcoran realized when faced with It in the guise of the Swamp Thing, "it was real enough, this Creature. After all, it was killing him."[29] Refusing to consider the fact that the strange happenings around town are caused by vampires, shape-shifters, or cars that can drive themselves in favor of searching for a "reasonable" explanation often means simply playing into the antagonist's hands.

Characters who most rigidly cling to the belief that the world should be explicable and scientific are the ones who are also most in need of a metaphorical slap to the face if they are to triumph as the book's protagonists. Ben Mears, the author in 'Salem's Lot, has a much harder time accepting the existence of the vampires then either the English teacher, the twelve-year-old boy, or the physician. His unbelief is only superseded by that of his girlfriend, Susan, who first finds herself captured by the vampire's assistant and then cannot free herself in time to escape her undead fate. Both Susan and Ben approached their first possible vampire without either a cross or a useful weapon, and it was only through the quick thinking and actions of their companions—the boy and the physician respectively—that anyone survived those encounters.

This is not to say that belief means salvation, or that imagination is "a viable commodity for routine existence."[30] Of the early vampire-believers, only young Mark survives to the end of the book. The English teacher dies in the hospital of another heart attack, and the physician falls into a booby-trap laid by the vampires. Because it was daylight, and because he had bought into the explanation completely, Jimmy forgot to think of any more mundane threats to his life and to look for passive protections. Still, his willingness to keep an open mind saved him from a previous encounter, during which he—and Ben—was then forced to admit the truth.

Along with intellect and belief, King's characters are most likely to survive if they also possess cunning intelligence and the ability to think on their feet. They need to be open to changes in plans as well as changes in their perception of the world. In this, King's Constant Reader has the advantage. Readers are fully aware that they are engrossed in a Stephen King novel, while the characters—outside of some in the Dark Tower series—are not.

Readers therefore approach the narrative expecting the supernatural to arise, while the characters, believing themselves to exist in the "real" world, must be convinced.

The Constant Reader is also in the position of self-selecting, making them more likely to believe in the supernatural, or at least to enjoy reading about such explanations, in the first place. The reader's prior knowledge of a book summary or even simply the author's name and reputation provide background information that the characters themselves do not possess. The inclusion or introduction of a previously known character, such as Holly Gibney, into a new and possibly up-until-then realistic narrative also offers these clues to returning readers but not necessarily to a story's characters.

A protagonist's resistance to belief in the face of such apparently overwhelming evidence is cause to fear for that character's life. Although children in King's books are more likely to understand and adapt faster than adults, even child characters can be threatened. Stan Uris, the only Loser not to return to Derry in 1985 and to choose suicide instead, is also shown to be one of the weaker members in 1958. His fears are different from the other children's, and he struggles to communicate them. Believing in It would, for Stan, be an offense, the way witnessing any of the miracles attributed to Jesus Christ would be an offense.[31] Stan understands the way belief would threaten his own sanity, even as the other Losers recognize that Stan's lack of belief could undermine their possibility of success. Because he does not return for the second half of the book, and because his own story of the years between 1958 and 1985 is told as his wife's story, Stan is less of a protagonist than the others, even though they understood that they needed all seven to face It as children. His lack of belief not only leads to his death, but to less of his life being explored, and he is almost stigmatized for it.

Belief and imagination are strong central themes in It because each is tied to confronting and defeating the monster. If the children and then the adults fully believe, then It knows that Its life is threatened. After all, if they only half-believe, It has nothing to fear.[32] In *The Outsider*, Holly Gibney tells Ralph Anderson that in order for them to succeed in their battle against their own supernatural foe, she needs him to "[b]elieve in this. If only for the next twenty-four hours."[33] Belief and imagination are different from physical strength, and allow even a character like Eddie Kaspbrak, with his asthma and his pharmacy of pills, to play a major role in the defeat of the monster. As a child, Eddie finds the courage to fight Its iteration as a giant eye when the others fall back in fear, and as an adult he uses both his imagination and his asthma inhaler to greatly weaken It during their final confrontation. Eddie dies despite his heroic efforts, but his death is meaningful because of the active role he plays.

In other narratives, the only belief necessary is that which allows the protagonists to recognize that there is in fact a possessed car, some form of vampire, shape-shifter, or other apparently impossible creature bent on killing them. Wit and cunning are needed to face the foe, and perhaps there was once a small child who dreamed up the stake and mallet necessary to kill a vampire,[34] but the destruction of the monster is largely based on damage to its physical form. Characters do not need to be asked to believe that driving a stake through vampire's heart will kill it because science has proven that driving a stake through a living creature's heart is deadly. These seem to be proven facts instead of the idea that an asthma inhaler might suddenly be filled with battery acid.

Again, just as King subverts generic expectations, he can also subvert those of the Constant Reader. After all, as the Turtle tells us, *"what can be done when you're eleven can often never be done again,"*[35] and things do not happen the same way twice. Although belief, imagination, and a strong moral conviction make it more likely that a character risking death will instead triumph over evil, there is always sacrifice, and always a risk. Even when aided by a benevolent and powerful Other, the protagonist is always chancing death, and therein lies the courage.

Mourning and Restoration

These characters see the risk as being worth it, however, because this also seems to be the only way for the world to make sense again. Something has disrupted their usual lives in such a way that it cannot be allowed to continue. The threat must be stopped, and things must be returned to normal, even at the cost of lives. Only then can the world begin to make sense again.

In the narratives where restoration seems to have occurred instead of remaining an unconfirmed possibility, there is frequently a time jump between the falling action and an epilogue. Restoration is not quick, even when the threat has really and truly been eradicated. Once the alien spaceship has been removed from planet Earth, or the last inhuman Other has died, there is still work to be done and a lingering threat to society and everyday life. Even those who simply know about the situation, rather than having lived through it, can be considered a threat to the government or to other organizations because of their knowledge. It is therefore difficult within King's books to fully declare that something is, in fact, over.

This break in the time line also allows for readers to reach a faster catharsis than the characters themselves. This jump can skip over the worst grief and the initial process of mourning so that, when the narrative checks back in, the remaining protagonist have more or less reached the state of acceptance. The characters have had the time to explain everything to themselves and to give their friends' deaths a measure of Purpose. Thus, when readers encounter them again, it is in this emotionally stable state and with a generally "feel-good" explanation for everything that happened.

The world is once again as it was, and the characters have had time to organize their thoughts and memories so that it makes sense again. A brief glimpse into their new everyday lives or into a conversation between survivors reassures readers that the restoration is complete. Whether or not a character's death served the Purpose, it can in fact be given purpose as surviving characters shape and reclaim their own narratives.

Although this same process of turning lived events into narrative happens in real life, the way these books are presented allow for readers to skip over the character's most emotional and most immediate responses to many of these deaths. Even if a death happened earlier in the novel, the stressful survival situation surrounding it means that remaining characters are in fight-or-flight mode and are unable to take the time to process their emotions. Such mundane questions as "What do we do with the body?" are rarely addressed, and any such queries after the climax go likewise unseen. It is enough for readers to see survivors emerging from the final confrontation, knowing that at least one person is left and still capable of pursuing happiness.

This does not mean that happiness is always present in the epilogue. Sue Snell has been hounded by the men on the White Commission, Edgar Freemantle recounts the death of his friend Jerome Wireman, and Dennis Guilder has more than a sneaking suspicion that Christine has somehow risen again, to name but three. The deaths encountered within the text still haunt the survivors and affect their lives. Characters may have done their best to make peace with it, but, especially in situations where the threat is a supernatural serial killer, there is always the chance that the cycle will begin again. This is, in itself, its own horror.

THE MANY HORRORS OF DEATH

Death is horrific, because in many ways it means the end of something. After all, "[t]he most obvious psychological pressure point is the fact of our own mortality,"[36] and King knows how to keep poking at our tender places. The end of a life also signifies the loss of potential. No new memories can be made, no old breaks healed, and there is no longer any chance for growth and change. The more a character was loved or known, the greater the loss.

Anticipated and unanticipated deaths are each horrific in their own way. When readers, especially Constant Readers, pick up on foreshadowing or are given more information than the characters, they can anticipate danger and possible death before a mortal confrontation happens. Readers can follow the paths of inquiry and investigation that protagonists undertake, anticipating which discoveries and conclusions might be accurate, and which inaccuracies might be deadly. In these instances of suspense, it seems to readers as though the protagonists should be able to avoid their own deaths, but instead find themselves making mistakes that lead to them.

The horror of a sudden or unexpected death does not carry with it the same possible sense of guilt. In these, there was nothing the characters could have done to prevent their deaths. Because they come as surprises to the reader as well as to the other characters, and they more often come in situations where the other characters are threatened and must react immediately, readers have less of a chance to experience, or anticipate the need for, catharsis.

To keep his readers capable of experiencing surprise, even after the introduction of suspense, King must vary his approaches to character deaths to keep his narratives from being predictable. Although death frequently sets the stage for similar deaths later, and all characters who turn their back on humanity or their community are likely to die, neither of these generalities is a failsafe conclusion. Even in the most likely scenarios of death, the timing and purpose attributed to those deaths can vary.

There is no one single meaning of death within King's works, especially because, for some of his characters, death is not in fact the end. They can continue the horror by threatening others with their same fate, thereby turning a single death into a series that must be understood so that they can first be identified and then stopped. King's undead or supernatural killers take up the role occupied by his and others' all-too-human serial killers, increasing both the danger and suspense until they are themselves stopped, this time hopefully forever.

While death itself can be anticipated as occurring in any of King's works, the timing and narrative meaning of that death changes from book to book. No one single character can be assumed to have a 100 percent chance of survival, and even those who are more than likely to die will not always do so in predictable ways. It is the complexity of these variations, the subversion of tropes, and the refusal to fall into the same patterns time after time that allows for these many functions of death to arise and to continue to horrify readers. In his approach, King maintains the childlike attitude of "those who feel they can examine death because it does not yet live in their own hearts"[37] as he continues to play with—and study—death from so many fictional angles while inviting his readers to come close and do the same.

NOTES

1. King, *Danse Macabre*, 195.

2. Lippert, "Traveling before the Storm," 161.
3. Russell, *Stephen King: A Critical Companion*, 23.
4. Magistrale, *Stephen King: America's Storyteller*, 71.
5. Strengell, *Dissecting Stephen King*, 101.
6. Simpson, "From the Meat World to Cyberspace," 118.
7. Frost, "A Different Breed," 120.
8. Ingebretsen, S.J., "Cotton Mather and Stephen King,"15.
9. McAleer, "Untangling the True Knot," 230.
10. McAleer, "Untangling the True Knot," 226.
11. Davis, *Stephen King's America*, 50.
12. Magistrale, *Stephen King: America's Storyteller*, 105.
13. Strengell, *Dissecting Stephen King*, 184.
14. Russell, *Stephen King: A Critical Companion*, 116.
15. Davis, *Stephen King's America*, 82.
16. Stephen King, *Needful Things* (New York: Signet Books, 1991) 655.
17. McAleer, "Untangling the True Knot," 219.
18. Strengell, *Dissecting Stephen King*, 203.
19. Russell, *Revisiting Stephen King: A Critical Companion*, 153.
20. Russell, *Stephen King: A Critical Companion*, 133.
21. King, *Cell*, 282. Italics in original.
22. Findley, "The World at Large, America in Particular," 60.
23. Magistrale, *Stephen King: America's Storyteller*, 152.
24. Russell, *Stephen King: A Critical Companion*, 146.
25. Strengell, *Dissecting Stephen King*, 174.
26. King, *The Stand*, 965.
27. Magistrale, *Stephen King: The Second Decade*, 110.
28. Strengell, *Dissecting Stephen King*, 91.
29. King, *It*, 253.
30. Leonard J. Heldreth, "Rising Like Old Corpses: Stephen King and the Horrors of Time-Past," *Journal of the Fantastic in the Arts* 2, no. 1 (1989): 12.
31. King, *It*, 412.
32. King, *It*, 590.
33. Stephen King. *The Outsider* (New York: Scribner, 2018), 478.
34. King, *It*, 974.
35. King, *It*, 1013, italics in original.
36. King, *Danse Macabre*, 68.
37. King, *Danse Macabre*, 199.

Bibliography

Alegre, Sara Martín. "Nightmares of Childhood: The Child and the Monster in Four Novels by Stephen King." *Atlantis* 23, no. 1 (2001): 105–114.
Barthes, Roland. *The Pleasure of the Text*. New York, Hill and Wang, 1975.
Beahm, George. *The Stephen King Companion: Four Decades of Fear from the Master of Horror.* New York: Thomas Dunne Books, 2015.
Beal, Kimberly. "Bachman's 'Found' Novels: *The Regulators*, *Blaze*, and Author Identity." *Stephen King's Contemporary Classics: Reflections on the Modern Master of Horror*. Lanham, MD: Rowman & Littlefield, 2015. 161–176.
———. "Monsters at Home: Representations of Domestic and Sexual Abuse in *Gerald's Game*, *Dolores Claiborne*, and *Rose Madder*." *The Modern Stephen King Canon: Beyond Horror*. Lanham, MD: Lexington Books, 2019. 61–82.
Brandt, Stefan L. "Time *Ravel*: History, Metafiction, and Immersion in Stephen King's *11/22/63*." *The Modern Stephen King Canon: Beyond Horror.* Lanham, MD: Lexington Books, 2019, 183–202.
Bruner, Jerome. "Life as Narrative." *Social Research* 54, no. 1 (1987): 11–32.
———. "The Narrative Construction of Reality." *Critical Inquiry* 18.1 (1991), 1–21.
Davis, Jonathan P. *Stephen King's America*. Bowling Green, OH: Bowling Green State University Popular Press, 1994.
Findley, Mary. "The World at Large, America in Particular: Cultural Fears and Societal Mayhem in King's Fiction since 1995." *Stephen King's Modern Macabre: Essays on the Later Works.* Jefferson, NC: McFarland & Company, Inc., 2014, 56–63.
Frost, Rebecca. "A Different Breed: Stephen King's Serial Killers." *Stephen King's Contemporary Classics: Reflections on the Modern Master of Horror*. Lanham, MD: Rowman & Littlefield, 2015, 117–132.
———. "Razors, Bumper Stickers, and Wheelchairs: Male Violence and Madness in *Rose Madder* and *Mr. Mercedes*." *The Modern Stephen King Canon: Beyond Horror.* Lanham, MD: Lexington Books, 2019, 83–97.
Goehring, Cory R. "Seven Children and *It*: Stephen King's *It* as Children's Story." *The Many Lives of IT: Essays on the Stephen King Horror Franchise.* Jefferson, NC: McFarland & Company, Inc, 2020, 18–31.

Haugen, Hayley Mitchell. "Horrific Sympathies: The Comingling of Violence and Mental Illness in Stephen King's *Mr. Mercedes*." *The Modern Stephen King Canon: Beyond Horror.* Lanham, MD: Lexington Books, 2019, 99–112.

———. "'Ordinary Miracles': Stephen King's Writing (and Painting) a 'Way Back to Life' in *Duma Key*." *Stephen King's Contemporary Classics: Reflections on the Modern Master of Horror*. Lanham, MD: Rowman & Littlefield, 2015, 3–12.

Heldreth, Leonard J. "Rising Like Old Corpses: Stephen King and the Horrors of Time-Past." *Journal of the Fantastic in the Arts* 2, no. 1 (1989): 5–13.

Hicks, James E. "Stephen King's Creation of Horror in *'Salem's Lot*: A Prolegomenon Towards a New Hermeneutic of the Gothic Novel." *The Gothic World of Stephen King: Landscape of Nightmares*. Bowling Green, OH: Bowling Green State University Popular Press, 1987, 75–83.

Hoppenstand, Gary. *Critical Insights: Stephen King*. Pasadena, California: Salem Press, 2011.

Ingebretsen, Edward J. S.J., "Cotton Mather and Stephen King: Writing/Righting the Body Politic." *Imagining the Worst: Stephen King and the Representation of Women*. Westport, CT: Greenwood Press, 1998, 11–30.

Jenkins, Jennifer. "Fantasy in Fiction: The Double-Edged Sword." *Stephen King's Modern Macabre: Essays on the Later Works*. Jefferson, NC: McFarland & Company, Inc., 2014, 10–23.

Keesey, Douglas. "Patriarchal Mediations of *Carrie*: The Book, the Movie, and the Musical." *Imagining the Worst: Stephen King and the Representation of Women*. Westport, CT: Greenwood Press, 1998, 31–46.

King, Stephen. *11/22/63*. New York: Gallery Books, 2012.

———. "A Good Marriage." *Full Dark, No Stars*. New York: Scribner, 2010.

———. *Cell*. New York: Pocket Books, 2006.

———. *Christine*. New York: Gallery Books, 1983.

———. *Cujo*. New York: Gallery Books, 1981.

———. *Danse Macabre*. New York: Berkely Books, 1983.

———. *The Dark Half*. New York: Signet Books, 1989.

———. *The Dead Zone*. New York: Signet Books, 1979.

———. *Desperation*. New York: Gallery Books, 1996.

———. *Doctor Sleep*. New York: Scribner, 2013.

———. *Dreamcatcher*. New York: Pocket Books, 2001.

———. *Duma Key*. New York: Pocket Books, 2008.

———. *Firestarter*. New York: Signet, 1980.

———. *Gerald's Game*. New York: Signet Books, 1992.

———. *The Green Mile*. New York: Pocket Books, 1996.

———. *The Institute*. New York: Scribner, 2019.

———. *It*. New York: Scribner, 1986.

———. *The Long Walk*. New York: Signet Books, 1979. Reissued 1999.

———. *Misery*. New York: Scribner, 1987.

———. *Needful Things*. New York: Signet Books, 1991.

———. *On Writing*. New York: Pocket Books, 2000.

———. *The Outsider*. New York: Scribner, 2018.

———. *Pet Sematary*. New York: Pocket Books, 1983.
———. *'Salem's Lot*. New York: Pocket Books, 1975.
———. *The Stand*. New York: Anchor Books, 1990.
———. *The Tommyknockers*. New York: Signet, 1987.
Lamarque, Peter, and Stein Haugam Olsen. *Truth, Fiction, and Literature: A Philosophical Perspective*. Oxford: Clarendon Press, 1994.
Landais, Clotilde. "Reading *Joyland* and *Doctor Sleep* as Complementary Stories." *Stephen King's Contemporary Classics: Reflections on the Modern Master of Horror*. Lanham, MD: Rowman & Littlefield, 2015, 41–53.
Lippert, Conny L. "Traveling before the Storm: Shades of the Lightening Rod Salesman in Stephen King's Gothic." *The Modern Stephen King Canon: Beyond Horror*. Lanham, MD: Lexington Books, 2019, 147–166.
Magistrale, Anthony. *The Moral Voyages of Stephen King*. USA: Wildside Press, LLC, this edition 2006. 1989.
Magistrale, Tony. *Landscape of Fear: Stephen King's American Gothic*. Madison: Popular Press, 1988.
———. "The Rehabilitation of Stephen King." *The Modern Stephen King Canon: Beyond Horror*. Lanham, MD: Lexington Books, 2019, 3–22.
———. *Stephen King: America's Storyteller*. Santa Barbara: Praeger, 2010.
———. *Stephen King: The Second Decade, Danse Macabre to the Dark Half*. New York: Twayne Publishers, 1992.
Marshall, Helen. "A Snapshot of an Age: The Publication History of *Carrie*." *Journal of Popular Culture* 53, no. 2 (2020): 284–302.
McAleer, Patrick. "The Fallen King(dom): Surviving Ruin and Decay from *The Stand* to *Cell*." *Stephen King's Modern Macabre: Essays on the Later Works*. Jefferson, NC: McFarland & Company, Inc., 2014, 168–184.
———. "Untangling the True Knot: Stephen King's (Accidental) Vegan Manifesto in *Doctor Sleep*." *The Modern Stephen King Canon: Beyond Horror*. Lanham, MD: Lexington Books, 2019, 219–233.
Mercer, Erin. "The Difference Between World and Want: Adulthood and the Horrors of History in Stephen King's *IT*." *Journal of Popular Culture* 52, no. 2 (2019): 315–329.
Mustazza, Leonard. "Fear and Pity: Tragic Horror in King's *Pet Sematary*." *The Dark Descent: Essays Defining Stephen King's Horrorscape*. New York: Greenwood Press, 1992, 73–82.
Nazare, Joe. "The Horror! The Horror? The Appropriation, and Reclamation, of Native American Mythology." *Journal of the Fantastic in the Arts* 11, no. 1 (41) (2000): 24–51.
Newhouse, Tom. "A Blind Date with Disaster: Adolescent Revolt in the Fiction of Stephen King." *Critical Insights: Stephen King*. Pasadena, California: Salem Press, 2011, 267–275.
Pharr, Mary. "Partners in the Danse: Women in Stephen King's Fiction," *The Dark Descent: Essays Defining Stephen King's Horrorscape*. New York: Greenwood Press, 1992, 19–32.

Reino, Joseph. *Stephen King: The First Decade,* Carrie *to* Pet Sematary. Boston: Twayne Publishers, 1988.
Reuber, Alexandra. "In Search of the Lost Object in a Bad Place: Stephen King's Contemporary Gothic." *Stephen King's Contemporary Classics: Reflections on the Modern Master of Horror*. Lanham, MD: Rowman & Littlefield, 2015, 101–115.
Russell, Sharon A. *Revisiting Stephen King: A Critical Companion.* Westport, CT: Greenwood Press, 2002.
———. *Stephen King: A Critical Companion.* Westport, CT: Greenwood Press, 1996.
Sears, John. *Stephen King's Gothic*. Cardiff: University of Wales Press, 2011.
Senf, Carol A. "*Gerald's Game* and *Dolores Claiborne*: Stephen King and the Evolution of an Authentic Female Narrative Voice." *Imagining the Worst: Stephen King and the Representation of Women*. Westport, CT: Greenwood Press, 1998, 91–107.
Simpson, Phillip L. "From the Meat World to Cyberspace: The Psychopath's Journey in *Mr. Mercedes* and *End of Watch*." *The Modern Stephen King Canon: Beyond Horror*. Lanham, MD: Lexington Books, 2019, 113–124.
Sternberg, Meir. "Telling in Time (II): Chronology, Narrative, Teleology." *Poetics Today* 13.3. (1992), 463–541.
Strengell, Heidi. *Dissecting Stephen King: From the Gothic to Literary Naturalism*. Madison: The University of Wisconsin Press, 2005.
Thoens, Karen. "It: A Sexual Fantasy." *Imagining the Worst: Stephen King and the Representation of Women*. Westport, CT: Greenwood Press, 1998, 127–140.
Vronsky, Peter. *Sons of Cain: A History of Serial Killers from the Stone Age to the Present.* New York: Berkley, 2019, 127–140.

Index

abortion, 173
Ackerman Field, 35
alcoholism, 12, 83, 104, 116, 158
alien, 3, 26, 35, 40, 45, 98, 99, 114, 125, 127–28, 141, 142, 144, 155, 161, 177, 178, 182
Alzheimer's, 178
Anderson, Bob, 4, 40, 49–50, 141, 149, 152–53, 155
Anderson, Bobbi, 74, 98, 101, 116–17, 161
Anderson, Darcy, 4, 40, 49–50, 58, 141, 142, 144, 152–53, 155
Anderson, Ralph, 28, 29, 97–98, 111, 181
Andros, Nick, 61, 112, 164, 172
"Apt Pupil," 136–37
Ardai, Charles "The Head," 85, 91, 166
Arthur ("I am the Doorway"), 127, 142, 144
Atropos, 134, 136

Bachman, Richard, 32
Bag of Bones, 14, 16, 86, 151, 179
"Bad Little Kid," 24, 34, 35, 36, 141, 142, 144
Bannerman, Sheriff George, 4, 41, 42, 44, 46–48, 107, 109–10, 122

Barlow, Kurt, 10–11, 20, 93–94, 95, 96, 97, 98, 100, 128, 156, 166
Bateman, Glen, 112–13, 114, 162
Bazaar of Bad Dreams, 34
"Beadie," 40, 49–50, 141, 144
Beahm, George, 17
Beal, Kimberly, 138
Beaumont, Liz, 67, 169
Beaumont, Thad, 65, 66–67, 68, 69, 74, 133–34, 163, 169–70, 171, 173
Bellamy, Morris, 9, 17, 21
"Big Driver," 80, 83–84, 87, 91, 141
Bissette, Antonia, 160, 166
Blackwood, Algernon, 51
"The Body," 10, 19, 20, 21, 100
Bolton, Claude, 28
Bonsaint, John, 35
Boulder, CO, 4, 62, 112, 113, 162, 164, 173
Boulder Free Zone, 112–13, 122, 164, 172
Bowden, Todd, 126, 136–37, 143
Bowers, Henry, 92, 95, 96, 97, 98, 100, 103
Bradley, Leonard, 35
Brentner, Ralph, 112–13, 114, 162, 164
Brown, George "Candy," 55–57
Bruner, Jerome, 5
BTK, 50, 141

191

bully, 19, 21, 25, 27, 43, 44, 80, 81, 95, 100, 150, 154, 163, 166, 171
Burke, Matt, 107, 108–9
Burlingame, Gerald, 16–17
Burlingame, Jessie, 9, 16–17, 20

Cabot, Leigh, 43, 44, 45, 58, 150, 166
Camber, Brett, 3, 42
Camber, Charity, 3, 42
Camber, Joe, 3, 42, 149
Campbell, Joseph, 109
Carrie, 79, 80–82, 87, 154, 171–72
Carver, David, 118, 119, 120
Castle Rock, ME, 3, 4, 41, 46, 47, 48, 50, 73, 100–101, 104, 152, 159, 167, 168, 171, 176, 178
catharsis, 148, 182, 184
Clavell, Douglas "Duddits," 107, 114, 119, 122, 162
Cell, 66, 72, 76, 80, 84–85, 87, 91, 163, 165–66, 169, 178
Chalmers, Polly, 74
Chamberlain, ME, 81, 154
Chicago, IL, 52
Christ, Jesus, 139, 143, 181
Christine (car), 43, 44, 45, 58, 149–50, 166, 183
Christine (novel), 39, 43, 45, 46, 166
Church (cat), 51–52, 58, 102
Churchill, Winston. *See* Church (cat)
Claiborne, Dolores, 80, 82–84, 88–89, 91
Clarendon, Joe "Beaver," 53
climax, 6, 7, 47, 48, 49, 63, 65, 70, 74, 76, 85, 98, 110, 112, 122, 148, 150, 153, 157, 166, 177, 183
Cody, Jimmy, 11, 14, 93, 97, 107, 109, 110, 111, 166, 180
Coffey, John, 126, 138–39, 143
Colorado, 9, 11, 48, 120
The Colorado Kid, 148
Constant Reader, 2, 29, 32, 57, 122, 129, 140, 148, 150, 152, 178, 180, 181, 182, 183
Corcoran, Eddie, 26, 180

Crandall, Jud, 51, 52, 53, 102, 103, 104, 159
Crandall, Norma, 51, 52
Creed, Ellie, 51, 52
Creed, Gage, 51, 52, 53, 58, 103
Creed, Louis, 40, 51, 52, 53, 102, 103, 159
Creed, Rachel, 51, 52
Cross, Nadine, 62
Cujo (dog), 3, 41, 42, 43, 45, 46 58, 107, 109–10, 149, 156
Cujo (novel), 2, 39, 41, 46, 109–10, 169
Cullen, Tom, 113
Cunningham, Arnie, 39, 43, 44, 45, 150, 166
Curley, 32, 33

Daniels, Norman, 65, 67–68, 76, 170–71
Danse Macabre, 1
The Dark Half, 65, 66–68, 74, 144, 163, 169–70, 173
the Dark Man. *See* Flagg, Randall
Dark Score Lake, ME, 15, 151, 179
the Dark Tower, 6, 121, 136, 140, 142, 143, 164, 167, 173, 180
Darnell, Will, 44, 45
The Dead Zone, 40, 46–49, 51, 53, 107, 113–14, 132
Deepneau, Ed, 126, 133, 134, 135, 136, 137, 143, 173–74
Deepneau, Natalie, 167
Denbrough, Bill, 25, 26, 29, 95–96
Denbrough, Georgie, 25
Derry, ME, 24, 25, 27, 28, 30, 33, 34, 94–95, 103–4, 110–11, 140, 173, 174, 175, 177, 181
Desperation, 117–18
Devlin, Henry, 53–55, 114, 162
Dixon, Avery, 107, 118–21, 122
Doctor Sleep, 23, 29, 33, 129–31, 157, 160, 168, 169
Dodd, Frank, 3, 4, 40, 46–49, 50, 149, 152, 153, 155, 156
Dodd, Henrietta, 48
Dolores Claiborne, 82–83

Donovan, Vera, 82–83
Dracula, 92, 108, 110
Drayton, David, 45–46, 58
Dreamcatcher, 40, 51, 53–55, 58, 107, 114, 115, 122, 150, 162, 176
Duddits. *See* Clavell, Douglas "Duddits"
Dufresne, Andy, 9, 10, 18–19, 20, 21
Duma Key (novel), 13–14, 51, 55–57, 58 65, 66, 68–69, 99–100, 147
Duma Key, FL, 9, 13, 40, 55, 56, 99, 100, 104, 157, 178
Dunning family, 126–27, 140, 143, 144
Dunning, Harry, 144

Eastlake, Elizabeth, 14, 69, 99, 178–79
Edgecombe, Paul, 138–39
11/22/63, 66, 72–73, 76, 127, 139–40, 143
Ellis, Luke, 9, 10, 17–18, 20, 21, 118, 119, 132, 151, 175
End of Watch, 135
Epping, Jake, 72–73, 140, 144
exposition, 5, 7, 148

falling action, 7, 19, 110, 182
Farris, Judge, 113, 114
FBI, 23, 46
Finders Keepers, 9, 17
Firestarter, 65, 66, 76, 158
Flagg, Randall, 62, 112–13, 173
Flint City, OK, 28, 47
Florida, 9, 13, 55
Free Zone. *See* Boulder Free Zone
Freeman, Andrew "Poke," 4
Freemantle, Abigail, 107, 112–13, 162, 163, 167, 173
Freemantle, Edgar, 13, 14, 15, 55–57, 65, 68–9, 99–100, 157, 178–79, 183
Freemantle, Ilse, 14
Full Dark, No Stars, 141

Gamache, Homer, 170
Gardener, Jim "Gard," 74–75, 77, 107, 116–20, 122, 127–28, 130, 131, 132, 161, 178

Garibaldi, Tina, 55–56
Garin, Audrey, 126, 138, 143
Garin, Seth, 126, 137–38, 139, 143
Gaunt, Leland, 74, 100–101, 102, 159–60, 167, 176, 177, 178
generic convention, 5, 7, 107, 144, 152, 153, 182
Gerald's Game, 9, 16
Gibney, Holly, 28, 29, 31, 98, 111, 181
God, 112–13, 118, 119, 137, 162, 164, 167
Gold, Howie, 107, 111
"A Good Marriage," 4, 40, 49–50, 51, 58, 141, 152–53
Grady, Delbert, 12
The Green Mile, 126, 138–39
gothic, 10, 16
Guilder, Dennis, 43, 44, 45, 58, 150, 166, 183

Hanlon, Mike, 25, 26, 27
Hanscom, Ben, 26, 111
Harker, Mina, 108
Hartsfield, Brady, 66, 75–76, 77, 126, 135–36, 137, 143, 152, 155, 156
Hartsfield, Deborah, 76
Haven, ME, 74–75, 98–99, 101, 104, 116–17, 120, 125, 127–28, 159, 160, 168
the Head. *See* Ardai, Charles
"The Head"
Henreid, Lloyd, 4
Hodges, Kermit William "Bill," 17, 75–76, 126, 135–36, 152, 155
Hopewell, Nick, 107, 114–15, 122
Hoskins, Jack, 97–98, 104, 160
Huizenga, Ray, 72, 76, 77, 84, 163, 166, 178

"I am the Doorway," 127, 141, 142
"If It Bleeds," 31
inciting incident, 6
Insomnia, 108, 120–21, 122, 133, 167, 173

The Institute (novel), 9, 17–18, 23, 34, 118–19, 131–32, 151, 158
the Institute (place), 17, 18, 21, 34, 36, 118–19, 120, 125, 131–32, 143, 175
introduction of conflict, 6, 148
It (creature), 24, 26, 27, 28, 30, 31, 33, 34, 35, 36, 47, 92, 95, 96, 97, 103, 107, 110–11, 122, 142, 149, 155, 174, 175, 177, 180, 181
It (novel), 23, 29, 30, 33, 94–95, 110–11

James, Arlette, 86, 89, 91
James, Henry "Hank," 86
James, Wilfred, 86, 89
Jones, Gary "Jonesy," 53–55
Jordan (*Cell*), 80, 84–85, 87, 88, 89, 91
Junkins, Rudolph, 44
Jurgens, Dayna, 113, 114
Just After Sunset, 34

Kaspbrak, Eddie, 96, 107, 110–11, 122, 181
ka-tet, 31, 97, 156
Keaton, Danforth, 100–101, 102
Kennedy, John Fitzgerald "JFK," 73, 139–40, 144
King, Owen, 53
Kurtz, Abraham, 54, 163
Kushner, Duane, 71, 74, 150

LaChance, Gordie, 19, 21
Landon, Lisey, 134–35, 136
Landon, Scott, 134, 135
"The Langoliers," 10, 20, 21, 107, 114–15, 122
Las Vegas, NV, 4, 32, 112, 113, 162, 164, 167
Lauder, Harold, 62, 172, 173, 174
LeBay, Roland, 44
"The Library Policeman," 23, 27–28
Lisey's Story, 134–35
Little Tall Island, ME, 89
The Long Walk, 23, 32, 33, 169, 174
Lortz, Ardelia, 27–28, 36

the Losers, 24, 25, 26, 27, 29, 95, 96, 103, 110–11, 175, 181
the Lot. *See* 'salem's Lot (town)

Magistrale, Tony, 11, 21, 25, 42, 49, 75, 92, 102, 115, 127
Maine, 9, 32, 34, 54, 93, 98, 118, 128, 129, 132, 143, 172, 175
Maitland, Terry, 28, 29, 96, 111
the Major, 32, 33, 34, 36
Marinville, Johnny, 107, 117–18, 119, 120, 122
Marsh, Beverly, "Bev," 95
mass death, 20
mass murder, 4, 5, 9, 24, 62, 66, 79, 85, 173, 174, 179
Maxwell, Alice (*Cell*), 85, 165–66
McAleer, Patrick, 30
McCarthy (*Dreamcatcher*), 53–55
McCausland, Ruth, 74–75, 77, 98, 160, 167–68
McClendon, Rosie, 65, 67–68, 134, 170–71
McCool, Zak, 126, 134–35, 136, 137, 143
McGee, Andy, 70–71, 74, 170
McGee, Charlie, 65, 66, 70–71, 74, 76, 158, 170, 171, 172
McGee, Vicky, 70, 170
Mears, Ben, 15, 93–94, 109, 128–29, 130, 131, 176, 180
Mellon, Adrian, 26
Merrill, Ace, 100–101, 160
Mexico, 128
Micmac, 51, 102, 103
Misery, 63, 65, 66, 71, 76, 134, 150
"The Mist," 40, 45, 58
Moore, Pete, 54
Mother Abigail. *See* Freemantle, Abigail
Mr. Gray, 55
Mr. Mercedes, 66, 75–76, 135, 152, 155
multiple murder, 3, 4, 23, 32, 125, 151

"N.," 24, 34, 35, 36

Needful Things, 66, 73–74, 77, 100–101, 159, 166, 167
New York City, 169
"1922," 80, 86, 89, 91
"Nona," 100
Noonan, Jo, 15, 16
Noonan, Mike, 14, 15, 16, 151, 179
Norton, Susan, 10–11, 12, 13, 93, 109, 180

Ohio, 28
Oklahoma, 28
On Writing, 6, 61, 62
"One for the Road," 129
Oswald, Lee Harvey, 73
the Outsider (creature), 28, 29, 31, 33, 34, 35, 36, 47, 81, 96, 97, 98, 104, 111, 122, 149, 155, 156, 174, 176, 177
The Outsider (novel), 23, 29, 33, 96–98, 111, 121, 181
the Overlook Hotel, 9, 11–14, 20–21, 92, 102–3, 107, 115–17, 118, 120, 157–59, 161

Pangborn, Sheriff Alan, 74, 75, 77, 100–101, 160, 167, 168, 176, 178
Pelly, Alec, 107, 111
Pennywise. *See* It (creature)
Perse, 13–14, 20, 21, 56–57, 65, 68–69, 76, 99–100, 104, 157, 178–79
Pervier, Gary, 41, 42, 149
Pet Sematary (novel), 40, 51–53, 58, 102–3
pet sematary (place), 40, 92, 102, 159
Peterson, Frankie, 28, 29, 33, 47
Peterson, Ollie, 29
Petrie, Mark, 93–94, 109, 128–29, 130, 131, 176, 180

Rainbird, John, 70, 74
Rainey, Mort, 126, 136–37, 143
Red ("Rita Hayworth and Shawshank Redemption"), 9, 18

Redman, Stuart, "Stu," 112–13, 162, 172
Reed, Cammie, 138
The Regulators, 126, 137–38
Repperton, Buddy, 166
resolution, 7, 20, 138, 144, 148
restoration, 3, 122, 123, 126, 131, 137–40, 143, 144, 165, 173, 182–83
Revival, 147
Riddell, Clay, 72, 73, 84, 85, 87, 178
rising action, 6, 148
"Rita Hayworth and Shawshank Redemption," 9, 18–19
Roberts, Ralph, 108, 120–21, 122, 167
Rogan, Tom, 95–96
Rolling Stone, 172
Rose Madder, 65, 67–68, 134, 170–71
Rose the Hat, 30, 31, 129–31, 132
Ross, Tommy, 81
Rothstein, John, 17
Rusk, Brian, 73–75, 77, 101, 167–68, 178
Rusk, Sean, 74, 167, 178
Russell, Sharon, 144

'Salem's Lot (novel), 9, 10, 12, 14, 21, 92–94, 100, 107, 108–9, 122, 128–29, 131, 166, 180
'salem's lot (town), 11, 13, 133, 125, 128, 129, 143, 156, 159, 176, 177
Samuels, Bill, 28
Saubers, Peter, 17, 20, 21
Sears, John, 13
"Secret Window, Secret Garden," 136
serial killer, 3, 23, 40, 50, 79, 127, 149, 152, 178, 183, 184
serial murder, 2, 4, 31, 173
Shawshank Prison, 18
Sheldon, Paul, 63, 65, 66, 71, 74, 76, 150
The Shining (novel), 11, 14, 29, 102, 115–16, 157, 161
the shining (power), 11, 12, 13, 29, 157
The Shop, 65, 70–71, 170
Sigsby, Mrs., 131, 175

Smith, Johnny, 40, 46–49, 58, 107,
    113–14, 122, 132, 155
Snakebite Andi, 31, 130, 156
"Sneakers," 10, 19, 21
Snell, Sue, 81, 87, 154, 171, 172, 183
spree murder, 4
The Stand, 4, 6, 42, 61–63, 107, 112–13,
    114, 115, 162, 167, 172
St. George, Joe, 82–83, 84, 88
St. George, Selena, 82–83, 88
St. Paul, MN, 13
Stark, George, 65, 66–67, 68, 74, 76,
    86, 126, 127, 133–34, 135, 136, 137,
    143, 163, 169–70, 171, 173, 174, 176
Stebbins (*The Long Walk*), 32
Sternberg, Meir, 5
Stillson, Greg, 47, 49, 113
Stoker, Bram, 92, 93, 108
Stone, Abra, 29, 30, 31, 130, 132, 169
Stengell, Heidi, 79, 110, 112, 127, 137
Straker, Richard Throckett,
    92–98, 101, 103
suicide, 11, 17, 50, 66, 69, 71, 72–75,
    76, 77, 85, 107, 135, 141, 142,
    155, 175, 178
surprise, 40, 63, 71, 91, 141, 184
suspense, 2, 3, 4, 5, 6, 10, 20, 24, 28,
    29, 36, 39–59, 62, 68, 76, 84, 88,
    108, 109, 148–51, 168, 184

taboo, 1, 147
Tak, 107, 117–18, 137–38, 143
telekinesis, 17, 79, 80, 87, 119, 131,
    132, 135, 154, 158
telepathy, 17, 55, 98, 101, 117, 119, 127,
    128, 131, 132, 135, 158, 176, 178
Tell, John, 19, 20, 21
Templeton, Al, 72–73, 76, 77
Tess ("Big Driver"), 80, 83–84, 87–88,
    89, 91, 141, 142, 144
Tidwell, Sara, 14–15, 16, 20,
    86, 151, 179
Tommyknockers (aliens), 75, 77, 92,
    98, 107, 116–17, 120, 125, 128, 129,
    130, 131, 132, 133, 143, 156, 159

The Tommyknockers (novel), 3, 66,
    74–75, 98–99, 101, 116–17, 127–28,
    131, 167–68, 178
Torrance, Dan "Danny," 11, 12, 13, 14,
    15, 29, 30, 102, 116, 117, 119, 120,
    130, 132, 157, 159, 161, 169
Torrance, Jack, 11, 12, 13, 14, 15, 102,
    103, 104, 107, 115–16, 117, 118,
    119, 120, 121, 122, 157, 158–59, 161
Torrance, Wendy, 12, 13, 15,
    120, 161, 163
Tozier, Richie, 26, 96, 111
TR-90, ME, 15
Trenton, Donna, 41, 42, 46, 50,
    109–10, 121
Trenton, Tad, 41, 42, 46, 58,
    109–10, 121
Trenton, Vic, 41
Trevor, Bradley, 30, 33, 168, 169
the True Knot, 29, 30, 31, 33, 35, 125,
    129–31, 132, 143, 149, 156, 158,
    160–61, 169, 176, 177
the Turtle, 31, 182

Under the Dome, 3, 4, 62
Underhill, Owen, 54, 114, 117, 162–63
Underwood, Larry, 62, 112–13, 114,
    162, 163, 164
Uris, Stan, 27, 29, 31, 143, 181

vampire, 9, 10, 11, 13, 15, 20, 81,
    91, 94, 99, 109, 125, 128–29, 130,
    131, 132, 133, 143, 156, 157, 159,
    176, 180, 182
Van Helsing, 108, 109
Vietnam, 89

Wendigo, 51
White, Carrie, 77, 79, 80–84, 87–89, 91,
    154, 171–72, 176
White Commission, 82, 87,
    154, 171, 183
Wilkes, Annie, 71, 150
Wireman, Jerome, 56–57, 183
writer's block, 61, 62, 172

About the Author

Rebecca Frost, PhD, is an independent scholar and cochair for the Stephen King Area of the National Popular Culture Association Conference. She is the author of *Surviving Stephen King: Reactions to the Supernatural in Works by the Master of Horror*.